Held in the Highest Esteem by All

The Civil War Letters of William B. Chilvers, 95th Illinois Infantry

Held in the Highest Esteem by All

The Civil War Letters of William B. Chilvers, 95th Illinois Infantry

Edited by
Thomas A. Pressly, III
and
Gary D. Joiner

State ✦ House
Press
Abilene, Texas

State ★ House Press

State House Press
1 McMurry University, #637
Abilene, Texas 79697-0001
325-793-4682
www.mcwhiney.org

Cataloging-in-Publication Data

Names: Chilvers, William B., author. | Pressly, Thomas A., III, editor. | Joiner, Gary D., editor.
Title: Held in the highest esteem by all: the Civil War letters of William B. Chilvers, 95th Illinois Infantry / edited by Thomas A. Pressly, III and Gary D. Joiner
Description: First edition. |Abilene, TX: State House Press, 2018. | Includes bibliographical references and index.
Identifiers: ISBN 9781933337784 (hardcover)
Subjects: LCSH: Chilvers, William B. – Correspondence. | United States. Army. Illinois Infantry Regiment, 95th (1862-1865). | Illinois – History – Civil War, 1861-1865 – Personal narratives. | United States – History – Civil War, 1861-1865 – Personal narratives.
Classification: LLC E505.595th2018 | DDC 973.7/473/092

This paper meets the requirements of ANSI/NISO, Z39.48-1992 (Permanence of Paper).
Binding materials have been chosen for durability.

First edition, reissue 2018

Book Design by Rosenbohm Graphic Design

Printed in the United States of America
Distributed by Texas A&M University Press Consortium
800-826-8911
www.tamupress.com

Contents

Maps and Illustrations

Unless otherwise noted, all illustrations are from the Thomas A. Pressly Collection.

Acknowledgements

I would like to thank C. Richard "Dick" Chilvers and his family for allowing me to publish this account of their relative. I also want to thank them for their patience with me in formulating this account and for traveling with me to Nebraska to meet Dick's uncle and aunt and to see his remarkable family legacy in Pierce and Plainview.

As a physician I'm sure that the reader has no patience with me noting that at times the penmanship was worse than mine. I thank my family, Tracy, Thomas, Maggie, Catherine, and Mason, and friend Maury Hicks for their assistance with deciphering the Chilvers family letters. I continue to be in gratitude to my wife, Tracy, for her love and support on another one of my ventures. I also thank Gary and Marilyn Joiner for their years of guidance, encouragement and expertise in publishing our book. This book has been tremendously improved by Gary's expertise as a noted and prolific Civil War author. I also thank Donald S. Frazier for his production of the detailed maps as well as his review and support of this project. I have certainly been blessed by having two civil war authorities assist me on completion of my first book. Several other people were of invaluable service. Ashley Dean at the Strategic Alternatives Consortium (SAC) at Louisiana State University in Shreveport, Gary's deputy, helped immensely in indexing the manuscript. I also deeply appreciate the editorial talents of Carly Kahl as well as the State House Press director, Scott Clowdus, for his patience and friendship. I certainly agree with Kent Bifle of the *Dallas Morning News* who said, "I never met a State House Book I didn't like." Finally, thanks to Gary S. Zaboly, the military illustrator, who the Chilvers family commissioned to paint our cover illustration.

Preface

In late 2012, a friend told me that he had a few letters that he thought I would be interested in reviewing. That friend, Dick Chilvers, brought to me a collection of one hundred and seventy letters from his great-grandfather, William Burnham Chilvers. This correspondence includes letters from his family in England, and the United States, as well as those to his aunt and uncle, Rebecca and George Burnham.

Will Chilvers had a limited education, but his strong character and an obviously brilliant intellect shine in the collection of letters as he provides an unique insight to life as an infantryman with the analysis of the war and people.

William Burnham Chilvers was born into a relatively impoverished, rural England in the 1830s and was orphaned by age seven. He moved as a teenager with his aunt and uncle, initially to Chicago and later to Boone County, Illinois, to farm.

When the war broke out Chilvers joined the Ninety-Fifth Illinois Infantry Regiment. William and his aunt and uncle were Anglophiles and abolitionists. He found that many of his fellow soldiers were indifferent to the institution of slavery and were suspicious of the English who by the mid-nineteenth century had become an economic rival to the United States. Chilvers felt discounted by fellow soldiers since he was an immigrant. He was appalled at the treatment of African Americans by Southerners as well as by his fellow Union soldiers. He describes episodes of abuses, including one where he single-handedly stood up to the defense of two newly freed African Americans who were assaulted by Union troops.

Chilvers extends empathy to his foe and mentions the massacre of Southerners at the Battle of Tupelo. Chilvers and his fellow comrades, including the woman Albert Cashier, were involved in seventy-five battles and traveled over nine thousand miles. They experienced disease, rugged weather, and the horrors of battles at Vicksburg, the Red River Campaign, Guntown, the Missouri Raid, Nashville, and Mobile. His dedication to the Union army is highlighted when he carried the colors over the parapet during the storming of the Spanish Fort during the Mobile Campaign.

Following discharge from the service and an initial stay in Chicago, he moved to northeastern Nebraska and worked as a carpenter in Pierce and Plainview. He married Nellie Picher and they had the first child of European ancestry in that part of the country. William Burnham Chilvers, an impoverished orphan, became a man that he could only have dreamed of as a child. Respect and fortune followed this remarkable man who was held in the highest esteem by all.

Growing up in San Antonio, a community full of historical vignettes, such as Davy Crockett and friends who defended the Alamo, Teddy Roosevelt who formed his Rough Riders, and characters such as John Wesley Hardin and his lawyer, Judge William Seat Fly, who helped tame the West, I learned that history mattered. In the early 1960s it was hard to escape the publications, movies, and stories that crept into my elementary school on the Civil War. Movies and television series such as *Shenandoah, How the West was Won, Johnny Shiloh,* and *Gone With the Wind* were featured films. A multitude of books were written on the topic and my favorites were *Rebel Rider,* and the *Civil War* by American Heritage Publications. My elementary school even furnished us with book covers featuring a map of the war. My interest in the conflict began with owning a "Johnny Reb's Cannon" by Remco. This progressed with a fascination of photographs depicting both the gallantry and tragedies of the Civil War. My beloved great-aunt, Zora Crews, told me stories of family members, both soldiers and civilians, whose lives were deeply affected by the war. During my adult life, I researched and documented several of the accounts of my family from the era and other figures that fascinated me, but never had enough information to publish a book.

CHAPTER 1

A "NORFOLK DUMPLING"

Opportunities for a poor, uneducated orphan born in 1835 in Great Britain were limited to tenant farming, working in the coal mines or a factory, and serving the Crown as a soldier or sailor. Western Europe and Britain had entered the Industrial Revolution with an explosion of inventions and mechanization that required copious amounts of raw materials from their numerous colonies which provided tremendous wealth for these European countries. The educated elite managed and developed industries. Manufactured goods such as ships, textiles, machinery, and tools were in great demand from a rapidly developing world. As the economies grew, so did the pressures to obtain greater quantities of raw materials and to improve workers' productivity. This desire for goods fueled many of the national conflicts and warfare that marked the next 120 years. The economic success of the elite failed to reach the working class and led to social discord and revolution in France and eventually Russia. Great Britain instigated reforms earlier than many of its European peers and thus avoided much of the turbulence that many European nations experienced. Important reforms in England in the 1830s included an update of the "Poor Law,"child labor restrictions, the abolition of slavery, and a revision of the election system.[1] Despite these reforms, a tremendous economic gap occurred between the wealthy and the poor, particularly those in the farmlands along the eastern coast of England.

William Burnham Chilvers was born on October 10, 1835, in Terrington, County Norfolk.[2] The land was known well by the English because it was the origin of the powerful and wealthy Earl of Norfolk, an active leader in the English Revolution as a key aide to Oliver Cromwell.[3] The county lay on the

Map by Donald S. Frazier.

east coast of England, alongside the North Sea. Just north of Norfolk was a series of swampy lowlands simply known as "the Wash."[4]

The people were sarcastically depicted as "normal for Norfolk" being typecast as incestuous, illiterate, and backwater.[5] These rural inhabitants were mocked and given the nickname of the "Norfolk Dumplings" due to their typical diet consisting of flour rolled into clumps. Most of the people lived as farmers or worked in the fishing industry. Social advancement in England at this time was blocked by limited educational opportunities, particularly in this relatively impoverished area.

William, an only child, was born to William Chilvers (1812–1844) and Marie Twelves Chilvers (1818–1843).[6] He was orphaned by age seven as his mother died in 1843 at age twenty-five and his father the following year at age thirty-two, of unknown causes.[7] Such early deaths in this pre-antibiotic age of infectious diseases like typhoid fever, measles, or pneumonia or perhaps complications of an injury, appendicitis, or childbirth were common. Will, as he was commonly called, lived with grandparents until he came to the United States in October 1851 with his uncle, George Burnham, and aunt, Rebecca Twelves Burnham. Several relatives joined their venture to America, including another uncle Mathew Twelves, his wife Mary, as well as second cousins with the surname Fillingham.[8]

Chilvers initially moved to Chicago, where at age sixteen he began a three-year stint as a carpenter's assistant. He then moved 100 miles west to Belvidere, Illinois, in 1855, still working as a carpenter.[9] He eventually entered the limestone business with his uncle George.[10] In 1861 they became full-time farmers and worked together until the summer of 1862 when Will entered the Army.[11] Despite its small size, Belvidere had a remarkable political presence in Illinois politics since it was the home of Maj. Gen. Stephen Hurlbut, as well as Attorney General Allan C. Fuller.[12]

Gen. Stephen Augustus Hurlbut was a forty-six-year-old attorney who is a native of Charleston, South Carolina, who moved to Belvidere, Illinois, in 1845. He entered politics and was a Republican member of the state legislature. Lincoln appointed him as a brigadier general of volunteers in June 1861 and he advanced to major general on September 17, 1862. He subsequently commanded the Fourth Division of the Army of the Tennessee, the Sixteenth Corps, and the Department of the Gulf. He was "honorably mustered out" of command of the department when a special commission was appointed when he was accused of corruption. After the war he returned to Belvidere and became the First Commander of the Grand Army of the Republic.[13]

Many Northerners were surprised that the war had not quickly ended in 1861. The South had put up a much stiffer resistance than thought possible, even though they were outnumbered and

Cpl. William Burnham Chilvers, Company B, Ninety-Fifth Illinois Infantry in uniform. [Photo from the Collection of C. Richard Chilvers]

Richard Yates served as the wartime governor of Illinois and was responsible for providing a quota of troops to the Union. He ordered the Ninety-Fifth Illinois Infantry to leave Camp Fuller and report to Columbus, Tennessee, to join Gen. Ulysses S. Grant's Army of the Tennessee on October 30, 1862.

had limited industrial resources and factories. The Rebels were more than holding their own in the East, winning the major battle First Manassas in July 1861, and achieving continued success in the Shenandoah Valley, Seven Days Campaigns, and Second Manassas in August 1862.[14]

The North secured victories in the West at Forts Henry and Donelson, and Island Number 10 in 1861. Other successes followed at Memphis in March and Shiloh in April. They captured the South's important commercial center, New Orleans, in May 1862. Obviously the General-in-Chief Winfield Scott's vision of the Anaconda Plan was going to take time. Scott's strategy included surrounding the South through a blockade of the coast, capturing the Mississippi River, and gradually squeezing inward. In order to fulfill this plan, war materials, a brown water navy, and a much larger army were needed to capture the strongly fortified citadels at Vicksburg and Port Hudson.

In the summer of 1862 Abraham Lincoln called for an additional 600,000 troops to put down the rebellion. Illinois was given a quota of the troops to provide the Union, but this farmland state in the Midwest did not fully support the war. Many Midwesterners were previous supporters of the American Party, better remembered as the "Know Nothings." This group was also known as "Northern Doughfaces." They were popular in Illinois and were not sure whether the preservation of the Union was worth the lives of their sons. Clement L. Vallandigham of Ohio was the leader of a group in the Midwest that advocated allowing the South to leave the Union peacefully if they did not desire to remain in the Union.[15]

Map by Donald S. Frazier.

This party was given the name "Copperheads." They had a strong presence in Illinois until the end of the war.

Illinois Gov. Richard Yates called for recruits from his state.[16] They were compensated by local and state money, earning an enlistment bonus as well as a monthly salary of thirteen dollars. Seven companies from McHenry County and three companies from neighboring Boone County were formed after enthusiastic recruiting efforts allowed them to reach maximum size by mid-August. Following a convention, election of officers, and acceptance by the governor, the Ninety-Fifth Illinois Regiment was formed to go "forth to the defense of the country, eloquently and with Patriotism."[17]

Officers of the Ninety-Fifth Illinois Regiment elected Lawrence S. Church as colonel, Thomas W. Humphrey as lieutenant colonel, Leander Blanden as major, and Wales Wood as adjutant. William B. Chilvers entered Company B as a private under the command of Capt. Charles B. Loop, 1st Lt. Milton Keeler, and 2nd Lt. Aaron F. Randall.[18]

The Ninety-Fifth Illinois marched to nearby Rockford and Camp Fuller, named for the attorney general. Three other northern Illinois regiments, the Seventy-Fourth, Ninety-Second, and Ninety-Sixth, joined the Ninety-Fifth. According to Wood, a "spirited rivalry sprang up," which was "commendable and beneficial" to their training.[19]

When the Seventy-Fourth was sent to the field, Colonel Church became commander of the post in a limited capacity due to his poor health. Lt. Alfred H. Sellers of the Thirty-Sixth Illinois Infantry was employed as drillmaster. Within a few weeks the soldiers could perform dress parade, guard mounting, and maneuvers prescribed in William Hardee's book *Tactics*.[20]

Following are two letters in full which are indicative of Will's early experiences in the field:

Jackson, Tenn[21]

Nov 9, [18]62

Dear Uncle & Aunt

I take this opportunity of writing a few lines to find you both in good health as it leaves me at present. When last I wrote I was on the steam boat and did not know where we where going to. I am on guard today at general headquarters so I have a little time to write. I suppose you would like to know how we got along after we left Woodstock.[22] Well we had a pleasant time of it to Chicago. Every house we past the people wave their hankerchiefs and cheer. We arrived at Chicago at dusk & the major lost his horse.[23] That is all the accidents we had until we arrived at Jackson. One man got his foot run over with the cars but the doctor thinks he will not lose it.[24] After we arrived at Chicago we marched from the depot across Randolph Street Bridge to the Central Depot. The people was perfectly crazy with eccitement cheering and waving hats & flags the whole way. I heard several of the citizens remark that it was the best looking regt. that ever passed through Chicago. When we got to the depot we occupied the whole building & staid there 3 hours. A wagon came round with hot coffee. We had all we wanted to drink. We had a very good car to ride in on the central road.[25] We had to sea a peace. The road is a very good one but the country is not very interesting. Nothing but low pararie uncultivated & unsettled until we got to Kankakee which is a very nice thriveing city.[26] We met Gen Fuller at the intersection of the Ill Central & Ohio & Miss railroad and he treated the officer to a breakfast.[27] We started on & arrived at Centralia at twilight & got hot coffee & crackers.[28] There was some 3 hundred secesh there.[29] I had quite a talk with a few. They seam to have great confidence in gaining there independence. We arrived at Cairo about 3 o'clock in the morning & staid on the cars until eight when we embarked on the Ohio River on board the steamboat Dacotah.[30] Cairo is a busy place. We saw the old gunboat Tyler & several ironclad boats & the steamboat Desota & another large one, the Memphis, taken at Memphis from the Rebels.[31] We where all put on board one boat and went down the river to Columbus.[32] We had commenced to unload when we where ordered back on board, & a guard placed around the boat to keep us from landing. Columbus is situated close to a high bluff which commands the Mississippi. It seems to be strongly fortified. It was here the Rebels put the chains across the river. I saw the chain it is a very large one it is about 3 miles long. Right across the river is the Belmont Battlefield.[33] We left Columbus in the evening & arrived at Jackson on Friday morning at 2 o'clock.[34] The boys was very glad we where ordered to Jackson it being in command of Gen Hurlbut. We unloaded from the cars & took our traps on a vacant lot and the Col. placed a guard over us until morning.[35] In the morning Gen Hurlbut told the col. he has a good looking lot of prisoners but the sooner he took the guard from us the better and we have never had a guard. Since the soldiers . . . the bugle is blowing to assemble and I must go.

William B. Chilvers

Dec 24, 1862

Great Confusion[36]

We tore down nice pickett fences, window blinds, and everything we can get hold of to make fires of, and lay on. The next morning we where ordered to leave our knapsacks & be ready to march out at daylight. We stacked our knapsacks in a pile & took our blankets & started in a northeast direction. Some said we was going to Corinth & some one place and some other but the general impression is that we was going to Corinth but after marching about 15 miles we halted at a small ancient looking place . . . Salem.[37] Planted the battery, stacked arms in a good position & broke ranks but was ordered not to stray away but the boys began to look around & to see what the chances where to get something to eat, seeing our haversacks where not very heavy. We had 3 crackers which lasted us four days. The first thing I came across was some sweet potatos. The next thing was to find something to carrying them in. I found an old box that was used for a doorstep. I froze to that very sudden & the young lady looked quite pitiful but I did not stop to make any apologys. After carrying them to camp I started again & found a flock of geese in the lane. They where very wild but I managed to secure two and sent them to camp by one of the boys of our mess and make tracks for a large brick . . . About ¾ of a mile I found a large plantation with lots of slick looking darkies & any amount of provisions. There was about 5 cords of side pork stacked up in an outhouse and the hams & shoulders etc from the same and such like after finding a pail. I impressed a darkie in my service and armed with a candel and pail we explored the cellar & found a molasses barrel store in the bung & fill the pail then started for the pork house. I got a fence stake & stuck it through a big side; and got a big chunk of salt which was very scarce for us and started for the camp. Some of the other boys had got dried fruit and other little [illegible]. all together we made out very well. The next morning we had to fall in at 5 o'clock in line of battle (until after daylight) expecting to be attacked by Van Dorn & we not being very strong did not want to be surprised.[38] There was only one brigade in all about 14 hundred infantry & a battery of 4 guns but we had a very good position. Comp B had the 3rd largest comp in the reg. We numbered 67 men fit for duty. Co G 68 co F 71. The others were smaller than ours. We stayed there all the following day. December 24th in the morning about 10 o'clock went to my old acquaintance at the large brick house. I was sitting in the kitchen eating sweet potatos when I see the pickets legging it for camp. I run out to see what was the matter they said there was a large body of Rebel cavelry coming slowly through the woods. I pilled up my best pail and made tracks for camp at my best gait. I run through their fruit garden. There was some white children playing around the house. The old butternut said if you are a going to fight here for God's sake look out for these children.[39] I told him I was not going to do any fighting if I could help it for I was going to evacuate his premises as quick as possible seeing I was not very well prepared to fight being armed with a tin pail only. After running about half a mile I ventured to look back to see who was coming. Not seeing anybody following I took it a little more leisurely. It turned out to be a body of our cavalry coming in with a couple of prisoners. The pickets were told in the morning we had no calvelry in that direction. If they saw any outside they was to run and inform the Col. which accounted for my mistake.[40] I went back filled my pail with sweet potatos, and shouldered another side of pork. The next morning we was in line at 5 as usual when we where ordered to march by daylight towards Ripley. Van Dorn heering of our being in Salem took another road to Ripley.[41] We marched about 8 miles to cut him off when we found we was to late he had about 10 hours ahead. We had about 100 cavelry with us. They followed them to Ripley and took a few prisoners.

CHAPTER 2

"THE HIRELING"

As the year 1863 began, William Burnham Chilvers had indeed become a soldier. He enjoyed the drill and dress and was initially proud of the Ninety-Fifth Illinois Infantry's soldierly abilities. The Ninety-Fifth traveled across several states, and Chilvers became quite successful as a forager, which supplemented his government issued rations. He heard about fighting that occurred close to him at Holly Springs in December 1862. At the beginning of 1863, Chilvers and his regiment had not seen significant combat, but 1863 would prove to be a decisive year for the Ninety-Fifth as the men became part of the ever-tightening siege around the last nail holding the South together—the citadel of Vicksburg.

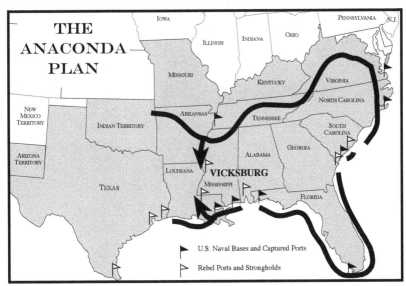

Early in the war, Gen. Winfield Scott formulated the Anaconda Plan as a strategy to suppress the Confederacy. *Map by Donald S. Frazier.*

APPROACHING VICKSBURG

ARKANSAS

BATTLE OF ARKANSAS POST, JANUARY 11, 1863:

Union Gen. John McClernand captured this point to eliminate its potential threat to the Vicksburg operations

Memphis

Corinth

Holly Springs

Helena

Yazoo Pass

Cold Water River

Yalobusha R.

Grenada

4

HOLLY SPRINGS RAID:

Confederate Gen. Earl Van Dorn led a cavalry raid, December 17-20, 1862, destroying the Union depot at Holly Springs and stopping the advance of Federal troops along the Mississippi Central Railroad

Mississippi River

Sunflower River

Ouachita River

Bayou Bartholomew

Bayou Macon

3   **5**

Yazoo River

Big Black River

MISSISSIPPI CENTRAL R. R.

MISSISSIPPI

Monroe

×1   Jackson

LOUISIANA

Tensas River

2   **VICKSBURG**

THE NAVAL SIEGE:

Union Adm. David Farragut attempts to bombard Vicksburg into submission, May-July 1862

Natchez

ATTEMPTS TO BY-PASS VICKSBURG

1. Battle of Chickasaw Bluffs, December 29, 1862: Union Gen. William Sherman fails to breach the Vicksburg defenses

2. Two different canals are attempted across DeSoto Point, but neither are completed.

3. A canal connecting the Mississippi to the Louisiana bayous via Lake Providence also fails, February 2-March 29, 1863

4. The advance by the Yazoo Pass Route is blocked by Confederates at Fort Pemberton, February 3-April 4, 1863

5. Adm. David Porter's attempts to pass up Steele Bayou to the Yazoo River is blocked by Confederates, March 16-27, 1863

Red River

PORT HUDSON

BATTLE OF BATON ROUGE, AUGUST 5, 1862

× Baton Rouge

New Orleans

Map by Donald S. Frazier.

Through the North's grand plan of Winfield Scott, best remembered as the Anaconda Plan, controlling the Mississippi River would split the South and give the North the control of commerce from the Midwest to the Gulf of Mexico. Grant sent William T. Sherman down from Memphis in the fall of 1862 to attack Vicksburg, the citadel fortress lying about half way between Memphis and New Orleans. Sherman's forces were stopped at Chickasaw Bluffs at the end of December 1862. Between this defeat and the destruction of the supply depot at Holly Springs on December 20, Grant's efforts had been completely stymied.

A river approach on Vicksburg seemed difficult due to the swampy low ground on the west bank of the Mississippi River. Options included a direct river attack, digging canals to reroute the river to bypass Vicksburg, or joining Nathaniel Banks' forces at Port Hudson and attacking from the South. The spring of 1863 would reveal the persistence and innovation of the Department Commander of Memphis, Ulysses S. Grant. Grant would live through seven failures before achieving eventual success.[1]

In January 1863, Chilvers started out the year on a surveillance expedition with the Ninety-Fifth, looking for the Southern raiders who had, just weeks before, destroyed Gen. Ulysses Grant's major supply depot at Holly Springs. On January 3, 1863, Will wrote to his uncle while at a camp near Collierville, Tennessee, about his experiences in northern Mississippi. Even though Grant captured the town of Oxford, he was far from capturing the hearts of the citizens as Chilvers noted:

> We marched 8 miles the first day & the next we whent [went] through Oxford, Miss which at that time was General Grant's headquarters. Oxford is a very pretty place almost as large as Rockford. We had marched past Gen[eral] Grant's headquarters, which took us a mile out of our road. The boys did some tall grumbling about it. As we passed through the town one lady stood at her garden gate waveing her hankerchief with a little boy by her side dressed in red, white & blue. That was about all the Union feelings I saw in the town.[2]

On December 20, 1862, Confederate forces launched two raids against their Northern foe. Gen. Nathan Bedford Forrest's troops attacked the west

Lt. Gen. Bedford Forrest was called "that devil Forrest" and "the most remarkable man our civil war produced on either side" according to Union Gen. William Tecumseh Sherman.

Tennessee towns of Carroll, Humboldt, and Trenton. The second forces were under Gen. Earl Van Dorn who successfully destroyed the main Union depot base at Holly Springs, Mississippi. Van Dorn's raid devastated Grant's efforts to advance further south on the Mississippi Central Railroad heading to Jackson, the capitol of the state. Further along in his letter dated January 3, Chilvers continued:

When we reached Holly Springs we where [were] awful tired. Some gave out before we got there. We found the town in a different state than what we left it. All the principal business part of the town was burned. The magazine was blown up, and the railroad buildings with a large amount of army stores burned or carried off. Holly Springs was one of the if not the best-looking town I ever saw.[3]

Will celebrated Christmas 1862 in a simple fashion, writing:

we halted in the woods by the side of a little slough to eat our Christmas dinner. Mine consisted of a small piece of mutton broiled by the fire with a sharp stick & a little tea. After dinner we marched back to Salem. Some of us fell out about two miles from camp to scout around. I found a lot of molasses at one house. After looking around a little while I found a two-gallon jug. A darkie woman washed it out for me.[4]

Private Chilvers interviewed some captured Southerners at Salem, Mississippi: "I had quight [quite] an interesting chat with the secesh. They were the men that was at Holly Springs."[5]

The following letter from Chilvers to the Burnhams described a previously written letter from Rebecca's sister-in-law, Mary Woodward. In her letter to the Burnhams, Mary, the wife of Rebecca's only brother George Woodward, described how her husband George was about to lose his job as a blacksmith near Sheffield. The conditions in England must have been horrific, as this young couple beg for travel expenses for themselves and their young son to America from the Burnhams, who themselves were struggling in America.

Camp Near Memphis[6]   Jan 14, 1863

Dear Uncle & Aunt

I embrace this opportunity to write these few lines to you hoping they will find you both in good health as it leaves me at present. I received a letter from you today dated Jan 4th & two yesterday dated Dec 19th & 26th & two standards dated Dec 16th & 30th.[7] I received a letter & paper at Colliersville Jan 7th which was the first we received since we left Abbeville over 3 weeks.

I don't think I was ever so glad to get hold of a letter before and I was glad to hear you was both well & having such a fine month. You say you received no letters from me since the 9th of Dec at Abbeville. I wrote you one if not two dates later. That before Abbeville & one a few days later before Oxford but the Rebels may have destroyed them at Holly Springs. They destroyed a great deal of mail there but I believe I received all of your letters & all of your stamps. I received 3 in one and 2 in another, 4 yesterday & 4 today. This will leave me 6 to the good & out of debt. I received a letter from cousin John yesterday.[8] He is at St. Louis yet. He thinks he will stay there all winter. He has got well again yesterday. I went to Memphis. I found it quight a place. It is a great business place. A great deal larger than I had any idea it was.

John Galbrath is here.[9] Some of the boys saw him but I did not. They say he is in the quartermaster department & Capt. Cringle has his finger in the pie.[10]

We hear the Democrats are kicking up quight a ruckus at home. They say the Democrats want the Governor to call the Ills. Troops home & the Chicago & Galena RR Company refuse the Treasury notes but I have seen no papers lately.[11] The Standard is the latest paper I have seen except for a little paper published in Memphis and that is not much of an account. I expect the Northern doughfaces will do all they can to oppose the government & they may carry there point & let the war last so long that the people will get tired of it & let the South have there own terms.[12] I begin to think they will get their independence for we are getting whipped on all sides. They tell us so much about whipping England.[13] I don't believe they can [do] anything. I begin to be ashamed in being in such an army. If they would only do something there would be some encouragement but they seem to be the [most] miserable set of imbeciles in the world. I have but little faith in any of them. They are in for making money & that is as far as their patriotism goes.[14]

The Rebels came across the river a few days ago and took a steamboat right from under our guns. [They] took her across the river & set fire to her and left.[15] There seems to be no enterprise in our side. If you was to hear them talk as I do you would become disgusted with them. They used to all pitch on to one at first. They use to blow so much about England. I used to take them of[f] a little now and then. You had ought to hear them blow about how many English.

You said you received a letter. . . . Mary and they would like to come to America.[16] I would like to help if I could to send something to them to come with. There is some hopes of our getting our pay about the first of next month but I don't know if we will get it at all or not & when we do I don't know how I will send it home without somebody was a comeing. I have had 6 dollars from the sutler but Capt. Loop owes me $5 which I think I shall get when we are pay'd.[17] He has had no pay at all yet. He is sick at Memphis at present. We had a letter from him the other day. He says he is getting better. I think he will get a furlough for a few days. Since I am late and super is most ready. I don't know if I can ever finish this so as to mail it or not. I have just received a letters from you dated Feb 7th & 2 stamps in it. I think I have received all the letters & stamps you sent up to the 7th Feb. I am glad to hear you still remain in good health but am sorry to hear of uncle & aunt Twelves being sick. I find according to your report that there is no raise in grain in reality if is the money that is falling. If gold is worth 56 cents premium the farmers don't get much for their grain after all. You said some of the boys has got home and represent the reg[iment] to be half sick. There is no body got home from the Reg[iment].

. . . much about the health of . . . if you have received half the letters I sent you. Randall left us a Memphis when . . . as not as comfortable a[s] usual.[18] Isaac Conner is kind of a half wited [witted] fellow and has never been worth anything to his company since he enlisted.[19] George Griffin has never been with us since we left Abbeville.[20] So he knows nothing about our health only by report. The boys was sick a great many of them when we left the boat at the Yazoo River but most of them has recovered since. I think the boys are healthier with a few exceptions then they have been since we left Collierville & they are certainly feeling better. Pete Cramer has got his discharge and started for home.[21] Edd Barker, O. Allen, W. Harder and several others are playing for a discharge.[22] I think George Marvin & Draper will get theirs.[23] I have never been excused from duty or been to the Dr. since I have been in the service. Some have been pretty lucky. I am the only man in the company [that] can say I have never had my knapsack carried but once when the whole reg[iment] had them carried. The afternoon we was comeing to Memphis. We had marched 15 miles in the morning an[d] we was rear guard that day which is the worst place to march in. You need not take too much notice of what these invalids tell when they come home. I will tell you when I write just as it is far as I know and I have a great deal better opportunity to know than a man that has been in the hospital a month or two. Wm. Stevenson is well [and] never was in better health.[24] He is awful mad at Houghman.[25] Remember me to Mr. & Mrs. Robinson & family. I am sorry that Mrs. Robinson has the ague. Remember me to Uncle & Aunt Twelves. Tell them to write. I remain as ever your affectionate nephew. W. B. Chilvers

Write soon & give me all the news. Don't waite until you get a letter from me because the mails are very uncertain her[e]. Good by

As evidenced in his letter dated January 14, 1863, Chilvers enjoyed discussing politics with his family. Both Chilvers and his uncle maintained strong abolitionist viewpoints, and, as natives of England, had Anglophile sentiments. In the fall election of 1862, the anti-war Democratic Party won the governorships of New Jersey and New York, added thirty-four seats in the House of Representatives, and gained legislative control of the state houses in New Jersey, Illinois, and Indiana. Illinois Republican Gov. Richard Yates depicted the Illinois legislature as a "wild, rampant, revolutionary body" that sought to remove his executive power.[26]

On January 25, 1863, Chilvers described an unpleasant problem that he and his fellow soldiers experienced:

Sunday Jan 25th[27]

I will try to finish this now. I have never had time to write since Wednesday we was just leaving Helena. We had a pleasant trip that afternoon & met no accidents. Two or three of our boats was fired unto while passing a small village & some two or three wounded but none dangerously. We saw them lay behind the levey when we passed but thought it was nothing strange. I thought they had been fired into some time by our own men when passing and [were] afraid to show themselves. But it proved that they were afraid to interfere with us. We had a section of artillery in sight. We tied up on the Mississippi side Thursday night and burned some houses down. We started again Friday morning quight early. The banks of the river is pretty thickly dotted with plantations from here down. We frequently see negros on the banks of the river wherever they can get out of sight of the houses waving white rags for us to come and take them. But of cours we payed no attention to them.[28] About 9 o'clock we was fired into while passing a plantation. The bullets struck the band on the wheelhouse & [to] the right of it no other damage. About 10 o'clock the flag ship saw a band of guerillas on the Arkansas shore. They dismounted & got behind the levey. But the ships have too & waited for the other boats to come up. So they could not have a chance to pitch on a single boat which of course is their best hope. They let us pass unmolested.

About 2 o'clock we come in sight of a very large fleet of boats laying in the bend of the river which proved to be the Vicksburgh expedition. There seems to be a very large fleet of boats.[29] The river is full as far down as I can see but I have no means of knowing how many there is or how many troops there is here. You will probably know a great deal better by reading the newspapers than I do.

At 9 o'clock Co. B was ordered out on picket. We was stationed at a plantation owned by Dewitt Abbers cousin.[30]

Our co. was divided into two squads. One under Lieu Keeler & the other under the capt.[31] I was with the capt. We had a very good place to stay when we was not on pickett. We had 2 picketts out at a time & there was 14 of us. It rained most of the night & all day Saturday & it was foggy. We could see more [than] 5 or 6 rods.[32] It reminded me of the banks of New Foundland. We was relieved from picket about 8 o'clock Saturday evening. It has rained so much of late and the ground is so low. The mud is about a foot deep & like walking on greese. When we got back to the boat it was all covered with mud & slush. I slept all night in a cracker box & the capt's mess chest. The cracker box was about 4 inches the lowest but I managed to lay pretty comfortable.

This morning we was ordered off the boat and marched about a mile up the river where we found a very pleasant camping ground. It is level & grassy & dry for this country. After we stacked arms the sun came out and things began to look quight cheerful. The boys are washing themselves and hunting graybacks with pretty good luck.[33] The whole regt is covered by them. It is the first time we have been troubled by such things. But if we happen to go on the boats much we shall have plenty of them in the future.

Our 2nd Lieu has gone out & has either got a discharge or a fareway to get one.[34] I don't believe the lieu has much pluck & besides he was not very well used by his superiors & he had no way of resenting it. So I can't blame him so much for getting discouraged.

Pete Cramer shot his thumb off at Memphis in a very singular way.[35] He was cleaning his gun & shot his right thumb. The boys some of them accuse him of doing it on purpose. It is a pretty hard thing to accuse a man of but he has been one of the most home sick men I ever saw & the married men generally they don't make so much blow as they used to. I never hear them threaten England now which is a good sign that they are not as war like.

Remember me to all enquiring friends & give my love to Uncle & Aunt Twelves & receive the same yourselves. Write soon we don't get our mail very regular but when they do come I am always glad to get a letter if they are a long time coming anymore at present.

Wm. B. Chilvers

Chilvers reported to his uncle in March 1863 that he enjoyed his new duty:

> I am cook this week for the first time I have been in the
> service. I would like for Aunt to tell me how to make beef
> pudding & pork dumplings. I would like to try my hand
> at it. We have lots of meat of all kinds except – mutton &
> we all draw flour So if I was any cook I could make lots of
> luxuries. We can buy salerus [celery] of[f] the sutler. We
> eat considerable rice & pancakes[36]

On March 16, 1863, Chilvers expressed to his uncle the anti-copperhead speech that Colonel Humphrey gave to his troops. The war resistance in the Midwest had recently been hotly debated in Springfield, Illinois. On January 5, the Illinois "house of representatives began adopting a series of resolutions that condemned the Emancipation Proclamation, the suspension of habeas corpus, and the administration's conduct of the war and called for an armistice and a national convention to negotiate terms of reunion."[37] A fatal illness of a Democratic member prevented the adoption of these anti-administration resolutions from being passed in the closely divided state senate. State Senator Isaac Funk delivered a fiery speech to the Illinois State Senate in January 1863 entitled, "these traitors right here."[38] The commander of the Ninety-Fifth Illinois Infantry addressed his troops regarding dissension of the war effort in their state. According to Chilvers:

> the col got up and made a short speech & told the boys
> if they ever heard a man in Ills [Illinois] say a word in
> favor of the accursed rebellion after we get home, God
> dam them, shoot them.[39] We appointed a committee of 11.
> One from each co & one from the staff to draft resolutions
> expressing the feeling of the reg toward the Union men of
> Ills & the Copperheads to be published in the Woodstock
> Sentinel & Belvidere Standard.[40] You probably will se[e]
> all the proceedings in the Standard.[41]

Pvt. William Chilvers, like many soldiers through the ages, wrote often about his commanding officers, most often in an uncomplimentary fashion. As expressed in his letter of January 25, Chilvers was frustrated by his friend 2nd Lt. Aaron F. Randall's ability to obtain a furlough. In February Chilvers noted to his uncle his ambivalent feelings towards his captain:

> Captain Loop is going home on a furlough.[42] I don't think he would take much persuadein to resign. I have no doubt but he is sick but he is sorry for the war (as the boys used to say whenever we had a tough march). In short I think he has got any too much backbone. But I may judge him harshly. He is a pretty good commander in smooth water but I have whatched him closely & have been afraid he would be found wanting in a tight spot. But I hope you will not let anyone but yourself se[e] this for I may be entirely mistaken. He has used me well.[43]

One of Grant's eight attempts to take Vicksburg was through connecting the Mississippi River to the oxbow Lake Providence and then digging a canal from this formation to Bayou Macon, which flowed into the Red River and could lead the Union ships below Vicksburg. This would then bypass the heavily fortified Confederate position. While stationed at the post of Lake Providence in March 1863, Chilvers commented on the ambitions of his officers:

> Our brigade commander is commander of the post.[44] But he is ambitious to a Brigadier commission and he thinks he has one of the best brigades in the service to

Gen. John McArthur was born in Scotland on November 17, 1826. He became a blacksmith and moved to the United States at age twenty-three. He established the Excelsior Iron Works and was captain of a Chicago Militia Unit known as the "Chicago Highland Guards." He became colonel of the Twelfth Illinois Infantry until April 1862 when he was promoted to brigadier general and placed in command of Gen. W. H. L. Wallace's troops after that officer was mortally wounded at the Battle of Shiloh in April 1862. He commanded troops at Vicksburg, Chattanooga, and Nashville. He was brevetted major general. He returned to business after the war. He died May 15, 1906, and was buried in Rosehill Cemetery in Chicago. Gen. John McArthur's division was composed of the Eleventh, Twelfth, Seventeenth, and Ninety-Fifth Illinois, the Fourteenth, Sixteenth, and Seventeenth Wisconsin, the Eleventh, Thirteenth, Fifteenth, and Sixteenth Iowa, and the First Kansas Regiments. The unit was re-designated in January 1863 in Memphis as the Sixth Division of the Seventeenth Army Corps. The corps was commanded by Maj. Gen. James. B. McPherson.

fight, and if he can get a chance to get into a fieght he would think it a good string of luck. Gen McArthur & Col Humphrey are just like him.[45] Neither of them will take any pains to keep out of a fight. There is one thing certain. They will never sell us out as Col Murphy did at Holly Springs.[46]

Throughout his letters, Chilvers wrote his uncle about his thoughts on black people. He stayed consistent in his abolitionist viewpoints and this was the reason he fought in the war. He was appalled by the poor treatment that slaves received from their liberators:

The banks of the river is pretty thickly dotted with plantations from here down. We frequently see negros on the banks of the river wherever they can get out of sight of the houses waving white rags for us to come and take them. But of cours[e] we payed no attention to them.[47]

Chilvers became frequently criticized for being an abolitionist. Most of the men in the Ninety-Fifth Infantry fought to preserve the Union, or for excitement, the lure of far places, the desire for change, patriotism, adventure, or simply for the money.[48] According to historian Bell Wiley, "a polling of the rank and file through their letters and diaries indicates that those whose primary object was the liberation of Negroes comprised only a small part of the fighting forces. A considerable number originally indifferent or favorable to slavery eventually accepted emancipation as a necessary war measure, but in most cases their support appeared lukewarm."[49] In February 1863 Chilvers wrote:

I attended in the evening & was well satisfied with the discourse but he was denounced by most of the boys as a dam[ne]d abolitionist. You would be surprised to hear the boys talk about the darkies. The most of them are so home sick they don't know what to do with themselves & they have got it into their heads that the Negroes are to blame for the war & they think they are not worth fighting for.[50] So they are continually cursing at them. If a Negro passes a white man with anything they whant they are pretty shure to take it from them. They are the smallest lot of men I ever saw.[51]

Chilvers noted that many black people came into the Union lines to perform heavy manual work in order to escape slavery. He wrote that some people even drowned in an attempt to avoid being captured and taken back to the plantation:

> Our work is progressing slowly but shure here we have no diggin[g] to do the darkies does all that. They keep coming into our lines every day there is right smart of them. Here now we have 4 of them in our company as cooks. 3 of them are young fellows from one plantation. A couple more attempted to run away and come to us. They chased them so hard with dogs they jumped into Bayou Mason & drowned rather than go back. They were cousins of our boy. There master had run them from the river to Bayou Mason– where they are fortifying.[52]

Pvt. Will Chilvers supported the idea of newly freed black men entering the service. This policy, proposed by Secretary Edwin M. Stanton, was implemented by Gen. Lorenzo Thomas.[53]

Camp at Lake Providence, Louisiana

Mar 20th 1863[54]

Dear Uncle & Aunt,

> I just received a letter from you dated March. I was glad to hear you was both well, as it leaves me at present, you said the boys are leaving pretty fast on account of the conscript bill they might just as well leave as not for all the good they would be in the army there is enough such men in the army now, I don't think much of the conscript bill anyhow.
> I think it very bad policy to drain all the men from the country and fetch them down here where there is so many able bodied negros all through the south that would be glad to enlist & I belove [believe] one negro is worth 3 white men to the government any reasons may not be very good but I have looked at it from every side, in the first place if a reg of negros was musterd in to the service here, there would be no expence of running all over the north &

offering extra bounties and the cost of transportation is no small sum, for men from the north down here, & enlist a reg of negros here & put white men over them to drill them, that would have as much patience as they would have with white men & enlist a reg of white men up north (or draft them which is worse) and in 9 months from the time they enlist (if they put them in the field & treat them equally). The negros reg would be able to work three of the white because the negro reg would be full, as there would always be a chance to recruit and fill up the place of them that died by disease or killed in battle, whereas if the white reg had not seen any very hard battles they might be able to muster 300 hundred men & another by no means a small one is the negros are in the south & they must live with us, or the south. If we invite them to come into our lines we have got to keep them & they are a burden to us if we don't use them & if we drive them from us they have got to stay with there masters & raise corn for the rebel army & I believe one able bodied negro will raise corn & pork enough to support at least 6 soldiers & what reasonable loyal man in the face of all these facts can condemn the emancipation proclamation, it is there strength & if we could brake up the institution of slavery the rebels would be whipt at once. But my advice to you is not to be drafted they cant draft you anyhow & keep out of it, this is not place for you & I know your disposition so well that if you was in my [illegible] you would be entirely out of place, soldiering is so much defendant from anyone would imagine without they try it now it just suits me to nicely as Johnny Martin says I never was more contented in my life, but dispositions are so diferant [different] you know, now if you was a single man as I am with your turn of mind I could tell you of a job to suit you exactly, but as you are situated you cant do better then to stay where you are. [part missing][55]

In April 1863, soldiers from the Ninety-Fifth Illinois Infantry were requested to volunteer to become officers of the newly formed United States Colored Troop Regiments. The organization of negro troops began at Lake Providence and Adj. Gen. Lorenzo Thomas was sent down from Washington, D.C., to instigate this government policy by commissioning and mustering in

Lorenzo Thomas, adjutant general, of the army from 1861 through 1869 was born in New Castle, Delaware, in 1804 and graduated from West Point in 1823. He did not meet the tremendous demands of that office and was demoted from Washington, D.C., to organize colored regiments in the Military Division of the Mississippi. Thomas inspected the newly created national cemeteries after the war. When President Andrew Johnson dismissed Secretary of War Stanton he replaced him with Thomas. However, Stanton refused to vacate the position by barricading himself behind the door and the process stopped by the impeachment proceedings against Johnson. Lorenzo Thomas died on March 2, 1875, and is buried in Oak Hill Cemetery, Georgetown.

the new colored regiments into the United States service. The officers were white soldiers who came from other regiments, including the Ninety-Fifth Illinois Infantry.[56] As a strong abolitionist, Chilvers seemed an ideal candidate for a position working with these newly freed men. He wrote:

> after we got back to camp the Col[onel] requested Lieu[tenant] Keeler to get a list of names of those that would like a commission.[57] Those men who had always condemned the arming of black men where the first to put their names down. When we whent to headquarters there was so many of us that the Col[onel] sent us back & told the lieu to select 4 names out of the list. One for capt[ain], two for lieu[tenant] & one for orderly seargent. There was so many at Lieu[tenant] Pells.[58] I saw there no chance for a commission. So I put my name down for orderly.[59]

Chilvers wrote his uncle about the terrible treatment that Union soldiers gave former slaves:

> Lake Providence   April th 1863[60]
>
> Dear Uncle & Aunt.
>
> I embrace this opportunity to write you once more & I hope these few lines will find you both in good health as it leaves me at present.
>   I received a letter from you dated April 12th and a paper, cap & loop arrived Monday night. He brought the letter and medicine you sent. I was very glad you sent the

Thomas Humphrey was elected as the lieutenant colonel of the Ninety-Fifth Illinois in August 1862. He was promoted to colonel at Lake Providence, Louisiana, after the resignation of Lawrence Church in January 1863. He was popular with the troops he led during the Vicksburg, Red River, Missouri, and Nashville Campaigns. He was killed at the debacle at the Battle of Guntown (Brice's Cross Roads).

medicine but I did not expect it so soon. I think I am going to have a touch of the piles again but I shall not take anything until it troubles me.[61]

Capt. Loop looks well.[62] You would have been amused to have seem how some of them acted when he come back they "flock" around him as if they whant to kiss him. They yell & hooted and jumped around him as if they were crazy & some of them (& not a few either) got so drunk they could not navigate & I am sorry to say the Capt. & Liet. Was not a bit better then the rest.[63] The officer of the day ordered them to their quarters once or twice but they did not heed him. The Col. sent a man down to request them to make less noise.[64] The only satisfaction he got was vulgar insulting reply from the Capt. Now I have always like the Capt. For a commander because he has a military turn with him and on the whole is a good man to get along with a Company but such disgraceful conduct (in my opinion) ill becomes an officer. And any man guilty of such conduct looses the esteem & respect of all sober and sensible men. But I hope it will not be repeated.

You said you wished I could get a furlough. I should like to come home and see you but that is impossible. There was some talk of giving furloughs so as to let 5 percent away at a time that would give our company about 3 a month. & I would be one of the last so you may see ho much of a chance I would have. If they was to commence right off. But they have not commenced yet. The Col. told us on batallion drill one day that there was some chance of getting furloughs but they was for men that had don't their duty and behaved themselves well in every respect & no other man should get one if he could help it. But we all know how such things go. They are always recommended by the commanders of the Co. and the men that does the least duty are generally the ones to get the most favours.

But thank god I ask no odds of any of them. As long as my health continues good I have never had to ask any favors of them yet and I don't intend to until I am obliged. We have not moved yet. The impression is that we shall stay here after all but of course we never know.

There is a great deal of drunkenness here at present. The first Kansas has got back again.[65] They have been on old river most all the time we have been here. They are a miserable drunken low life set. They are always drunk when they can get anything to drink. You cant walk on the levey at any time without seeing a squad of them drunk and cu___ around. And abusing every darkey they meet. It is nothing for them to shove a darky in the river or kick him when they meet them I was on the levey this morning I saw one of the Kansas blackguards walking on the levee. He met an old lame black man with a walking stick, which he at once took away from him. The old man begged him to give it back to him as he was lame. But he walked off with a god damn you I am lame too. After carrying It a little way he would probably [throw] it away as it was of no use to him. Such things are of frequent occurancy and some things a great deal worse.

Chilvers commented on the recently approved draft to Burnham.[66] The draft became a frequent topic between men throughout both the North and the South. There was a sense of despair particularly in the winter of 1862–1863 in the North due to a series of military reverses. These included a failure to take Richmond, the humiliating loss at Fredericksburg, a bogged down advance by Rosecrans following the Battle of Murfreesboro, and failure to capture Vicksburg. Twice the Confederates had stymied Grant that winter through the Holly Springs Raid as well as Sherman's failure at Chickasaw Bluffs.[67]

If George Burnham was drafted, it would be devastating to the property which Chilvers and the Burnhams owned as there would not be a man to farm the land. Chilvers seemed to mock the manhood of some of the draftees, particularly the wealthy, that would be forced into the war:

> There prospects looks bad now congress has pass'd that naughty conscript bill to frighten all the young gentlemen away from there Mamas.[68] Poor things I don't know what will become of them.[69]

Chilvers frequently took care of his own medical problems, and often requested home remedies from his aunt, Rebecca Burnham:

> Some of the boys has the piles pretty bad & we can't get the stuff here.[70] If you would mix up a mess and put it in a tin box of some kind & send me enough of the syrup of buckthorn for two or three messes I think I can get the other things of[f] the Dr.[71]

Chilvers wrote about illnesses that beset the Illinois troops. Infectious diseases ran rampant with soldiers in close quarters as disorders such as measles and respiratory illnesses were easily transmitted. Other problem disorders included typhoid fever, waterborne illnesses, and mosquito-borne diseases such as malaria and yellow fever that were quite common in the rivers and swamps of the Mississippi basin. He also mentioned self-inflicted injuries and ways soldiers caught the white feather of cowardice.

Wiley wrote that, "dissatisfaction with army service became so great during this period that a rash of self-mutilation broke out among the soldiers. An Illinois Yank shot off the trigger finger of his right hand and a Vermont soldier got rid of three fingers while on picket by setting off his musket with a stick. A Massachusetts private, after failing in an effort in blowing his toe off, succeeded a few days later in injuring his right forefinger to such an extent that it had to be amputated. The evil of self-injury became so widespread that authorities ceased granting discharges to those guilty of the practice."[72]

Obtaining news was particularly difficult for soldiers fighting in the Trans-Mississippi area. Private Chilvers noted:

> We heard all kinds of rumors here. Richmond was taken & Vicksburgh & all the states had come back in the Union.[73] You have no idea what while lots of stories circulates through a camp when they are cut off from communication with the world.[74]

In March, Will described two of his friends who are improving from illnesses. He also informed his uncle to be wary of stories that are circulating in Boone County from homesick soldiers who he did not think were reliable sources of the army's activities:

> Cordiean is getting better but he has the rumatism yet.[75] But he looks a great deal better. Wm. Stevenson is well & harty [hearty].[76] You need not believe any of the stories you hear from the homesick chickens that has come home. For they are sure to make the worst of it. I will always try to keep you well informed but it seems you don't get my letters.[77]

The Holly Springs Raid led by Gen. Earl Van Dorn was a major setback for the Northern invaders as their forward supply depot was destroyed. Chilvers wrote:

> The col commanding had warning in time to have barricaded the streets with cotton bales.[78] There being plenty of it there. But he made no effort what ever to defend the place. The Rebels under Van Dorn all calvery came in a little before daylight and all our men was scattered all over the city and completely surprised.[79] There were only two companys that showed any fight at all.[80] The others never formed a line. What few calvery was there charged on them and done nobly but they where only a handful. They fought until they were surrounded when they cut there way out. But lost 5 killed and a great many wounded (some has since died of their wounds) & about 90 prisoners. The Rebels took Dr. Jones & all the sutlers in town prisoners.[81] But Dr. Jones told them he was a surgeon in the army & Van Dorn set him at liberty – but he lost most of his stock. The Rebels held the place all day (Dec 20th). They paroled all our men before they left. While they where [sic] in town the city made a great deal of fuss over them.[82]

In late January 1863, Chilvers participated in a scouting and raiding party in north Louisiana:[83]

> But I must tell you of a little bit of a skirmish I was in the other day about 200 of us was mounted on mules & about

50 of the 3rd Ills, cavalry.[84] There was from each co. from our reg. & I happened to be one of them. We started on a scout to pick up cattle & se[e] if we could run a cross any of the butternut gentry proleing around after traveling about 12 miles or advance saw a couple of secesh scouts.[85] I had just made up my mind to examine the contents of my haversack when I heard awful yelling ahead I ever heard. We all started forward but my mule was the slowest in our company & I soon fell a little behind. But he proved to have a good bottom & after we had run about a mile I began to gain ground. You should have seen the mule fly and some of the boys was laughing . . . I came with no damage but lost of my dinner which was no small loss as I had rather an extra one.[86]

Being stationed in the swamps of Louisiana and Mississippi made it difficult for the troops to obtain reliable information and decipher the ultimate plans of General Grant. Eight different attempts at capturing Vicksburg were formulated. Chilvers stated on March 31:

Some think there is going to be a fight in a few days & some think there will not be a fight at all at Vicksburgh. They think the intention is to run past . . . troops below Vicksburgh . . . mouth of the Red River & . . . it so the Rebels can't get supplies from Texas and start an expedition from the Yazoo across the country to the Jackson & Vicksburgh which is the principal & only road they can get supplies or reinforcements from the east to any amount. They say there is 4 or 5 miles of tressel work at one place and if that can be destroyed it could not be repaired in time to be of any use to them.[87]

In January, Will wrote his uncle about mutual friends:

Remember me to Stephen Stork & family when you see them.[88] I wrote to them but received no answer. Give my respects to the Robinsons. I have not seen George since I was at Waterford.[89] William Stephenson is well the same with Bruce & Butler.[90]

H. Houghman was one of the spectators. He had come in with his wife & child a day or two before and saw us coming into town. He has been with us ever since but I have not had a chance to talk with him. I saw Harriet two or three times in their carriage when we had been marching passed them. But I had never had a chance to speak to her. She looked quight natural. She had a young child in her arms. They have a very nice looking carriage and two mules. I don't know whether they are with us now or going to Memphis. I have not seen them since we first came to Collierville but they may be here now.[91]

Chilvers wrote frequently to comment on their farm operations. He was usually encouraging and uplifting to his uncle:

I am glad the colts are doing well and I wish you would keep them. I think they will be worth something some time. I think Illinois is ahead of any country I have seen yet. All things considered & the prospects are certainly better for Ills than any other state in the Union in case of peace being restored. I think I will like Ills better when I come home than I did before.[92]

In an early February letter to his uncle, Chilvers discussed a letter from a girlfriend who informed him of life back home in Illinois:

Hattie tells me there has been a great wolf hunt this winter some where in your neighborhood.[93] I did not think there were any wolf there worth bothering about. Enclosed is Hattie's letter. I got a few lines from person which I shall enclose to Aunt. Tell her she must not make too much fun because I am foolish enough to let her know who I corispond with. The last line I wrote to Hattie I thought I would have a little fun with Esther & she saw fit to notice it. I think I shall improve the opportunity now. Perhaps I can do better than I did before[94]

Grain seems to be very high this winter. I expect neighbor Strait will come out pretty good after all if he only held out long enough with his corn. I wish you and Steven had bought me out but I suppose we have got to wait awhile before our luck turns but I find it is a good thing to keep a stiff upper lip. We may come out all right after all I don't feel discouraged yet.[95]

Chilvers and his unit then became part of the great movement to capture Fortress Vicksburg. The maneuvers involved were anything but direct and the Union had great difficulty and preparing for their final assault on the city.

CHAPTER 3

"MOST FOOLISH PIECE OF BUSINESS"

The siege of Vicksburg began on May 19, 1863, when Gen. Ulysses S. Grant crossed the Mississippi River and, through a series of moves, isolated the city from the rest of the Confederacy. The six-week siege was fought by the Ninety-Fifth Illinois Infantry including Pvt. William B. Chilvers. Chilvers was often under fire as he was stationed at an entrenchment outside the Confederate forces near the Third Louisiana Redan.[1] Chilvers experienced the horrors of war as well as the excitement of victory during the largest battle of his military career.

Through a massive attack, the Union troops entered Mississippi at Grand Gulf and moved east.[2] They won the Battle of Raymond and then proceeded to capture another capitol of the South—Jackson.[3] The capitol of the state of Mississippi was defended marginally by Confederate Gen. Joseph E. Johnston, the commander of the Department of the West.[4] Grant's forces easily routed the Southern forces. After burning Jackson on May 14, 1863, the Northern troops began tightening the noose around its ultimate target—Vicksburg. Southern forces attempted to prevent Grant's army from moving towards Vicksburg at the battles of Champion Hill and the Big Black River Bridge.[5] However, they were unable to stop the eventual siege of this citadel on the Mississippi by the Northern forces, who were well led, maneuverable, and lived off the land. Lt. Gen. John Pemberton received conflicting orders between the District Commander, Johnston, who told Pemberton to leave Vicksburg and save his troops, and President Jefferson Davis who ordered him to hold the citadel at all costs.[6]

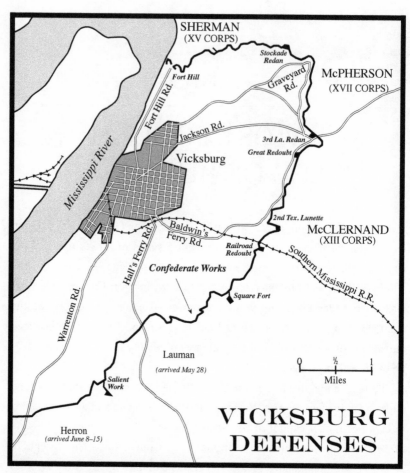

Map by Donald S. Frazier.

Upon arriving at Vicksburg, General Grant attempted massive assaults on May 19 and May 22.[7] The Ninety-Fifth Illinois Infantry suffered heavy casualties both of these days. Chilvers wrote to his aunt and uncle a few days after the second assault, stating:

> Camp in rear of Vicksburg[8]   May 27th 1863
> Dear Uncle & Aunt
>
>   I take this opportunity to drop you a few lines to let you
> [know] where I am & that I am well & hope these few lines

will find you both enjoying the same blessing. I found my regt last Saturday evening after a great deal of trouble & I tell you I found an awful hard looking regt. They had to march 9 days in succession before they got here & the day before I found them they had been in an awful fight. They had to charge up one of the worst hills. I even say it was completely covered with fallen timber. It was almost impossible for a man to climb up it and bullets fell among them like hail stones. I heard the battery men say it was the worst place they ever saw for a lot of men to charge.[9]

It seems to me it was the most foolish piece of business I ever saw. Our men was cut all to piece without accomplishing anything or even firing a gun. Out of the 14 in our mess was badly wounded and one killed (Jot. Westbury).[10] I was not there so there was only 13 in the fight. Wm Stevenson got two musket balls through the thigh & his finger grazed John Horan musket-ball in both shoulders–bad, Orlando Loper–Bad-musket–ball in shoulder, David Cox finger off, John Saxton thumb off, Alex Cummings in forehead, John Martin in shoulder bad, James Maning in shoulder bad, Ben Easton thigh bad, Alfred Horton thigh.[11] A great many others struck with spent balls and holes through their cloths, hats, haversacks, canteens & such things. Walt Harder put his foot under a wagon wheel & got it jam'd up pretty bad.[12] Charley Shockly stuck the bayonet through his foot yesterday & gone to the hospital.[13] Cordiean Bruce got hit in the shoulder but stay'd with his company.[14] Basset of Bonus was killed dead.[15] Capt Cornwell killed.[16] Capt Manyor of Harvard was mortally wounded & died before they got him to the hospital.[17] Capt Cook is suppose'd mortally wounded.[18]

Col Humphrey got wounded in the left foot in the first days fight but left the regt the next day is now in the hospital.[19] Everyone in the regt loves him. They are continually praising him for his bravery on the field & for the way he worked the boys on the march. He would ride around the boys most of the night while the boys was resting for battle & salt which they where greatly in need of. Having only 1/2 rations with them. The general said a braver man never live'd.

Last Sunday I was over to the hospital all day visiting the wounded. They all appeared cheerful. Wm. Stevenson takes it first rate. I think he will soon get well if he has good luck although he is wounded very bad, right through the thick of the thigh but no bones broke. Our boys are most of them bad but no bones broke. Schyler Wakefield lost his leg above the knee.[20] They had taken him down to the river before I got there. It was an awful sight to se[e] them laying on the ground. They had built a shade over them with brush.

The surgeons was cutting and slashing them around on a table and the poor fellows a groneing [groaning] and grateing their teeth. It was enough to make a grown man's hair stand stait [straight] on his hair.[21] There was several ladies around waiting on them & dressing their wounds. The boys used to wonder what use them women was following the army around last winter when we was on the march. They have found out now.[22]

But I must conclude. Remember me to all enquirering friends. Give my love to Uncle & Aunt Twelves. Except [Accept] my love & best wishes for yourselves, write soon.

I remain your affectionate nephew.

With the unsuccessful attacks, the Federals built fortifications of their own to prevent the Southerners leaving Vicksburg, as well as positioning troops to prevent a force under Johnston from coming to Pemberston's aid, a relief force that never materialized. After the quick attack when the Union troops reached Vicksburg, rumors ran rampant about further massive frontal assaults as the Northerners inched forward to reach the Southern entrenchments.

I should think the citizens of Harvard would waite & find out their information is correct before they made so much fuss.[23] They may have to waite some time yet before Vicksburg falls if it ever do. Although we are confident of our ultimate success. Yet we don't know but some unforeseen events may defeat us yet. In short we are never shure of anything until we get it. We still hold our old position we keep building roads & breastworks. I was at work this morning from 4 to 9. We keep planting batteries. We was a cutting a road around a hill about 300 yards from the Reb works. The Rebel sharp shooters were on one side of us and our men on the other. The bullets kept whistling over us pretty sharp but we were out of danger being about 50 ft. below the range.[24]

I should think it was rather scaley business to get up so close to the Rebels works. There is a good deal of interest felt here about the termination of the siege.[25]

It is the general opinion that it will nearly end the war but the Army in the East lets the Rebels go more they please. I think the war will last till we whipe [wipe] them out in the West and go down there and help them out of the scrape for I don't believe they will ever get out of themselves.[26]

Chilvers, positioned in the trenches and rifle pits which surrounded the Southerners, was often under fire, and used this time of prolonged sitting to write letters back home. He mentioned friends and girlfriends in Illinois, family in England, and occasionally his thoughts on existing on the front line in battle. The hardships of battle combined with boredom produced a sense of isolation, and Chilvers noted:

In Rear of Vicksburgh[27]

June 5th 1863

I again seat myself to write you a few lines which I hope will find you in good health & spirits as it leaves me at present. I suppose you are aware we not got Vicksburgh yet but you may rest assured we will have it and the nest of traitors inside. Since I have returned to the army I have more faith in Grant than I ever had before. I think he is persuing the right course now he has the enemy so entirely surrounded. That it seems impossible for them to get away & in my humble opinion it would be bad gener-alship to crowd them too hard while there is any chance to strengthen our position. The enemy has a very strong position & one very easy to defend against immense odds. On the other hand our position is almost or quight as strong as theirs & would give us almost the same odds as them where they to take to cut their way out. So you se[e] after we have strengthened our position as much as possible we run less risk in case we make an assault & get repulsed as we did before. But I tell you it is awful tiresome to lay around here doing nothing. If we had our tents & knapsacks it would not be as bad but we have nothing with us not even a second shirt. I took mine last night & washed it but we have a very poor chance to wash our cloths. A small brook with less water in it than what Mr. Robinson's ditch at any time during last summer has to serve us all to wash in.[28] So you may judge it is not very clean. It smells more like sink than anything else but I managed to get it cleaner than I expected under the circumstances. I had to go without a shirt until it dried which was quight a risk to run for we never know the moment we may be called upon. Although we have layd here for 2 weeks we may have to leave at a moments notice.

I could not have believed how lonesome I am without Wm. Stevenson.[29] You se[e] we have always been together since we have been in the service & it doesn't seem like the same co. to me. Everything seems so odd. I hope he & the rest of the boys will soon be back again with us. Smith Marvin is my partner now.[30] He whent out last night as guard to the Pioneer Corps and was ordered to come in just before daylight so as to get in before the enemy could se[e] them.[31] But he & Henery Munger & a corporeal from co. E are missing.[32] It is thought they stayd too long to get in without being seen & so had to stay all day. If they did they will be likely to suffer a great deal from heat & thirst or it may be that they are wounded or kill'd. A party of us intend to go out & search for them as soon as dark unless they return sooner. But it is probably some blunder of the officers as usual. I suppose you are all eager to get the papers & se[e] what is going on. You will probably be bother'd to know exactly where to find our position. From the reports of the newspapers our regt has been in the 2nd brigade (since we left Providence), of McArthur's Division. Under Gen Ranson we are on the extreme right of McPherson's [17th] Army Corps.[33] The 8th Missouri are on our right being on the extreme left of Sherman's Corps who holds the right. McPherson the center & McClerndand the left.[34]

Gen McArthur is gone with his 3rd brigade to the rear with Frank Blair to watch for Johnston or any other Gen that may attempt to reinforce Vicksburg or attack us in the rear.[35] There was a rumor in camp yesterday that McArthur had come in collision with a small force of Rebels & they had put a flag of truce on the house in the viscinity, & the gen sent a capt with his co. to acertain what was wanted when the enemy fired on them from behind the house &

Gen McArthur order'd a battery to open on the house.[36]
Which they did, destroying the house & killing several
women who was in the house at the time. You have the
story for what it is worth. I got it from Adgt Keeler. But if
it is true you will hear about it through the papers.

The 13th is on the left. Their Col is here today visiting
our officers. There has been a great number of the boys
to visit us but it is so far of I have not been down to see
them yet. They came without leave but they are the greatest regt to run around I ever saw. If we was to go of[f]
from our regt without leave as they do, we would have old
Tom after us with sharp sticks.[37] I have not seen George
Robinson.[38] I stood on the side of the road when his regt
passed us Sunday the 24th but they was scater'd so much I
did not se[e] him. I enquired after his health & was told he
as well. I received a letter from Canton last evening they
was all well. But Edmund had lost his eldest boy.[39] He had
always been subject to fits & they kept getting worse as he
grew older until they finaly kill'd him.[40] I just heard some
of the boys say a mail had come but [I] think it is a false
report as I don't hear any more of it. I have not got that
letter from grandfather spoke of in yours yet I have only
received one from you since I left home & that I was a
very small one. I received a notice from the Memphis Post
Office a few days a[go] that there was a letter bearing my
adress at that office without a stamp. I thought it must be
the letter from England but as they only call'd for a 3 cent
stamp concluded it could not be it. I began to despair of
getting it as it has been so long on the road. I believe I will
walk a while and se[e] if we get a mail this evening before
I seal this. June 6th There was no mail last night so I concluded to waite any longer so you will have to be satisfied
with this. For I can't think of anything else without tell[ing]
you about the fruit which I believe I have never mention'd
yet. Well plums are some of them ripe and them that is not
ripe are just right to be stew. Apples are large enough to
make sauce & we have a good supply of sugar so we have
fruit every meal. The woods are intersperced with black
mulberry trees & they are ripe.[41] When I was at Young's
Point I could get all the blackberries I whanted. The boys
would go and gather a pattend pail full of large berries in
an incredible short time & sell them on the boats for 75

cents. The corn on these hills is not very large but in the little swails it is about tasseling out, & I expects it is about to silk on the Louisiana low lands opposite Vicksburg. Smith Marvin & Henery Munger came in after dark last evening.[42] They stayd toolate so had to lay under the enemys works all day with nothing to hide them from view but some small brush & a little stunted cane. They saw some Rebs during the day but dare not fire on them for fear of exposing themselves. They suffer'd considerable for water during the time. Some of the boys say's our mail is not sent North but detain at head quarters until we occupy the city but I shall continue to write as opportunity offers whither they come through or not.

Remember me to the Robinson's & all enquiring friends. Give my love to Uncle & Aunt Twelves. Write often & tell me all the news & how your crops get alone & the price of produce & how far they are getting a long with the conscripture. I still think you will be to blame to stand the draft as it will be the means of making you looseing your home. Under any other circumstances it would be different. No more at present Accept the love & best wishes of your nephew.

Wm. B. Chilvers

This is the 7th since I left home. I am a going to se[e] if I can't tire you a reading my letters. If I whant you try and tire me first (good bye)

His boredom was intermittently and abruptly interrupted by the whiz of bullets and projectiles that barely missed him in his tenuous position on the front line. Despite vicious fighting during the day, Chilvers described:

the Rebs & our boys talk across the lines every night but our officers won't allow our men to meet them between their lines & ours any more as they often propose. But they each get on top of the pits in plain view of each other these moon light nights and they never fire without giving each other time to hunt their holes. They are very sociable with us but always take pain to find out whether we are from. Ill or not they won't speak to the Wisconsin troops if they know it.[43] They got the Rebs up two or three times & then fired on them.[44]

He wrote that some Southerners deserted and crossed the lines.[45] He later penned, however, that some of the men presumed to have given up their will to fight turned out to be spies.

Despite the siege of Vicksburg in June 1863 with its hopes of a Northern victory, there was a lot of dissension in Illinois. Many Midwesterners were not convinced that the sacrifices of war were worth preventing the South from having it's independence. Chilvers wrote his uncle:

> they tell me there is likely to be trouble in Ills with the cop-
> perheads again.[46] I hope the Union men will handle them
> without gloves if they undertake to kick up any rumpus.
> There will be a great many of our boys home after we get
> Vicksburg & you can count on them for help. Men that has
> gone through the hardships and privation incident to a sol-
> diers life to sustain their government are not the men to put
> up with the foul mouth traitors at home. You may depend
> upon it the Copperheads of Belvidere will have a hard road
> to travel when our boys get home if they don't keep mute.
> We are in a place to see the effect of their disloyalty.[47]

After weeks of siege, Vicksburg finally fell to Union forces. Following the surrender of General Pemberton to Grant, the previously "bloodless 95th" Illinois was one of the first Union troops to march into the captured city on July 4, 1863.[48]

> We marched through the town about noon. The streets
> & windows was crowded to see the Yankees come in to
> town. The citizens seem to be surprised to see us march
> into town in such order & without molesting either per-
> sons or property. When they found out we was not going
> to disturb them they treated us very kindly many of them
> carrying water for us to drink & waveing hankerchiefs.[49]

Chilvers wrote the Burnhams in the summer of 1863 about the ambiguity of love, as he tried to decipher his romantic feelings concerning a girlfriend:

You said Richard Sinten was disappointed because I did not go to se[e] them.[50] You know if he don't that I could not go to see them all in the little time I was at home & such bad weather too. I supose there is some that will feel more disappointed than they do & now I am away & think more about I think I use one person in particular very mean & I tell you I feel ashamed of it. After pretending to entertain diferant feelings toward her.[51] You probably know who I refer to. I received a letter from her since I have been here. One she wrote before I come home & I am at loss what to do. I am ashamed to answer it & yet I feel as if I have ought. I don't see what possessed me while I was at home. That I did not call on her. It could not have done any harm but I am an odd kind of fellow. Anyway, always doing something I don't mean too. But I suppose she won't care much about it, but that don't make my unmanly treatment of her any better. You said you thought Israel Wood had a great mind to marry Hattie.[52] Now I don't think anyone that would advice him different (after what had pass'd) would do right. Because if it is true what was told about her it is his duty to marry her. Let her be what she will and he is & imprincibel'd man if he don't do it. We all know he was continually with her.[53]

In late May 1863, Chilvers updated the Burnhams on his cousins, the Fillinghams, who lived in Canton, Illinois.

I received a letter from Canton last Monday.[54] They was all well at the time. John was at home yet.[55] I wish I could have made them a visit while I was at home but you know it was impossible. But I am afraid they will feel disappointed when they know I've been home without visiting them. I wrote to them today. I received a letter & paper you sent me before I come home.[56]

Chilvers mentioned his family back in England to the Burnhams. Chilvers had a large extended family despite being an orphan.

I received a letter from grandfather the 8th Grandfather & Spooner where improving.[57] The others where all well.

Grandfather was at work on the roads for 9 shillings a week. The letter was written by two different persons. One part was written by a lady & I think it was your daughter Maria [that] wrote it.[58] At all events it was a very good hand. She will be 15 years old in July. Next Grandfather says they are spoiling her. She goes to saboth school & meeting twice of a Sunday but they don't know about her to go anywhere much which was enough I think to spoil any young girl. But old folks will have their notions.

My Aunt Susan is married again to Isaac Watson & has one child.[59] Uncle Thomas is married & lives at Wisbeach & works on the railroad.[60] They have two children. Cousin Lidda is married to Bartlett Bailey.[61] They Have 3 children. Wm. Spooner has 3 & James & Esther 4.[62] So you se[e] they are all prosperous if they don't get sick.[63]

Private Chilvers acknowledged in a letter in the summer of 1863 that his relative, Matthew Twelves, was an alcoholic, and assured George that he was not naïve to Twelves' attempts at manipulation.

I would send a rose this time but my paper is heavier then usual so I shall have to wait until next time, in your last letter you spoke of Matthew guarding with you on my accord.[64] I think you had ought to know me better then to think I would bare anything about what he said or so take any notice of him yourselves. You know I have always tried to use him as well as I could notwithstanding his bad habits of drinking. I have always thought it was our duty to try and reform him by setting a good example ourselves & I think if nothing else would keep me from drink, seeing my friends & relatives Drunk would.[65]

The Ninety-Fifth Illinois Infantry stayed in Vicksburg briefly. As part of Ransom's brigade, the regiment left Vicksburg and entered Natchez on July 13.[66] No opposition met the Northerners in Natchez, and most of the citizens seemed to support the victors, particularly when they discovered that their town would neither be ransacked nor burnt. The Confederates used Natchez as a post where cattle from Texas were driven to feed Gen. Joseph E. Johnston's army in the East.[67]

Brig. Gen. T. E. G. Ransom's command included the Ninety-Fifth Illinois during the Vicksburg and Red River Campaigns. Gen. William T. Sherman wrote, "I saw Ransom during the assault of the 22nd of May . . . I then marked him as of the kind of whom heroes are made."

While in Natchez, Chilvers received a letter from his friend and former officer, Lieutenant Randall.[68] 2nd Lt. Aaron Randall left the service several months prior to the Vicksburg siege. Randall wrote Chilvers and congratulated his victorious former compatriots.

Wm. B. Chilvers Esq.[69]

Belvidere, Ills   July 12 / 63

My dear friend and comrade

Your truly kind and interesting letter bearing date June 30 was received yesterday on my return home from an absence of a week at Maringo where I am now engaged in the capacity of a clerk in the office of the Provost Marshall for the 2nd Congressional District of this state.[70] So great a length of time had elapsed since I bade you adieu in Chicago without receiving any letter from you that I had about given up all expectations of hearing from you - but I am happy to learn that I have not yet been forgotten by my old comrades in Co. B. Rest assured that none of you are forgotten by me and it is my sincere hope that you and every one of you will be permitted again to return home to your friends crowned with honor and the laurels of victory. The glad news has been received that Vicksburg has fallen after a long and bloody siege and we must admit a brave defense on the part of its garrison rebels though they were. It must have been a proud and glorious hour to you and all of you on the 4th of July when you saw the stars and bars lowered and the glorious of flag come up in place of that emblem of treason. I felt proud that my old regiment was one of the first that entered that rebel stronghold and have often wished that I could have stand with you in the exciting scenes which preceded its final surrender. It was worth a lifetime to have been permitted to have seen the surrender, the capture of Vicksburg and the terrible defeat that Lee's army suffered in Pennsylvania on one day accompanied with the bloody repulse of the rebels in their attack upon Helena.[71]

All upon the 4th has put a very different complexion upon affairs in the north. Copperhead stock has gone out of sight and there are now none who will admit that they ever owed any interest to in the corrupt party. All is rejoicing and hope bright with a prospect of a speedy and near close of the war and a safe return of you all. God speed the day when this unholy rebellion will have been crushed as it [illegible] bids fair to be and the ringleaders will have received their justly merited deserts.

But to come to others matters. It is painful to learn of the death of so many of my old comrades on the field of battle or of wounds received while making that unfortunate assault on the 22nd of May.[72] A day that will long be remembered with painful reflections by many in Boone County. Horan and Easton died at Memphis. Sometime since the former was brought home and buried.[73] A brave soldier was killed when David Steed [illegible] was fall in the rifle pit.[74] Poor fellow his heart was filled unto hope and sight [illegible] anticipations of a safe return home. When I last saw him a happy reunion with his family when the war was over. Say for Charley for me that he has my fullest smpathies in his loss. I can not say more. So many of Co. B have gone that it makes me feel sad to think that so many of those brave boys who stand [illegible] with me during the many miles the hardships of the campaign in Central Mississippi have gone whose no noville [illegible] will amise [illegible] there. Though they are gone and will never return their heroic deeds will be ever tranince [illegible] up and rememberance by a grateful country and may God deal midly [illegible] with their friends in their losses.

Mr-an about ready for making a draft in Boone County and undoubtedly several days before this will have [illegible] you it will have taken place. The draft will be very heavy and some of the Copperheads will have the opportunity to either shell out $300 with which to procure their exemption or else shoulder a musket along side of those whom they have [illegible] Sought to discourage or have styled as hired [illegible] of a despotic administration when they do come handle their rough [illegible]. Still many good men will be drawn who are true and willing comrades by your side on all occasions men who will go willingly. This class you will welcome as volunteers. I have made application to again enter service and am expecting daily to receive my papers and orders to report to duty. When I shall go is now impossible to guess. My health is not as good as when you last saw me and I am now under a strict course of treatment and it is very doubtful if I am ever again a well man.[75] B. Woodward has made application for a position in the Invalid Corps and will lungs being very much afflicted.

I saw Siutenmauth [illegible], Van Eason [illegible], Walker and Dow yesterday in Marringo.[76] Walker will soon be able to return to his regiment. Maj. Avery is at home doing well and will soon be able to report for duty.[77]

Say to all of my friends in Co B and you know who they are that I would write to each and all of them but one letter must do for all. I will try and get [illegible] around in the course of time. Tell them that Dr. Mimm is very sick with little prospect of recovery and that we heard that he was wounded in the fauteuil.[78] How much commissary did he lose? Also that his people have a contraband at work for Steve. Ask him if he intends keeping his resolution of last winter in that aspect. Tell him also that I saw Addie Little today.[79] She looked smiling and happy and in fact all of the girls of his acquaintance are looking as well as could be expected while he is absent. Give my respects to Corporal Webb and Mosby [illegible], Stevenson (S & W), Shorty Curtis and to all as if received [illegible].[80] Write me and give me some incidences of the siege and I will try to keep you posted on matters and things here. If you can I wish you would send me a revolver of the navy size from the spoils captured in Vicksburg if you can obtain one, if not, that something as a memento of the place.[81] Send it by express at my expense. But I must close with the urge to write soon and often and believe me.

Ever Your Sincere Friend
A. W. Randall Jr.

After entering Natchez, the regiment stayed in that location for a few months.[82] The troops speculated on what Southern location would be their next target.

Natchez, Miss[83]   Aug 12th 63

Dear Uncle & Aunt

I received your of July 30th & was glad to hear you was both well & getting along so well with your harvest. Since I last wrote you my health has improved rapidly. I commenced to do duty last Sunday. Our duty has been very light. We have had nothing much to do but tend our horses. We whent out 5 or 6 miles after cattle Monday. We have not been out since. We expect to get two months pay tomorrow. Our knapsacks came this morning & six of our convalescents that had been left behind at Vicksburg. The band has all come down but there is talk again of our going back to Vicksburg. The 45th has come down & two boat loads of troops besides. The boys dread to go back to Vicksburg so much.[84]

They think any time any troops come down they are come to relieve us. We had rather go to Mobile than Vicksburg but there is no place [that] suit[s] us like Natchez. In the first place we have such a beautiful camp ground lit up with gas every night to say nothing of the nice shade trees & the air seems so pure. Some of the residence is paradise compared with anything of the kind in the North & they most of all are neat & pretty with nice hedges trimmed neatly with arches over the gate & beautiful shrubbery. In short I think I could content myself here if I owned a little place. & the institutions where changed. But I could never live contented where the accursed institution of slavery existed. The more I se[e] of it the more I hate it. I have seen scores of men, women, & children whiter than I am in slavery. I saw beautiful looking young girls at church last Sunday sitting with others black as a stove pipe. Some of them where free born & some slaves. But all call'd niggers. They dress very rich (they seem to have a great taste for dress). I noticed one woman in particular her hair was long & black. I should judge she was about 25 years old. She had two little boys with her which I took to be her children. One of the boys was whiter than I am & his hair was long & light colourd. The other was most as white but his hair was black. In any other country but this they would pass for hansome white boys. The woman herself was very hansome. It is almost impossible to find any of the features or characteristics of the African race about her. But she is a damned nigger for all that. I tell you it is awful to witness the effects of slavery.

I will tell you of a little incident as one of our boys told it to me. When the company came in from pickett one morning he said when they was on their post a black boy came riding up the road. He was met by a white boy some two or three years older than himself close to the pickett. The white boy haled him in the following language. Where did you get that horse you damn'd nigger. I didn't get him from you answered the black boy. Don't you sauce me you damn'd nigger said the white boy & ask him the same question over again & received the same answer when he started after him with a blade swearing he would learn him better than to sauce him & the boys had to cock their guns and threaten to shoot him before he would let the boy go. The boys said he thought he was awfully injured because they would not let him beat the Negro. Such is the natural effects of slavery. James Stevenson came down today from Vicksburg to join his company.[85] He looks fat & well. Remember me to all enquiring friends. Write soon tell aunt the rose she sent me smells beautiful. I have put it in her likeness case. Ever Yours

Wm. B. Chilvers

While stationed in Natchez, Chilvers observed the newly freed people. He was amazed at both the attitudes of the Southern whites as well as by the Illinois troops to these human beings.[86] Chilvers immigrated from England little more than a decade before, where he never lived where slavery was legal. England outlawed slavery in 1833, three years before Chilvers' birth.[87] Once he moved to the United States, Chilvers became a lifelong abolitionist. He was also amazed at the lack of support for abolition by the Illinois troops, and he commented, "It seems to me nothing could be too great" than "the freedom of all mankind."[88] He responded to his fellow Union soldiers in his letter to his uncle, George Burnham, on August 16, 1863:

O how I wished a poor bleeding slave would have appeared before them, Fresh from the last of the Driver or a poor mother pleading for her child about to be sold at the auction block. Slaves there where but they where Decked in their Holiday

Drepes & most of them House servants and & Gare better
then the Field Hands, but some of them Daribettes could tell
heart rending stories of their differings & wrongs, how Did I
know but a middle aged woman setting opposite me. (I almost
as white as anyone in the Church) had a child sold from her
& perhaps have never seen it for years. It might perhaps be a
bright child & some aristocrats take a fancy to it, as we would
a bolt or a nice horse. Such cases are very numerous Down
South, or was before the war broke out.

Give me war with all its horrors rather than Peace coupled with slavery, but some says you are Free. You are not
fighting for your freedom but for the Dam'd nigger. But if
we all look to our personal interest & day at home instead
of taken up arms in defense of our principals or Country
where would we find any patriots. We would all stay at
home for fear owe might be risking our lives to benefit
someone else that stayed at home. But as much as I love
home, I would do far more for principle then home. Yes I
would do more the Freedom of all mankind then anything
else. It seems to me nothing could be too great. Sacrifice
to make for such principle, but it seems as if very few
Americans had any principles at all & they do seem to me
to be a cowardly lot of people. There is some honorable
exception.[89] But I mean as a nation & the greatest imagination in the world, I have seen. Loh, if them frightened
out of their whits by imagination, I would bet I could have
[frightened] the whole Pickett Guard from their Post at
Vicksburg sometimes by making a little noise.[90]

Health was a common topic of discussion between Chilvers and his aunt
and uncle as death could occur rapidly in this pre-antibiotic age with limited
public sanitation. He wrote in the summer of 1863:

my appetite has been better today and I think on the whole I
feel better this afternoon. I can get a little milk most every
night and morning and I have it scalded and put a little
toasted bread in it. We had chicken soup for dinner today
and I done very well. The day before yesterday I tried to eat
a piece of chicken but failed entirely. I did not eat a mouth
full all day. They removed all the sick from the Reg. yesterday to the Marine Hospital.[91] The boys tried to persuade

me to go as they have such good accommodations but you know I always had an adversion to Drs. and Hospitals but I don't know but I shall have to go as they are taken all who are no fit for duty. For the reason our Dr. has no medicines but our Co. is all out on a Scout but a few of us that is complain. I am staying in the Captains tent while he is away.[92]

When Chilvers seemed healthy and not under the stress of battle, he preferred to stay with the army than to go home on furlough.

I don't think I shall stand any chance for a furlough this fall. But if my health keeps good I don't care so much about one at present. I should like to come & see you but I can't expect to be all the time at home or comeing & going. If we where at Camp Fuller it would be different.[93] I tell you it is a long & tedious journey to travel so far on the deck of a steamboat in all weathers. Nothing but the pleasure of seeing my home & friends would induce me to accept a furlough under such circumstances. I had rather stay where I am & do duty. But when I was sick I would have given everything I had in the world to have been at home. But I have recover'd so much quicker than I expected & I am glad I didn't get a furlough when the first lot was furlough'd but I should have been very glad at that time if I had got one.[94]

Clement Laird Vallandigham was a U.S Representative from Ohio who led the anti-war Democrats (nicknamed "Copperheads") during the American Civil War.

With a prolonged war that amassed large numbers of casualties, the federal government issued several drafts to fill their military needs. The draft proved particularly unpopular in New York City and in the Midwest, including Illinois, but the Union army needed additional troops to keep pressure on the South. Even the progressively lucrative bounty was not alluring enough to gain a large number of new recruits.[95]

Will Chilvers, and the Ninety-Fifth Illinois Infantry, had come through the lengthy siege of Vicksburg as heroes. The regiment participated in the two major assaults on the citadel taking significant casualties. The siege eventually took its toll with the Confederate surrender to General Grant on the Fourth of July 1863. Chilvers continued to be horrified by the treatment of Black people by both Southerners and his fellow Northern soldiers. Chilvers' resolve for fighting was strengthened as he wrote, "give me war with all its horrors than peace coupled with slavery."[96]

CHAPTER 4

"MOST POPULAR MAN I EVER SAW"

By Fall 1863, the Union's military attention in the western campaign turned from capturing fixed defenses to stopping the South's small raids. These assaults attempted to destroy the supply and communication routes of roads, rivers, and railroads. The Union had to avoid major mistakes which could create an opportunity for Richard Taylor's forces to recapture New Orleans or Nathan Bedford Forest to retake Memphis.[1] Another goal was to push the Confederates farther east in Mississippi and Tennessee with eventual goals to capture Atlanta and Mobile. Northern forces also were looking for opportunities to invade Texas.[2] This state had been left relatively unscathed from the two-year conflict, and was thriving with an open trade of cotton and cattle with Mexico and the outside world.[3]

In the meantime, Chilvers was stationed in Natchez or Vicksburg for most of the remainder of 1863. He commented on the conditions of army life, including unseasonably cold weather, boredom, rumors of the war, observing soldiers and citizens, and guard duty which is occasionally relieved by dress parades and skirmishes. His letters also contained his experiences with the newly formed colored troops, of whom he was proud.[4] Chilvers continued his correspondence with friends and family in Illinois. Much of the information that Chilvers obtained on the progression of the war came from these letters or correspondence received from fellow soldiers. Even away from home, Chilvers continued advising his uncle on farming techniques and business strategy. The fall of 1863 in Natchez, Mississippi was unseasonably cold as "the citizens says the coldest they have experienced for 21 years."[5] The tough weather made the

Map by Donald S. Frazier.

hardships of a soldier more difficult and "the fact is it is really trying on our patriotism."[6] Chilvers enjoyed Natchez, stating, "I have never seen a place in America I like as much" but "it is no place for a poor man to settle . . . unless engaged in a business besides farming."[7] Natchez seemed to not fit well for Chilvers' business interests, as "I certainly like my trade and take a great deal of pride in it. I would make a much better farmer than a mechanic."[8]

Natchez, Miss[9]   Oct 9th, [18]63

Dear Uncle & Aunt,

It is a long time since I hear from you, but I trust you are both well, as this leaves me at present. I have just come from guard. The weather is very pleasant here now. Rather bold nights but we manage to keep tolerable warm by doubling up. I think we shall move in a day or two up the river, eighteen to Vicksburg or some intermediate point. Someday we are going to Rodney, a little place 25 miles above this place. But we shall know when we get there & not before. The Rebs have been very bold around Rodney a long time. Some time since they captured a gunboat officer & 8 or 9 men while they where attending [a] meeting & they have fired into our transport several times. But I don't think there will be much of a force sent there, without there is a chance to get some cotton.

But I don't care much where we go. I am getting tired of this camp, although I don't think we will ever get a better one. But a soldier's life is too monotonous without a change once in a while. Although we shall have to leave lots of little notions behind. They could just as well spare us from this place as not. The whole of the 4 divisions would be left.[10] Besides a couple of regt of color'd men. Although I don't believe the colord regt would amount to much in a fight. In the first place their officers don't amount to much. They are mostly men that has gone in for pay & position. Their col. is drunk most of the time on whiskey that is drawn by the doctor for the sick. There is a great deal of sickness among them. The measles having got among them. They are dieing very fast.[11]

A great amount of them are discouraged on account of their family. It seems the recruiting officers told them that their familys would be provided for & have houses to live in but as soon as their regt was full the genl. Commanding issued an order to have all colord people removed from the city to the corral where they are pend up like a lot of hogs & the consequence is they are dieing of[f] like rotton sheep & who can blame the men for being dishartend when they have been so much deceived.

I was on guard yesterday with Jeff Brown.[12] He is good company. I had known him by sight a long time but I did not know his name until he was telling about breaking for Robinson.[13] He has been sick a great deal since he has been in the service but he looks well now.

I have got a few cockspur seeds to send you & a few castor beens. The cockspurs are the finest I ever saw. Remember me to all. I remain your affectionate nephew.

Wm. B. Chilvers

P.S. Since writing the above we have received a mail. I got one letter from you & two papers in one wrapper & another letter from Cheming. Good bye

Ambrotype of a soldier in the United States Colored Troops. These troops were actively involved in combat in the Trans-Mississippi Campaign from Milliken's Bend to the end of the war.

Chilvers visited the camps of the newly formed Sixth Mississippi Regiment—the colored regiment.[14] As a strong abolitionist, he was proud of these newly freed men, noting: "they will make good looking soldiers, and will fight well."[15] He also held some concerns with the way the black soldiers were treated, as evidenced in the previous excerpt from his letter dated October 9, 1863.

Many of Chilvers' correspondence described health issues from illness and battle. An interesting letter was sent to Will Chilvers from his friend, William Stevenson, who was improving from a leg wound at a hospital in St. Louis. Stevenson anticipated being transferred to an invalid corp.[16] These units were used by both sides, but more frequently by the South, for prison guards, and to protect fixed defensive positions. Stevenson was one of many soldiers from the Ninety-Fifth Regiment who was wounded in the Vicksburg Campaign. Three of Chilvers friends, including Stevenson, returned to duty by the end of September 1863. Will noted it "makes us glad to see them returned with their wounds healed and the flush of health on their faces ready to take part in and share with us the dutys [*sic*] and dangers of a soldiers life."[17] Will has several episodes of painful hemorrhoids noting that he was in "some trouble" and desired from home "a little of that pile medicine . . . as the doctors here can't do anything."[18] Chilvers wrote about the death of a soldier to dysentery, "Sergeant Locke died of the bloody gilux [which] no one of the company thought he was seriously sick."[19] In November, the "regt has been healthy . . . only one man in hospital (Harvey Smith)."[20] Smith was the "first man in since we carried poor lock (Locke) out. John Merrill & Roberrt Horan (Co G) will probably go home when they get to Cairo . . . Heren has gone to work taking pictures . . . the boys would like to see him put into the ranks . . . I guess his age will excuse him."[21]

In Fall 1863, Ulysses S. Grant was promoted to command the whole southwest. With this news there were high hopes for a quick end to the war in the Ninety-Fifth Illinois Regiment. The North won the two major campaigns of the summer of 1863. In the East, the Federals handed Robert E. Lee a major defeat where he lost his last chance for an offensive option. In the western campaign, Vicksburg and Port Hudson were taken and the Mississippi River became open to Union shipping. These forces also captured an army of more than twenty thousand men with large numbers of artillery, arms, and munitions.[22]

According to Chilvers, many rumors circulated among the Union troops that they were "winding up the Confederacy this next-winters campaign," and he added, "it looks to me as if we might."[23] "False news" of the fall of Fort Sumter and Fort Wagner led Chilvers to anxiously anticipate the "fall of Charleston but I suppose it will be [a] slow job like Vicksburg but we can wait a little while if they are crowned with success at last."[24] Chilvers expected action in the west "with some talk of us being mounted for a winter campaign."[25] Chilvers desired to see some new country and hoped to be mounted for a "tramp into Texas."[26]

Minor skirmishes occurred around Natchez during the fall of 1863. Vidalia was across the river from Natchez, and in a raid, the pickets were driven in. The Ninety-Fifth Illinois Regiment was sent up river to Vicksburg later that fall to combat these raiders. Chilvers reported that "the Rebs had been very bold around Rodney for a very long time."[27] They had captured a gunboat with eight or nine men and "had fired into our transport several times."[28] Will did "not think that much of a force" would "be sent there" unless "there is a chance to get some cotton."[29] This prize would be sent to the desperate textile mills in New England whose output had been markedly restricted by shortages of the war as well as naval forces who could capture cotton and be directed paid for their captured booty.[30] There were rumors of Southern forces retaking Vicksburg. Chilvers was not sure if the rumors were true, but it was "clearly evident our commanders expect an attack."[31] The

Contraband driving a wagon in the Baton Rouge area. [Courtesy of the John Nau Collection.]

Ninety-Fifth was ordered to build "first class fortifications nearer town then the old line of works and mounting siege guns"[32] on sites such as Fort Hill on this once thought to be impregnable citadel.[33] Vicksburg overlooked the artery of supplies and communication of the invading army to their homes upstream.

In October 1863, Chilvers wrote his uncle that, according to the Memphis newspaper, our boys had a fight at Collierville on the Memphis and Charleston Rail Road.[34] He noted "that I guess my cousin John was in it [as he] . . . received a letter f[r]om him 11 days ago that he had been sent from LaGrange to Collierville." Chilvers added that the "papers don't give the names of killed and wounded."[35] Chilvers' cousins, the Fillinghams, wrote Chilvers more specifics on Collierville, noting:

> they have had 2 or 3 fights there of late . . . and on one of the skirmishes the rebs drove them out of the camp into the fort and burned the camp. . . . that was the time Gen[eral] Sherman was there [and] our men had no artillery ...but the rebs were not satisfied and so they attacked them again. [By this time] our men had 4 pieces of artillery [and] the rebs attacked the pickett who checked them for about an hour. . . . [This delaying action] allowed the 2nd iowa cav[alry] to come in from the west of the fort and reinforce our men.[36] [The Iowans] dismounted and lay down behind the railroad track. The rebs charged and when they got within 200 yard our boys they had them in a cross fire. The rebs broke and

run. Their general's horse run from him and run into our lines . . . our boys captured him and 3 others with him.[37] [He reports] the rebs lost 200 killed and wounded.[38] Heard from others that [John Fillingham] came out of the fights [they have had at Collierville] all right.

A change in the command of the army was reported by Chilvers in late October 1863:

> Gen[eral] Grant has command of the middle division including Burnside, Rosecrans & army of Tenn[essee] and Missouri.[39] Sherman commands our army & McPherson is district commander as far as Napoleon, Arkansas and then Hurlbut has command.[40] [And] that McArthur is post commander of Vicksburg and that General Dennis commands the division.[41] Our division is now the first division and our brigade is the 2nd in the 17th Army corps.[42]

In the fall of 1863, many of the troops were allowed to go home to Illinois on furlough. Chilvers wrote his uncle about his friend:

> I suppose Cordean Bruce is about ready to start back . . . [I] hope he had a good time at home.[43] [A] man pays pretty high for a visit home & if he don't have a good time he is the looser. . . . capt loop by all accounts is getting a great many recruits up north . . . he sent one of his advertisements . . . and wrote to lt. keeler that he had 40.[44] The 302 dollars [in bounty] is quite a bait . . . but I'm sure some will regret taking hold of it if it is like last winter and spring.[45]

In mid-November a rumor circulated "that the boat the boys went up on was burned and boys were all captured buy guerillas."[46] It turned out that the Confederates captured and burnt another boat which was carrying the "old colors" of the Ninety-Fifth Illinois Infantry.

Cousin John Fillingham wrote Will Chilvers on December 16, 1863, about a skirmish near LaGrange, Tennessee. Cousin John noted:

> glad to hear you was having good times at Vicksburg . . . had fight with rebels on the 4th at Moscow . . . the rebels

tried to cross Wolf River (they call it Flint River) at the bridge at Moscow . . . hard fighting for one hour and half.[47] [P]retty heavy loss they left 28 killled and about half as many wounded on the field . . . we lost 4 killed and 13 wounded including Col Hatch of the 2nd Iowa Cavalry who was commanding our brigade . . . severely wounded in the breast but is getting better fast . . . since then rebs have kept a respectful distance from the railroad.[48]

Chilvers, like many soldiers of the Civil War and of all wars, wrote extensively about the officers that commanded him. By the fall of 1863, Will respected the leadership of Col. Thomas Humphrey. The commander of the Ninety-Fifth had gone back to Illinois during the latter part of 1863 to recruit. He blamed Lt. Col. Leander Blanden for the choice of a "very bad camp ground" when the Ninety-Fifth Illinois was transferred to Vicksburg.[49] Chilvers noted:

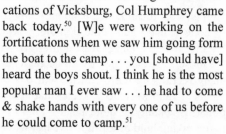

I don't believe we should have camped here if Col Humphrey was here . . . he would get us a better camp. In October, while the 95th Illinois was working on the fortications of Vicksburg, Col Humphrey came back today.[50] [W]e were working on the fortifications when we saw him going form the boat to the camp . . . you [should have] heard the boys shout. I think he is the most popular man I ever saw . . . he had to come & shake hands with every one of us before he could come to camp.[51]

Col. Frederick Augustus Starring of the Seventy-Second Illinois Infantry became a brigade commander of which the Ninety-Fifth Illinois was appointed. He was not popular with the troops and was replaced by Col. Thomas Humphrey.

Chilvers noted that Colonel Humphrey has command of our brigade, and "I think he will wear a star before he is much older."[52]

Col. Frederick Starring of the Seventy-Second Illinois Infantry first commanded the brigade in which the Ninety-Fifth Illinois was assigned.[53] However, "the officers refused to serve under him."[54] Gen. John McArthur adjusted the situation by placing the Seventy-Second into another brigade and "gave our Colonel Humphrey command." On his return, Humphrey moved the camp site of the brigade, and Will wrote, "we like the new camp better than the first. [M]ore convenient to picket lines and town" and we "get our mail regular and quicker."[55]

Will Chilvers was not as complementary about many of his other officers, noting in a letter dated October 22, 1863, that "all our officers seem to care about . . . is to get a drink [and] they are drunk two-thirds of the time.[56] He continued his thoughts in a letter dated a couple weeks later:

Pvt. Albert Cashier, Company G, Ninety-Fifth Illinois, fought throughout the enlistment of the regiment. When an accident occurred in the early twentieth century it was discovered that Albert Cashier was a woman. The former soldier's real name was Jenny Hodgers. [Images from the *Journal of the Illinois State Historical Society*.]

> a man has to get drunk half the time, or run around with miserable negro women and get some bad disease before they are thought anything of [by the officers]. [S]ome of the boys hope Capt [Loop] and Jim [Tisdel] never come back [and most of the troops want] someone who will get whiskey when they want it. I don't think Jim will stay long in the service if he gets his commission [particularly] if we have another Vicksburg affair [as he] is not the most courageous or patriotic man in the world. [A petition was sent to the colonel to allow] James Tisdel to resign.[57]

Chilvers wrote on November 23, 1863, that Lt. Jim Tisdel "is better anywhere else than a fight[,] but them that stand up to the rack best are not the ones who get the honors."[58]

The American Civil War was the first conflict in which a draft occurred to recruit soldiers in America. The North used this vehicle to bring over a million soldiers into the war and assessed a quota to each state including Illinois. The draft was a frequent topic of conversation between Will Chilvers and his family. Cousin James Fillingham wrote to Chilvers:

> they have opened a recruiting office in Canton. [I] have not learned how fast recruits are coming in . . . [and] cannot tell

> if there will be a draft in illinois. . . . for the people want
> some of the copperheads to go and try how they like the
> hardships that the boys which they denounce are patiently
> enduring to protect them and then they will see whether it
> is as easy to live as the soldier does as it is to set at home
> and tell long yarns about Lincolns thieves stealing things
> from their friends in the south.[59]

Will wrote his uncle frequently about farming, encouraging George
Burnham's hard work in Illinois by stating, "I would feel disappointed and
chagrin'd if we was to fail to make it work after so much has been said about
it."[60] Chilvers sent George Burnham a variety of seeds while he was stationed
in Natchez, including muscadine, which he described as "large but have very
tough skins. I think they are hardy and might do well, [okra] I think it will grow
up without any trouble [and] I think it is a great thing, cockspur, castor beans,
eggplant."[61] He later wrote from Vicksburg, "that this is a bad place for seeds
as the gardens were all destroyed during the siege."[62]

Chilvers gave Burnham detailed advice on farming, "you must remember
that manure is a great stimulant . . . every shovel full you can get hold of is
money."[63] He continued his suggestions in a later letter with, "I am glad you
got your garden fenced . . . if it is plowed . . . and manured it will give you
a good start in the spring."[64] A few months later he wrote a longer passage:

> I think if you could leave home this winter you might do
> well here . . . but you would have to get protection papers
> . . . in case of a draft . . . you would be foolish to stand the
> chance of being drafted while so many Yankees sneek out
> of it . . . it is your duty yourself and your wife to make
> something to help you in old age . . . if you w[e]re drafted
> you would not be able to save your place which is your
> only hope to make a home . . . you could make a lot more
> money out of the army than in it . . . you could get 40 dol-
> lars a month to work on a boat[65]

The Burnhams sent Chilvers a variety of items during his enlistment. Will
was particularly appreciative of food and clothing. He mentioned several food
items in particular on numerous occasions, first in October 27, 1863: "tell aunt

I and everyone who tasted her onions thought they were first rate, . . . [and] the currants and strawberries you sent w[e]re excellent," and then again on November 10, 1863, stating the food stuffs were "better than any I have seen sent down here."[66] He received a package just before Christmas 1863, and noted in a letter to his aunt and uncle, "[I] received your letter and plum pudding and butter you sent by Cordean Bruce. [A]lso pickle & dried fruit form Bogardus. [T]he butter and culiflowre are excellent. [I] saved the pudding for Christmas. . . . how shall I pay you for your kindness."[67] In a separate letter to just his uncle dated the same day, he confided that while William Stevenson had received a lot of clothing in a recent package, "I would not trade my little present for fancy fixings . . . I would rather have a plum pudding of my aunt's than a wagon load of sweet cake & caper coldan. [A]ll your presents remind me that I am an englishman yet I put on the shirt you made for me. [O]nly second I have owned because I lost one at Youngs Point . . . It is so comfortable."[68]

Chilvers mentioned letters he received from family in England as well as Illinois. He remained proud of his English heritage, noting that:

> the longer I live in America the more proud I am of my native land & country man . . . all the Yankee blow & bragadocia will neve[r] make me anything else . . . they won't find a half-starved and naked enemy to cope with . . . but a country the largest resources of any nation in the world and a good . . . men. [I] hope their conceit will not serve them into a war with England for it would place me in an awkward position.[69]

His English relatives were miserable according to a letter he received from Stephen Stork, who was "frustrated with farming as his crops are bad."[70] Stork lived in Wisbeach, County Norfolk, along with Will's uncle, Thomas. Uncle Thomas worked on the railroad and had two children, a boy and a girl. The boy was named for his father.[71]

Chilvers received letters from his cousins John and James Fillingham, who had moved from England to Illinois. John was a young cavalry trooper who informed Will about his military experiences as well as courting Southern women. James, like the Burnhams, was trying to survive the hard work required of being a small farmer.

John wrote Chilvers in November 1863 that he had been moving the last few days, "from Colliersville to La Grange Ten[nessee] and [was] busy putting up winter quarters . . . I would rather stay in collersvile for I have got the things all right with a southern belle out in the country. . . . She wanted to make me promise to return when my time [of enlistment was over] . . . She said she would go up north . . . but if she thinks I will take her up north she will have to wait a good while."[72]

John later wrote that he had not seen his southern belle "s[i]nce we left colliersville . . . [and that he will] try to get [a] pass for christmas day. My time will be up in 10 months . . . but as for taking a slave reared lady of the south I shall be far from it."[73] John Fillingham described that in the cavalry, "we have to do considerable scouting . . . [and] the infantry stands most of the picket. Since the last fight at colliersville the rebels have kept themselves at a safe distance . . . [as] they found the cavalry could fight behind breast works as well as any other way. [The] weather is getting pretty cold up here now . . . but as soon as we get our quarters fixed it may come as cool as it pleases for we will have good houses to live in."[74] John ended a later note by stating, "I am 21 years old today. I got some likeness taken the other day . . . I will send you one."[75]

In November 1863, James wrote from Banner, Illinois, responding to Chilvers complaints of not receiving any mail:

> You blame me (and justly too) for neglecting you . . . beg your pardon . . . truth is I was so bothered with things that I could not do anything but try [and] keep things in their place . . . the fences on tis farm were poor when we bought it . . . and needed repair. We have about 90 pigs which was about as hard to keep out of the corn field as it was for the rebels to keep you out of Vicksburg. [We have] got them stopped now . . . so I have a chance to write promptly and I hope you will do the same. We are obliged to sell our hogs on account of the scarcity of corn . . . [and] pork is at a pretty good price. [We have] first rate weather for gathering corn, and the farmers are getting it out pretty fast.[76]

Chilvers enjoyed his farming experiences in Mississippi, telling his uncle "I have done some farming this fall. I helped an old lady of the secesh . . . to harvest her peanuts. She had a fine crop and we saved her the trouble. The boys are always willing and ready to help on such occasions."[77]

By the end of 1863, Will Chilvers was proud of the development of the Ninety-Fifth Illinois Infantry Regiment. They had fought through the siege of Vicksburg, multiple skirmishes, solidified the defenses of forts, and served on provost and guard duty. He noted that:

> a year ago we was on our first march from Grand Junction. how small our regt looks . . . but as small as we are we are worth more to the service today then we was then. a large proportion of the men has been discharged.. of no use any-where are better out [o]f the service then in. but we have lost some of our soldiers . . . men both here & at home . . . I believe that the experience of the regt will more then make up for loss of numbers[78]

As the year ended, Chilvers was confident about his prospects of the New Year, and his survival, noting: "my health was never better . . . I feel 10 years younger than I did at Natchez."[79] He alluded to coming home soon and was disappointed that a former girlfriend was mentioned in the newspaper, the *Standard*, by noting to his aunt and uncle "Matilda Butler is married . . . which makes my chance of getting a wife considerably smaller . . . there will be lots of widows when this war is over . . . I may stand a better chance with them than with the girls."[80]

CHAPTER 5

"Second Potomac General Second Defeat"

The year 1864 began with people "froze to death" and "blood running out of cattles nostrils" for George and Rebecca Burnham who lived in the frigid state of Illinois.[1] Surprisingly, Rebecca ventured out to visit friends during this tumultuous winter and found herself unable to travel home until the roads were shoveled out. Conditions were not any better for Pvt. Will Chilvers who suffered from sickness, cold weather, and monotony while stationed in Vicksburg.

Chilvers performed garrison duty on the once thought of impregnable citadel of Vicksburg that Grant had captured six months before. Soldiers saw little action during this winter period. Both sides took a hiatus from the war as weather conditions proved unpredictable and travel treacherous. Chilvers commented to his uncle, "William Stevenson, Harvey & Alvin Smith, J Johnson, Tim Sergent & I built a shebang. We transformed a place 3 logs high & covered it over with shelter tent. It is very comfortable to sleep in. But it is not large enough to stay in the daytime."[2]

In February Chilvers noted, "I think the Rebs will make a desperate effort to keep us at bay until after another Presidential election hopeing the Copperheads may elect someone more favorable to their interests than Old Abe is. But they will find themselves slightly mistaken for Old Abe will be reelected if he runs."[3]

Chilvers described frequent military formal drills to encourage morale during these periods of inactivity. He penned, "we have had Brigade Dress Parade every Sunday & Regimental Parade every evening . . . We was reviewed yesterday by Major General Hunter, accompanied by Gens. McPherson, Lawler, Dennis, Smith, & two or three other Brigadiers."[4]

In January rumors floated through camp regarding where the troops would be sent for the spring campaign. Chilvers wrote:

> We have all sorts of rumors on leaving but we have too many such in camp to take much notice of any of them but I will give you two of them for what they are worth is that one Ill Regt from this Division has to go to Rocksland to do Garrison duty & that the 95th or the 72nd will go.[5] The same rumor has it that the 95th is recommended by Gen McArthur and that Col. Tom Humphrey is in favor of going & this is his present erran'd to Springfield.[6] But of course this is all conjecture. It is certain he took our muster rolls with him & that is all I know about it. Well the other rumor is the 15 corps under Logan is coming back here & the 17th (our corps) is going to Mobile.[7] You have them for what they are worth.[8]

The draft and how it would affect Boone County, Illinois, was regularly discussed by the two men. In January Chilvers noted, "I suppose you will know by this time whether there will be any draft in Boone county or not. The recruits came down slowly. We had two for our co. Last Sunday, one was Leacherson, the other a young chap from Calidonia by the name of Sergent.[9] Co. K got one, a brother to the Wakefields."[10] Burnham responded to Chilvers later that week, "we hear the President was a going to make another call for 300,000 more.[11] If he does there will be no chance to avoid the draft. I wish he may end the thing."[12]

In early February, troop movement began in anticipation for spring maneuvers. Chilvers wrote to his aunt and uncle:

> There is a great movement going on from this place. The troops are all leaving except our division. The 95th & 17th Wis. has all the pickett to do besides furnishing a permanent guard of 42 privates, 2 corp., 1 sergt. & one lieut.[13] From the 95th & 38 men, 3 non- commission & one capt from the 17th Wis. to guard ordinance stores.[14]

The next week, good news arrived from Illinois as new recruits and Col. Tom Humphrey joined the Ninety-Fifth Illinois Infantry. "We have considerable excitement for the last few days cause'd by the Arival of about 110 Recruits, also Col. Tom, I found a great many familiar faces among them."[15]

Burnham wrote his nephew about his hopes that Gen. Ulysses S. Grant would be as successful in his transfer to the eastern part of the war as he had been in the west:

> The rebels boasted of their strong holds in the west such as Columbus, Ky, Fort Donelson, Vicksburg & Chatanooga as being impregnable & could not be taken & also that they were the strongest positions in the South. Yet they are all taken never to be given up to rebels against our government. But in the east it has been different. They first tried Manasses and was defeated and then again before Richmond where they met with like results also twice at Fredricksburg where they was beaten both times.[16] I hope it may not be so any more for it would be a pity for Gen Grant to lose the honors he has won by hard fighting. You say that there are rumors of your regt marching. I hope you will go through the war safe.[17]

Newspapers and information on the outside world was scarce for these soldiers who saw little action during the winter of 1863–1864. Chilvers wrote his aunt and uncle about the newspaper report describing the first world prize fight between American John C. "Benica Boy" Heenan and Tom "Fighting sailor" King. Will was chided by his fellow soldiers for being an Englishman. Chilvers noted:

> Vicksburg, Miss Jan 4, 1864 [mistakenly written as 1863][18]
>
> My Dear Uncle & aunt
>
> I received your letter of Dec 20 on New Years Day. I was glad to hear you was well. I hope his letter will find you both in good health Uncle & Aunt Twelves also. I hope you will excuse my not writing sooner. The fact is I have been a little under the weather since Christmas Eve.[19] I have had a turn with the Dr. Again. He thinks I shall soon get out of his hands as I am feeling much better.
> You never said whether Cordean gave you that letter after all other barrage of old letters.[20] There is some talk of our goung up north to Rock Island to do garrison duty.[21] Col Tom has left us & gone home.[22] Some day to try I have us stay

One of the first World Champion Boxing matches, "the Great Prize Fight in England" was held on December 10, 1863. The contestants were the defending champion, the American, John C. "Benica Boy" Heenan and the English Challenger, Tom "Fighting Sailor" King. The challenger won in the twenty-second round.

here but I guess there are few that knows anything. I don't know whether there is anthing in the rumor on note. The boys is feeling very good. The news about the prizefight between Heenan & King.[23] The news has just come to camp that

Heenan came of victory. That is about all the news we have down here. We are having it very wet & cold weather here at present time & the river is raising fast. We have had lots of very cold weather. The weather around New Year's Day in particular. Colder than I ever thought it got this far South. But it is an awful place for [illegible] in the picket lines. A few haven't [illegible] is enough to a [illegible] bell of any fort where our picket posts are. But it dried up just as quick. Well news is very scarce here & I am so far behind with my gossip or fence. You will have to excuse me this time.

I will try to write again in a day or two remember me to all & believe me ever yours

Wm. B. Chilvers

The following week he recounted his news about the prize fight:

considerable fun about the prize fight.[24] The first news we got said King won the fight. A day or two after the boys got hold of a New Orleans paper, & they gave the victory to Heenan. Some of the boys were so tickled they did not know what to do & blow'd awfully. But when the Tribune confirmed the first report it was all hushed up in camp & you would think there had never been such a thing as a prize fight. I hear but very little about it now & I am shure I am very much obliged to King for thresh-ing Heenan. If it was only to stop the blow in camp. Otherwise it makes very little difference to me who whip'd.[25]

Chilvers and Burnham shared their Anglophile sentiments on the out-come of the prize fight as well as the possibilities of foreign countries becom-ing involved in the war. On an international scene, Lincoln held a difficult balance with France as he desired the forces of Napoleon III to leave Mexico but he also could not offend the French enough that they would recognize the Confederacy as a sovereign nation. As one historian noted: "England and France seriously considered some form of intervention based on allegedly altruistic reasons and if the Confederate States won international recogni-tion it could negotiate treaties of both commercial and military nature. The Emperor was strongly pro-South because of his country's need for cotton and his own desire to exploit the weaknesses of the United States to fulfill his

namesake's dream of establishing a French Empire in the New World."[26] In
March, Burnham wrote his nephew:

> You speak of a probable war with France & that the
> Catholics are always ready to support them but should
> such a thing happen there is no danger of the Northern
> Catholics at least siding with France.[27] If they did you
> bet I should not stay at home on that account but that
> would knock all the Irish plans in the head. Which is
> to stir up a war between the North & England & you
> can readily see such a course would bring England
> & the North in alliance with each other & then all
> dreams of Irish nationality would be at an end at once.
> There is not an Irish man (hardly) in the Union Army
> but what thinks America will help them whip England
> when this war is over but they will be disappointed.[28]

Chilvers wrote his family, "I take this opportunity to inform you I have
entirely recovered from my late spell of sickness. I am doing duty once more.
I had a very rough time for a few days with the Disentary.[29] The doctor gave
me salts, & opium & camphor powders.[30] I think I will stand it for a while."[31]

By the end of January the weather had become pleasant but a major health
issue faced the Ninety-Fifth Illinois. Many of the soldiers developed "sore
eyes" which was probably due to infectious conjunctivitis that the soldiers
transmitted to each other.

> We have beautiful weather now more like summer than win-
> ter. I like this place first rate when it is pleasant weather. We
> are having easy times now our sick boys are all returned to
> the G & with the exceptions of a few are doing duty. Sore
> eyes is the only trouble now & they are all getting better.[32]

Unlike the weather in Vicksburg, the winters in Illinois lasted longer, and
proved dreadfully challenging to early pioneers. Chilvers wrote a note of
encouragement to his uncle in March 1864:

> You seem to be discouraged some about farming in Illinois
> on account of the cold winters. Well it is discouraging.
> Such long winters. It seems one might find a pleasanter cli-

mate to settle in but it is mostly the case where the climate is moderate there is something else to make it disagreeable. It is either very sickly summer seasons or the inhabitants are such as we would not like to settle among.[33]

Throughout their writings, both Burnham and Chilvers consistently expressed their strong abolitionist thoughts deploring slavery. Chilvers wrote his uncle that his beliefs were challenged by a group of Union soldiers who threatened to harm two newly freed black men.

> I stood on the levee looking at 3 or 4 of the 17th playing with a dog.[34] A couple of darkies was crossing the bridge. They thought it would be good fun to shove the God Damn nigers in the water. So just as they got opposite to them they took them on awares and shove them both of[f] the bridge. One of them show fight. When they all pitched on to him I run down to the bridge but before I got there the darkie took to his heels. I told them that they had ought be ashamed of themselves. When they brusel'd up to me & ask me if I whanted to take it up I told them that I did not suppose 5 or 6 of them was afraid to pitch on to one man but I whip any one man that would take advantage of a poor niger. While I was talking another man came up and said he could whip half of them if I could take care of the rest of them and he being a large resolute looking fellow they backed off and mixt up with the crowd. I understand one of them was afterwards arrested. We have sent a guard down to the Negro quarters every night but the guard is most as bad as the rest.[35]

In the spring of 1864, several expeditions were sent out from the base at Vicksburg. In February, the Sixteenth Army Corps, under Maj. Gen. Stephen Hurlbut, and the Seventeenth Army Corps, under Maj. Gen. James McPherson, were sent east to Meridian, Mississippi. During the twenty-day expedition, the Confederate railroad communications, arsenal, and stores were destroyed.[36]

Col. James H. Coates, accompanied by the Eleventh Illinois Infantry, a small cavalry force, and a gunboat, ascended the Yazoo River. They defeated

Nathaniel Prentiss Banks, "the Bobbin Boy of Massachusetts," was a career politician and former U.S. Speaker of the House. In late 1862, he replaced Benjamin Butler as commander of the Department of the Gulf. Under his command Port Hudson was captured. He resigned after the ill-fated Red River Campaign of 1864.

Southern forces at Sartaria, and destroyed Fort Pemberton at the confluence of the Tallahatchie and Yazoo Rivers.

Later that spring an expedition was formed from New Orleans under the Commander of the Department of the Gulf, Gen. Nathaniel Banks, to ascend the Red River and enter Texas. Two divisions from the Sixteenth Corps and one from the Seventeenth Corps were selected for this force under the command of Brig. Gen. Andrew Jackson Smith. The Ninety-Fifth Illinois was temporarily detached from the Second Brigade, Seventeenth Army Corps, and assigned to a brigade commanded by Col. L. M. Ward, along with the Fourteenth Wisconsin and Eighty-First Illinois.

On March 9, the Ninety-Fifth Illinois boarded the steamer *John Raines* and headed south to Louisiana. Chilvers wrote:

> after leaving Vicksburg we run down to the mouth of the
> Red River & tied up on the west bank of the Mississippi.[37]
> On the evening of the 9th the boys burn'd a nice house

in the vicinity & plundered everything worth taken & some not worth taken.[38] The most disgraceful part was their taken or destroying everything belonging to the negros [illegible] On the morning of the 12th the gunboats some 22 in number started up the river, the transports following. Our boat was the last to start except for the hospital boat & one gun boat [illegible] After descending the river some 10 miles we tied up in a very pleasant country.[39] Both banks of the river had good houses on. The next morning (Sunday the 13th) we landed & fell into line and marched into a field [illegible] After drilling & laying around all day we was ordered to be ready march with two days rations. We lay around the levee until about 9 o'clock when we marched a few rods & halted again for the waggons.

In Spring 1864, N. P. Banks and staff planned an expedition from New Orleans to ascend the Red River and enter Texas.

We was on the road until 3 o'clock in the morning of the 14th & only gain'd 7 or 8 miles owing to the culvert & one large bridge being destroyed by the Rebs. We passed a fort on the edge of a bayou.[40] It was too dark to see how large it was. The brigade from the 16th Corps drove the Rebs out Sunday morning but could not follow them on account of a large bayou.[41] The Rebs having burn'd the bridges the morning of the 14th we started early but our brigade was in the rear & owing to the waggon train we made slow headway in the morning [illegible] About 12 o'clock we crossed Bayou Glaze & after having about a mile The inhabitants through this country is mainly French & Creoles.[42] Some of them claims French protection [illegible] Others hung out white flags. I only saw one Union flag hung out & that a very small one. I should like you to see this country. I think you would prefer it to Illinois. The inhabitants are very primitive as far as I could judge but I doubt not that they are as happy as people generally are [illegible] The Atchafalaya River emp-

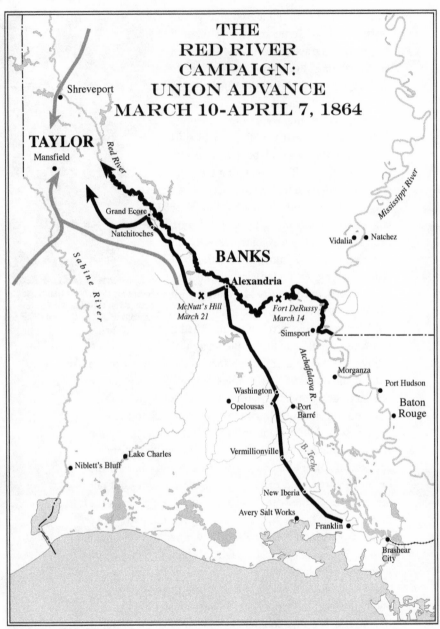

Map by Donald S. Frazier.

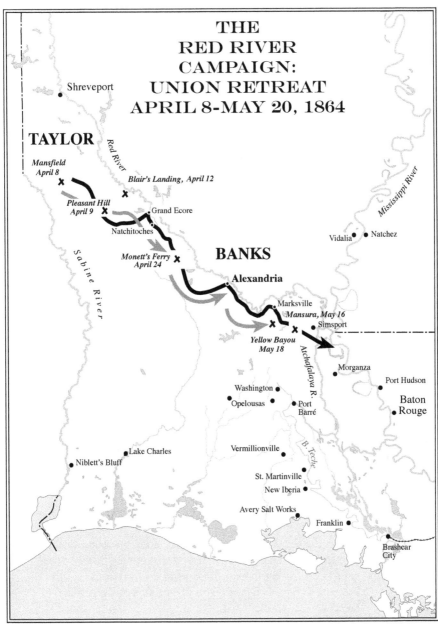

THE
RED RIVER
CAMPAIGN:
UNION RETREAT
APRIL 8–MAY 20, 1864

Map by Donald S. Frazier.

Edmund Kirby Smith took command of the Trans-Mississippi Department in February 1863, which became known as the Kirby Smithdom. He was successful as an administrator of the cotton trade that brought much needed war supplies through the blockade to trade with Mexico. Richard Taylor, who was Confederate President Jefferson Davis' brother-in-law, despised him.

ties into the Gulf & has been used in times past by blockade runners.

General Smith captured Fort DeRussy on March 14, 1864, and took three hundred prisoners. The Ninety-Fifth attempted to destroy the fortress and sustained casualties when the "magazines blew up with a terrific explosion."[43]

Banks' main force then followed a river road north from Alexandria towards Shreveport. The Ninety-Fifth Illinois was used to accompany Porter's fleet upstream, leaving Grand Ecore on April 8. "Companies 'B', 'E', 'G', 'H', 'I', and 'K,' boarded the 'Sioux City' with Companies 'B', and 'G' were detailed as sharpshooters. Company 'A' was placed as guard on the 'Black Hawk,' General Banks' head-quarters boat; 'F' on the 'Hastings,' General Kilby Smith's head-quarters; 'C' on the 'Meteor,' and 'D' on the 'Shreveport.'"[44]

Chilvers wrote Burnham on a regular basis, but in late March 1864 the flow of letters suddenly stopped. The Union fleet met strong opposition upstream from Alexandria by the Confederate forces of Gen. Richard Taylor and several ships including some carrying mail were captured or sunk.[45] Burnham wrote Chilvers:

> it has been reported you was at New Orleans but as we have no reliable news we must wait till we get another letter. we are sorry to hare [hear] of the Defeat & loss of part of the Expedtion & by the account of the papers it was through that miserable Gen. Stone the same that caused the defeat at balls bluf it is strange that such men keeps in command while such men as fremont is kept out it has always been so all through the war but I hope the Expedition will come out victoriou[s] yet.[46]

According to Adj. Wales Wood, the fleet ascended the Red River without much difficulty. "On the 10th intelligence was brought . . . that General

Gen. Charles Pomeroy Stone graduated from West Point in the class of 1845. He served in the Mexican War winning the brevets of first lieutenant and captain. In 1861, he served as inspector general of the Washington, D.C., militia and was responsible for the safety of the capitol and the president-elect, Abraham Lincoln. Lincoln came to "trust him implicitly." He was appointed brigadier general on August 6, 1861, and stood eighth in seniority of all those appointed. He was assigned a division of three brigades, a "corps of observation," on the Upper portion of the Potomac. "Through the rashness of a subordinate, Colonel (and Senator) Edward D. Baker, who was killed in the action, Stone was made to bear the burden of the Union disaster at Ball's Bluff." Stone was arrested and held at Fort Lafayette and Hamilton in February 1862. He was released on August 6, 1862, without formal charges being brought up or even an acknowledgement of error. In 1863 he was assigned to the Department of the Gulf under Gen. Nathaniel P. Banks "and served with gallantry at Port Hudson and in the Red River Campaign." After the war he served in Egypt for thirteen years as Chief of Staff of the Khedive. In his later life he was the engineer for the foundations for the Statue of Liberty.

Banks' army had been defeated at 'Pleasant Hill,' and was retreating on Grand Ecore." Adm. David Porter brought the fleet downstream. The Confederates built batteries to ensnare the returning transports, which the Union fleet passed on April 12 and 13. The Ninety-Fifth Illinois' Colonel Humphrey wrote, "On April thirteenth . . . I ran a gauntlet of a four gun battery (twelve-pounders) well posted, and musketry. The shots were fired at the pilot house 'Sioux City' with great precision."[47] No major damage occurred to this ship which Humphreys attributes to well-fortified decks and "the admirable coolness with which my sharpshooters played upon the enemy, I attribute, in a great measure, my escape with so little loss."[48]

On the Ninety-Fifth Illinois' return to Vicksburg it seemed that their status as being on loan from the Seventeenth Army Corps seemed forgotten. Instead of remaining in Vicksburg with the Seventeenth, the Ninety-Fifth moved upriver to Memphis, where

Adm. David Dixon Porter commanded the Mississippi River Squadron and worked well with both Gen. Ulysses S. Grant and Gen. William T. Sherman. He commanded the naval forces in N. P. Banks' unsuccessful Red River Campaign.

Samuel Davis Sturgis' disastrous loss to Nathan Bedford Forrest at Guntown in 1864 led to an official investigation. The Ninety-Fifth Illinois suffered tremendous losses at this battle.

Capt. E. N. Bush, Company G, briefly commanded the Ninety-Fifth Illinois after Colonel Humphrey was killed. After a short period he also was "stricken down."

the regiment arrived at the end of May. They were "turned over" to Brig. Gen. Samuel Davis Sturgis and were rushed into the battle on a venture into north Mississippi attempting to find and destroy the Southern forces of Gen. Nathan Forrest. Sturgis' men found Forest who turned their meeting into one of the biggest routs of the war. The Battle of Guntown, or Brice's Crossroads, was Forrest's biggest victory and led Sherman to say, "there never will be peace in Tennessee till [Gen. Nathan Bedford] Forrest is dead."[49] The Ninety-Fifth Illinois was particularly hard hit in this battle, and the regiment lost many men including Col. Tom Humphrey:

We have just returned from the worst expedition we ever saw. We have lost our Col & Capt. Bush & many others.[50] We left Sergt Rollins on the field so badly wounded that it was impossible for him to live long.[51] We had no means of carrying him off. Henery Williams was wounded (supposed mortally) just before we fell back. James Tisdel, Joseph Sweetapple & Washington Porter we brought off with us in our ambulances.[52] We was the only Inf Regt that brought any ambulances off. We brought both ours & our Colonels body. I will try & write you more particulars tomorrow or the next day. I am very [tired] now & dirty but my health is good. Cordien Bruce come through with us all right.[53] We have five missing [and] we don't have much hopes of their getting through. Their names is Frank Houck, Lyman Strong, James Goodman, William Tyler, & Mort Powel.[54]

A few weeks after his initial mention of the Battle of Guntown, Chilvers wrote a longer explanation to his aunt and uncle:

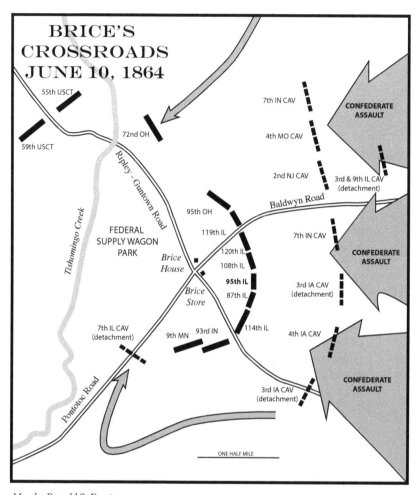

Map by Donald S. Frazier.

Memphis, Tenn[55]   June 22 1864

My Dear Uncle & Aunt,

I take this opportunity to write you a few lines which I hope will find you both in good health. We are still staying in Memphis but I don't know how long we will stay here for they are fitting up another expedition & we may possibly have to go.[56] We have got four months pay but we ow'd the sutler considerable & then we spen a great deal with the pedlars. It beats all how the money goes & we don't feel much like eating government rations while there is so many

nice things in camp. I believe the official report of our loss
at Guntown is 76 kill'd, wounded & missing, & I have no
doubt half of that number will turn up in the shape of prisoners.[57] Our co. is about equally divided. Albert Rollins brother
is here.[58] He is going out with Capt. Harper, 9th Cav., to see
if he can find out anything about him.[59] When our line fell
back he was quight rational. I staid as long as I dare & bathed
his forehead & wound. He was in a good place between two
houses & by the side of a well & in the shade. So he might
have a chance to be taken care of. I hope John will find him.
I believe our wounded corps here are all doing well. James
Tisdel is going home on a leave of absence.[60] I think the
affair at Guntown was the most shameful thing I ever heard
of.[61] I think there is the most cowards in the army of any
other army in the world.[62] A rebel looks as big as a hay stack
to some of them & the higher the position they hold the more
cowardly they act, and then they talk of whipping England.
I believe a half a dozen Englishmen would whip a regt. of
them. It is a hard thing to get half of them into line & when
a man is wounded two or three of them will throw their guns
down to help him to the rear. So if a dozen men is wounded
it puts 18 at least out of the ranks & it is very seldom that
any of them gets back to take part in the fight. When we
formed the 2nd line our regt. was very little larger than one
co. if any. There was only 4 or 5 in our co. besides the sergt.
& about half of them was so excited they didn't know what
they were about. They tell about the Rebs haveing such a
large force.[63] I don't believe they had much of a force but the
brush was so thick we could not see many of them anyway
& then theay our boys threw their guns & accoutrements
away was awful cowardly. Some of them I know was not
able to carry them but a great many threw them away for fear
they would have to use them. I saw two men in co. G empty-
ing their cartridge boxes & giveing them to the color'd men
& they had guns on their shoulders at the same time. I ask
them if they could not use them as well as a nigger but they
did not take much notice of it. They told the black soldiers
to go in & give them h__l.[64] But they took good care to get
pretty well in front everytime we was attack'd in the rear
where there is so many cowards & shirks. Men that stand up
to their duty stand a good chance to get kill'd or wounded.
Now there is Sergt. Rollins as brave a man as ever took hold

of a musket.[65] He is more a loss to the co. then all the shirks
& cowards together but they don't get hurt very often except
by a chance shot. I noticed those men that give out when we
was going into the fight stood it first rate comeing back with
the exception of one or two. The Rebs make a first rate rear
guard. Some of them that was not in the fight at all could
beat me comeing back. Co. A brought 4 guns into camp all
the rest was thrown away. Some of the other co. was not
much better. Co. B brought 12 or 13 in. I brought in two of
them. I stuck to my own accoutrements & pick'd up another
that was thrown away. Them that are short of guns will pay
23 dollars taken out of their next pay without our officers
find some way to evade the law. My cousin John is camp'd
within haldf a mile of us.[66] they have just returned from
home. I was over to see him once but he has not return'd the
visit. I guess he is a wild chap. He is downtown a great deal.
When you write again tell me what you think of Fremont's
chance for next president.[67] The papers we get down here are
all for Lincoln & Johnson.[68] They never mention Fremont
without it is to ridicule him. I think by the way they talk
they must be afraid of him. They stoop to the most low life
black guardism. What arguments they have are the most silly
absurd things I ever heard. In short they have no argument
at all. If I vote at all I shall vote for the only political man in
the United [that is a candidate for the presidency] that dare
to stand up for his princepals against all opposition & that is
Fremont. If we ever succeed in putting down this rebellion
we must have diferant men to lead us. We want a bold dare-
ing, energetic man. One who puts more faith in bullets to
win battles then bombast. A man won't sell & barter men's
lives for cotton or greenbacks. A man that will see that our
fighting generals has command of the army instead of a lot
of cowardly sneaks that holds position through the influence
of political wire pulling friends. The most of them was never
worth a cent until they came into the army & as long as they
stay in we may expect nothing but defeats such as Guntown.
I don't think there was a man in his [Sturgis] command
that had any confidence in him from the first & I am shure
he had none in himself or he never would have done as he
did.[69] If you can get hold of any Fremont papers I wish you
would send me some. I hope you have had rains since you
last wrote. If you have had as much as we have here I don't

Union Engineer George P. Hunt of the U.S.S. *Metacomet* wrote of the Union massacre of Southern forces after the defenses of Fort Blakely were breached.

think your crops will suffer much. There is talk this morning in camp that we stand a chance to stay here some time. Dr. Green & Quartermaster Southworth have started out with the 16 Corps under A. J. Smith.[70] There is two or three regt. of Hundred Day men who are doing pickett duty. I suppose you have new potatoes by this time. We can get them here for 60 cents a peck. I think this is the healthiest part of the United States I was ever in & some very good land. It is an excellent place for fruit but I have not seen a currant bush or much pie [illegible] plant since I have been South. But I must close. Remember me to Uncle & Aunt Twelves, Mr. & Mrs. Robinson & family, also Mr. Richard Sinten & family. I remain your affectionate nephew.

Wm. B. Chilvers

The Battle of Guntown had been particularly brutal, in part due to recent atrocities that occurred against black troops at Milliken's Bend and at Fort Pillow.[71] In mid-April 1864, news of the massacre of the largely black garrison reportedly by Gen. Nathan Bedford Forrest's troops reached the Ninety-Fifth.[72] Guntown was the first battle since Fort Pillow, and white Union soldiers, including Col. Tom Humphrey, encouraged retribution against the Confederates.[73] Massacres of captured soldiers occurred in other incidences in the war against Northern and Southern troops.[74] Pvt. Samuel Pepper, Company G, Ninety-Fifth Illinois Infantry, wrote, "I am passing thro a very severe trial amongst wicked men."[75]

The Ninety-Fifth Infantry was in shambles as the regiment stumbled back to Memphis. Their colonel, officers, troops, and *esprit de corps* were shattered by Nathan B. Forrest. Sgt. Onley Andrus, Ninety-Fifth Illinois Infantry, wrote, "we have been and seen the elephant and returned and I hope that they will let us rest enough to get our allowance of greenbacks before starting out on an other wild goose chase."[76] Pvt. Samuel Pepper noted, "This is the second Potomac General and the second defeat we have suffered her[e]."[77]

CHAPTER 6

"STERLING PRICE, BEDFORD FORREST, AND THE DRAFT"

After the fierce exploits of the Red River Campaign, and the debacle of the Battle of Brice's Crossroads, the Ninety-Fifth Illinois was left as a dejected unit with little confidence in its leadership.[1] This was particularly evident with the death of Col. Tom Humphrey, a key leader of the troops since its inception. The Ninety-Fifth was sent to Memphis for garrison duty to rest and recover its *esprit de corps*, which the regiment formed during their fighting at Vicksburg. After their time in Memphis, regimental leaders hoped the group would be ready if another Confederate breakthrough occurred.

While in Memphis, Chilvers wrote his uncle about his life in camp:

> Dear friends accept my sincere thanks for the two dollars you sent. Although I did not need it at the time it told me I was not forgot at home. At the time I got it I had my pocket full of money & was calculating to surprise you but things took a change. To tell you the truth I had been gameing & won a great deal but I could not be satisfied until my luck turn'd & I lost it all again. But luckily I had lent some around to the boys while I had plenty which I will get next pay day. But it leaves me scanty now. I lent more than enough to make me good with the game so I never lost anything in reality but won about 10 or 11 dollars.[2]

Chilvers' note was not well received by his uncle. Burnham responded:

> William sorry to hare you have changed so much as to
> go into gambling or speculation. It is a hablet that is hard
> to leave of[f]. it is poor busness any time. I suppose if
> I was thare I would be worse then you as I was always
> more inclind to it than you was & I was some little of a
> hand at it but with all I never maid much in the long run
> & my advise would be if you are right keep so as thare
> must be some quite sharpers with you. you never men-
> tioned wither you got the socks from Lut. Farham.[3] I am
> afraid as he had left befor your return you mist them.[4]

Chilvers was disgruntled with his duties in the summer of 1864. He noted
in a letter to his uncle:

> I don't think I shall reenlist without things changes greatly.
> The paper that we signed at Vicksburg agreeing to reenlist
> again has been destroy'd. So you se[e] I am under no obli-
> gation to stay longer than the three years & I can most se[e]
> the end of it a little over a year more. I think I will let some-
> one else take my place some of the natives of the soil for
> I se[e] they already take what little credit the Union army
> has gain'd to themselves & are quight willing to throw the
> blame of the many disasters on the foreign hirelings as
> many of the cowardly wretches that are staying at home
> see fit to call the men of foreign birth that are fighting their
> battles. I may stay here while the war lasts or a bullet ends
> my life & those miserable sneaks will take all the credit &
> consider that I am well paid for the hardships of a soldiers
> life. Don't they feed me & clothe & pay me for what little
> sacrifice I have to make & why should I complain if I am
> call'd hireling or if I should loose my life. I am paid for
> that too, that is part of the bargain but I have made up my
> mind not to be call'd a Hessian anymore. The fact is there
> was a slight mistake made when I enlisted. I thought I had a
> duty to perform but a hireling has no principals to fight for
> nor can expect any credit for what he does. His employers
> should have all the credit. In short I have found I am in
> the wrong place. I have hired out to murder my master's
> enemy. It may seem hard to you to think your nephew has

become a murderer but the American people accuses me of all that when they call me a hireling. Can you longer wonder why I have frequently tried to persuade you to apply for British protection so as to keep you out of the army. I don't whant my friends to sell their honor for Yankee Shinplasters especially now they are beginning to find out that foreigners are such bad fighting men.[5]

Chilvers frequently discussed rumors and politics of the day. He thought the war was not close to being completed:

but I hope they will never draft in Ills. but let me ashure you that the war is not a going to end in a day as some suppose & Guntown will be more frequent than ever.[6] Richmond is not taken yet or Atlanta either nor would the fall of either one or both end the war by any means.[7] Although I admit it would be a great help to our cause. But let me tell you the Southern people are not a going to lay down their arms as long as there is a shadow of a chance for them & I believe they have more confidence today in their ultimate success than at any other time since the war commenced. Their soldiers are better fed, better clothed & better disciplined than they ever was before. The prisoners we take now a days as a general thing [are] clean, healthy, hearty looking men. A year ago they where dirty, filthy & half starved, ready to do most anything for hard tack. In fack't the look like a different race of men. Which shows they profit by experience & every new campaign finds them improved as soldiers while I can't se[e] we gain any. In short I think we waste our time in euligizeing our favorite generals & expect too much from them. The American people as a general thing seem to put more confidence in newspaper fights than in bayonets. One would think the many failures in this war would open their eyes to the simple fact that one musket properly used would availe more towards defeating an enemy than all the newspaper bombast in the world. Old Abe's little jokes, or the color of Genl. Grant's horse, or the peculiar way he holds his tail ef.fects Genl. Lee's battalions but mighty little. Nor does Old Abe's honesty & patriotism secure him from a miserable corrupt cabinet. If the old saying that birds of a feather flock together is true what can we think of our president when he gathers such men as the Blairs & Bates of Mo. around him & by that means drives such a man as Chase from the cabinet & then ask the people to keep him there another four years & I have no doubt he will succeed.[8] But woe be to America if the people don't break from the minds of blood suckers now in office. What interest can it be to the shoddy merchant & all the other thousands of speculators to have the war end. They may enlist hundred day men & 3 year men but if such blood suckers are allowed to control the army as they have done the Rebellion will never be put down.[9] But such disasters as the Red River expedition & Guntown will be more frequent than ever. When I think of the way this war is conducted it makes my face burn with shame to think I am made a tool of by such wretches but I can only hope that something will turn up to place this war on a right footing. I have despair of the present administration entirely for every day only develops some new corruption.[10]

It is awfull how theas miserable scoundrels of money brokers controwls the country. Tha will use this country up intirerly. It looks to me as it is allread gone now. Fesenton has got it in his hands.[11] He allways was in favor of given the bankers thare own way. He wants the government to issue bonds & sell them at what tha will fetch & take bankers shinplasters the same as greenbacks. So you see how rotten the government is. It looks to me worse than the French revolution because thare armys was led by a diferant class of generals. I wish your time was out but all we can do is to hoope for the best.[12]

Uncle George Burnham predicted an economic crash due to the war, and the poor leadership of the government.

I tell you will be thare will be an awfull crash befor long. Every poor man that's in debt ma calculate to keep in. if we had the farm paid for thare would be a home for us but depend on it thare will bee such hard times as have never been seen on this continant & com it must sooner or late. The prospects look very dark to me. We scarcely dare alow our selves to think of the state the country is in. Everything looks dark but time will tell. The greenback falls very low in the exchange. Thare

Map by Donald S. Frazier.

does not seem to bee much confidence in the government &
some of our neighbours thinks I am a copperhead because I
said if I was a voter I would vote for Freemont. The mount
of it is tha vow he would hirt slavery if he was elected. Silas
Stevenson told me he was glad I cold not vote because I spoke
of Freemont. Will it is my opinion if he was in my place he
would be gladder still for his great patriotism does not amount
to much. He kept 300 dollars by him all the time tha expected
the draft. Now that is taken of[f] he don't say much about
it but when the hundred days men was in roling one of his
wanted to go & he would not let him but said tha would stay at
home and rais grain for the boys that would go. That is as far
as his patriotism goes. Tha would like me to goe or any other
farmer but stand you back you can't vote you g. d. furiner.[13]
But I do not trouble about voting nor that do not trouble me.[14]

While the Ninety-Fifth Infantry was recuperating from their dismal experiences at the Battle of Guntown, part of their division participated in the Union victory over Confederate generals Stephen D. Lee and Bedford Forrest at the Battle of Tupelo. Chilvers wrote about atrocities committed by Union troops upon their Southern foes which were in part due to poor behavior of Southerners at Fort Pillow. These conflicts progressed to several black flag fights during the Missouri Raid in the fall of 1864.

Memphis, Tenn.[15]   July 24th 1864

My Dear Uncle & Aunt,

I take this opportunity to let you know I am well & I hope these few lines will find you both enjoying the same blessing. There is some talk of us moveing from here but we don't know where we will go too or when we will start.[16] But I think we will be likely to go down the river to Vicksburg or Morganza or possibly to Little Rock, Arkansas but there is so many expeditions on foot that we can't tell where we will be whanted next. But I can't believe they will keep us here all summer without doing something. I think we may calculate on moveing somewhere soon.

The balance of our division returned last Friday evening from Tupelo where they had a fight with Forest.[17] According to their tell they whip'd Forest bad. The 14th Wis. (the only regt. from our bigade out with the expedition) brought in a Reb flag captured by them from the enemy when they charged our train while the 33rd Wis. & them was train guard.[18] The Col. that brought our party in from Guntown (Col Wilken of the Ninth Minnesota) was kill'd on this expedition.[19] His regt. was train guard at the time & the Rebs made a sudden dash on them when they was not prepared for them. They broke for the woods & the col. had just rallied them & got them into line again when he was shot through the heart (the 9th was the regt. that Ab Enoch was Capt. in).[20] The boys of the 14th says the slaughter among the Rebs was terrible. They was ordered to take no prisoners & when our boys drove them they never ask for quarter. They was so tired & worn down that they took no pains to shelter themselves from the bullets but walked away as unconcerned as if no enemy was near & our boys shot them down by scores. When they was wounded they would try to hide away in the brush. Those that could not get away would beg for their lives as soon as our men came near them. They thought the boys would show them no quarter because they had murdered so many of our comrades after the defeat at Guntown. Well they might think so if all accounts are true & I have no doubt but they felt guilty. Our men was unable to followup the advantage they had gained for whant of rations. The men had been on half rations for several days before the fight. The country here has been laid waste so many times by both armies that there is but very little to forage which is always a great disadvantage to an invading army. If they take a train large enough to last any length of time it always hampers their movement & is often is the means of defeating an army by blocking up the roads & it takes more generalship to handle a train in some country then the troops but it seems Smith understands both for he is always successful.[21] I don't get any letters from you or anybody else. Remember me to all.

Yours Wm. B. Chilvers

Stephen Dill Lee was the youngest lieutenant general of the Confederacy. He commanded troops at Tupelo and strongly complained to the Union command when captured Southern soldiers were slaughtered after the Battle of Tupelo. This battle occurred after the Fort Pillow massacre in which General Forrest had commanded troops.

Will kept well informed of the "March to the Sea" as part of the Ninety-Fifth had been transferred to Sherman's Army. Chilvers wrote his uncle about the fighting at the Battle of Atlanta:

We have just got news of a terrible fight in which our old General McPherson was kill'd.[22] He was considered one of the best genls. in the service & has been very popular especial with the soldiers & subordinate offi-cers of the 17th Corps which he has commanded for 2 years until he was promoted (while we was on the Red River Campaign) to the command of the Army of the Tennessee. His loss is deeply felt by all who knew him.

The American or Union Army can ill afford to loose such men at a time like this but I am afraid many of our bravest men will follow him before this war is over. We have not heard from the detachment from our regt. since the Atlanta fight. I expect they was in it. Capt. [Charles B.] Loop is on Genl. Legget's staff as engineer & I believe Capt. Stewart is Division Quartermaster.[23] Asa Farnam is with the detachment.[24] I don't know whether I will get them socks or not. We are expecting Major Avery back in a few days with our camp & garrison equipage & knapsacks & co. from Huntsville, Ala.[25] It will seem strange to have our tents once more.[26]

Chilvers continued his thoughts on the possibility of the regiment moving in the same letter as well, "We don't hear anything about moveing for the last few days. I would like to make you a visit & eat some of your currants but I suppose I shall make up for lost time when I get home."[27]

Chilvers wrote his uncle about the raid of Forrest in August 1864, as well as his lack of confidence in the competence of the Union generals at Memphis:

They have has a great scare at Memphis a few days ago. The Rebs come clear through the town. It is no more than might be expected at any town [as] Fort Pickering never protected the town. There is not a particle of fortifications around the town to protect it in the least. Fort Pickering is a strong work & very extensive, capable if properly defended to resist any force that can possibly be brought against it by the Rebels. But it is situated south of town on the river bank & any force coming in on any of the rear east & north of town are protected by the town. For the town is full of women & children to say nothing of the large hospitals all over town is fill'd with our sick & wounded soldiers. Besides all of the army supplies are in the town & steamboats all exposed. I think it is the weakest idea in the world to build such an extensive work where it can't be used. If they had two or three small works on the different approaches to town Forrest would never make a raid but it does seem like we have the poores[t] excuses for genls. That any army was ever curse'd with. What can we expect from such men. The affairs at Memphis are an example of a good many other places. There is some talk of our having to leave here & go to Little Rock. We have had orders to go but Adgt. Warner has gone to se[e] the Genl. about it. We are in line every morning at 4 o'clock expecting to be attacked. We have about half the men on pickett & the others working on breast works. We have no officer worth a cent or they would not weaken the garrison by sending so many men on pickett. All that can be expected of the pickett is to give the alarm & they are worth nothing to speak of in case the enemy made a sudden dash. They are so far from camp they could never get in. Whereas if they had a light pickett line & not move them half the distance from the works they could alarm the garrison and stand some chance to get in themselves. We have a guard on the breast works as well as the pickett. There is a ditch 16 foot wide on the outside of the ditch. So take it all round I think at least half of the men on pickett would be as good as the whole & the others would be in the fort to help defend the works but I suppose they will take their own way about it.[28]

After several weeks of inaction, the Ninety-Fifth Illinois was sent out from Memphis to fortify positions in Mississippi and Arkansas to protect positions from Southern raiders.[29] In August 1864, Chilvers wrote his uncle that the Ninety-Fifth Illinois had recovered enough from its losses to be sent to Arkansas:

We left Memphis on 3 o'clock on the morning of the 4th & landed at White River Station 10 o'clock the same night. The balance of the evening was consumed bringing a fleet for White River. Some of the boats was unloaded & others loaded. We left co. H & 15 men from the other cos. to garrison the place. Julius Bishop, E. A. Tyler & A. Farnsworth staid from our co.[30] We left there the next morning & arrived here yesterday afternoon (somewhere from 80 to 100 miles from the mouth). The river flows through a very uninteresting country. Here to the mouth the shores is too flat & swampy to build on or cultivate. We never saw a clearing. The whole way it is a continual forest. I saw more fish comeing up than I ever saw in a stream in my life before.

This place is a high bluff.[31] If there ever was a town here it is badly tore up now for there is not more than a dozen houses in the whole place. When we landed last evening the boys felt rather discouraged. The place look'd so much worse than we expected but the troops that we relieved did not like to leave very well. They say the country back from the river is thickly settled & they can get fruit & vegetables. The 37 Ills. has been here some time but I believe they go down the river this morning.[32] There was 12 men from a co. detailed as soon as we landed for pickett. I was one of them. I suppose our

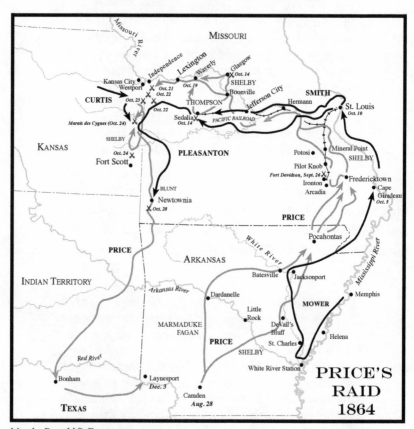

Map by Donald S. Frazier.

duty here will be pickett & work on the fortifications. This place is noted for blowing up one of our gunboats & scalding two or three hundred men. A little while after Memphis & Helena fell into our hands. Perhaps you recollect it. I forget the name of the boat. The woods here on the high ground is mostly white & black oak with very thick underbrush. The mosquitoes are intolerable. I was nearly eaten up with them last night. I think I should like this place better in the winter season but I can't tell yet. I don't like the idea of having to dig in this hot weather. The ground is very hard. About half the fortifications are completed.[33]

The troops left Memphis on August 3 and arrived at St. Charles, Arkansas, on August 16, 1864, where Chilvers wrote his uncle a week later:[34]

There is a boat at the landing ready to leave for the Mississippi. Some of our boys goes down on it for home recruiting. Sergt. Curtis goes from our co. & Sergt. Andrews from E. Co.[35] We have had a very wet time here of late but it has clear'd off at last. I was on pickett yesterday. Last night was one of the pleasantest nights I ever saw on pickett. The moon shone bright & the coons came & pick'd up pieces of bread within 9 yards of us. We caught one large one. We live a great deal better here than we did at Memphis. We get some good beef occasionally & sometimes fish. We had catfish for dinner yesterday & again today. They are opening the muster roles for veteran volunteers again but I don't think I shall enlist tis time. So you need not expect to se[e] me home inside a year from Sept. 4th without I should get sick. So I am better off here. We don't get much news here.[36]

John Sappington Marmaduke of Missouri studied at Yale and Harvard prior to graduating from West Point in 1857. A capable commander he served at Shiloh, Prairie Grove, Helena, and the Red River command. He led his command through the Missouri Raid where he was captured at Mine Creek. After the war he served as a governor of Missouri.

In the same letter, Chilvers wrote his uncle about Confederate forces in Arkansas: "A citizen come in yesterday & reported Marmaduke within 5 hours march with 9 thousand men but it is regarded here as unreliable.[37] A forage train has gone out with a small escort. If there is so many Rebs around they may get gobbled. Since the boys shot that deserter outside of the pickett lines we have had no alarms."[38]

Joseph Orville (J. O.) Shelby was one of the war's best cavalry commanders. He led the "Iron Brigade" through multiple raids into Arkansas and Missouri in 1863 and 1864. He saved the remnant of Sterling Price's forces following the Battle of Mine Creek. After the war he took his command to Mexico and allied with Emperor Maximilian. After the collapse of the French government in Mexico he returned to Missouri and served as a U.S. Marshal.

Chilvers grew accustomed to the terrain and weather by mid-September, and wrote Burnham about the beautiful land in Arkansas:

I have just got back from the bluff where I have been unloading hay. I wish you could se[e] the beautiful pararia between this place & the bluff. I think you would [be] pleased with it. It is quight as pretty as Grand Prarie & resembles it very much in appearance except some beautiful groves of live oak all around it. I have never seen any county in Illinois that I would as leave settled in, besides the climate is much better. It is entirely unsettled at present. Only once in a while [you will see] a house on the edge of the grove. Fruit seems to [do] well here. I have seen some of the finest apples & peaches here that I ever saw in my life. The rail road is straight as a line all the way across & the deepest cuts is about 2 feet but they have raised the graid to suit the ground. Dinner is ready & we have got all our things pack'd for a march so you must excuse me if I don't write a long letter this time.

The teams are now hauling our tents & co. to division headquarters. There is quight a large expedition fitting out here under Genl. Mower for some point.[39] Time alone will tell.[40]

Chilvers guessed that the Ninety-Fifth Illinois would soon be part of an expedition, and in a letter dated September 20 stated: "The genl. opinion is that we shall strike White River at Jacksonporte. If we meet resistance [we will] go as far as Batesville. Some say another force is comeing up the river & another from Little Rock & we will form a junction at Jacksonporte. If so I will get a chance to mail my letters."[41]

Chilvers' intuition was correct as Mower's army soon marched through Arkansas. A raid of more than 10,000 troops, through Arkansas and into Missouri, had been initiated by the Confederates under the command of

(seated left to right) Generals Cadmus Wilcox, Sterling Price, Thomas Hindman, (standing left to right) John B. Magruder and William Hardeman went to Mexico following the war and joined the Imperial Forces.

former Missouri governor, Gen. Sterling Price. Several smaller raids into Arkansas occurred in 1863 and 1864 under the commands of Confederate generals J. O. Shelby, Marmaduke, and Fagan. These three generals headed Price's brigades. Private Chilvers wrote on September 20:

> I think we are in for a hard march this time but I don't know how long it will last. We are some 60 miles from Brownsville station in the roughest country I ever traveled in (a foot).[42] It is very hilly & the surface is covered with large slabs of stone of iron color. They are very smooth pretty building stones but they make a dreadful rough road

James Fleming Fagan was born in Kentucky and moved to Arkansas at age ten. He led the First Arkansas Infantry at Shiloh and then was transferred to the Trans-Mississippi Department. He fought at Prairie Grove, Helena, the Red River, and Camden campaigns. He commanded the Arkansas division of cavalry during Price's Missouri Raid and was captured at the Battle of Mine Creek. After the war he served as a U.S. Marshal in Arkansas.

to travel on. The country is necessarily very thinly populated but we occasionally pass a good farm & a great many peach & apple orchards which look very thrifty & nice. We pass'd one orchard today that had at least 100 bushels of apples on the trees but they was gather'd very quick I assure you. The peaches are all gather'd & most of the apples through the country. We have pass'd a couple of good looking villages on our march but they look the worse for the war. The stores are all empty & deserted also a great many of the dwellings. Last night we bivouacked on [the] Little Red River. We crossed about 3 o'clock but it took the train most of the night to cross. It is about as wide as the Kishwaukee at the bridge & knee deep. We had to ford it. The bottom is all stone which was hard for sore feet. We have only travel'd about 15 miles today. The train could not keep up so we halted here by the side of a little brook of good water with big hills on both sides of us. The woods here has some grapes which is all the wild fruit I seen all the way. Yesterday we saw lots of Chinquapins (a nut some like a chestnut) but they are hardly ripe & some walnuts. We killed some excellent beef tonight. In short the beef in this country is all good.[43]

In the same letter, Chilvers noted some clothing difficulties he experienced during the long marches in Arkansas:

I have stood the march well so far but my socks are giving out. I started with a new pair of government socks but they are awful things. I wish I had brought them you sent me but I whant to save them for winter. The nights are very cold now for our thin coverings. My partner & I has a rubber each & a woolen between us. It is about time to pick out a soft place among those rocks to sleep on. So I will close for tonight . . . I have worn the shirt I have on for 19 days.

I have been wet for a dozen times since. So you may guess what kind of a looking thing it is.[44]

Chilvers also mentioned how hard it was to keep valuables on the long marches in Arkansas:

Gen. John Anthony Mower was a division commander under Gen. A. J. Smith's corps during Sterling Price's raid through Missouri in 1864.

> When you get the package of letters I sent you by James Manning I wish you would look them over & se[e] if there is two photographs in one & the receipt you sent me. I pick'd them up in such a hurry I forgot to take them out. I whant you to put the letters in my trunk & send one, the beer receipt, back. Please take care of the photos. They are my cousins, John & Mary Fillingham. The case with aunt's likeness got broke in my satchel but I got another to put it in. I have got to leave it again in my knapsack as we march in light order[45]

Health was a major concern for all Will's correspondents during this time. Chilvers wrote to his uncle:

> We had another man return to the co. yesterday from the St. Louis Hospital. His name is John Martin.[46] He was wounded in the rear of Vicksburg & has been away ever since. I have to go on guard at 9 o'clock & they are now beating tattoo half past eight so I guess I had better conclude for this time.[47] James Manning got his discharge yesterday & started for home [48]

Chilvers and Burnham wrote often to relatives in England as well as frequently discussing with each other family who lived in England. He mentioned one such correspondence on August 7, 1864: "I received alot of old mail before I left Memphis & one letter from you dated June 26th. I learned for the first time of the death of little Mary and her mother. Poor Mary, our ties to England are removeing one by one."[49]

Health could also be a precarious situation in Illinois. Burnham and Chilvers corresponded about Aunt Rebecca being involved in an accident. Burnham wrote:

> Rebecca & I are not very well. Hers was partley caused by a little accident in wich happened last Saturday. She went to Chemung for mail but was disepointed as usual not getting any. Well coming back she stopt a few minutes at Mrs. Woods will thare the horses got thare halters loose and run of[f] and broke everything all to peaces. Thare is not a whole part of buggy left everything slick and clean of[f]. It is destroyed except the base but no one was to blame. The flys are so bad it is impossible for horses to stand still without fly cloths on. The harness is old and tha broke that all together. It is quite a loss as much as 35 dollars but it might have happened with me.[50]

Chilvers wrote back to his uncle, "I am sorry to hear of the accident but I think it is lucky aunt was not in the buggy at the time. You will have to be careful in the future for they will be apt to take the first opportunity to run again."[51]

Will's uncle often requested Chilvers input on farming. In one such instance, Chilvers responded:

> I am sorry your crops are so bad but I hope the late rains has improved them. I have fail'd to get all your letters for I know nothing about your crops or what was sown on the bottom lands. I never had much faith in the bottoms. For spring graining I think it would be a good plan to seed it down until we could get a chance to drain it. If it was seed'd down & drag'd level so a reeper could run over it might be worth something for hay & then it would always be in good condition to break up at any time. Don't you think if it was well dran'd so it could be work'd early in the spring the drought would effect the crops less because they would get a good start before the dry weather commenced. Now you have to wait till all the spring rains are all over before you can get on the ground to work it & your grain has but a very poor start. I think corn is as good a thing as could be put on it. But the land being so wet it takes but a very light frost to kill the young plants in the spring. I think as you do about your farming under the present circum-

stances. I think you could make a great deal more at something else but whether you could save more is the question . . . I se[e] no reason why a man commonly smart might not do well in most any business he might choose to engage in. I think if you could seed your little farm down this fall & sell your stock with the exception perhaps of a good cow you might do well down here next winter without indead things change wounderfully before then & if they change you could easily plow your high land up again. You would not be oblige'd to sell your stock until you got ready to leave home. Aunt could manage to live alone for a little while until you would have an opportunity to look around a little for yourself & the you could determine whether you could get along better to have her with you or not & then again if you was drafted as you may be at anytime your affairs would be in better shape to leave.[52]

George wrote about the results of his farming efforts in the summer of 1864:

I thought the crops looked as thow thare would be a half a crop but if you cold the country hare now you would pittey the farmers splendid wheat fields until destroyed by the bugs that are so thick in some places you might shovel them up. Tha have spild all the wheat & barley & tha have commenced on corn & potatos. In short it looks as thow nothing woold escape them. Even Alexander's rye is destroyed. Mine is the best grain round for miles.[53] I think I shall git a paseable [passable] good crop of wheat & corn & potatos. In fact thare is not as many bugs on all our land at present as most all the others has on a half acre. Thear is none to speak about on the bottom land and I think I may cut the other tomorrow if it is fine. I would be cutting now only it rains. It rains about every other day now. So you se[e] it is catching time but I have put right in to it the last two weeks. I have cut an stacked 23 loads of hay. I have a splendid crop and it is selling from 10 to 13 dollars per tun. Thare is no tame hay in the country & cattle being so poor last spring people turnd thare cattle out on the slews in the spring & eat all the slew grass as fast as it grew. Then the drought set in in wich almost used the slews up so you can se[e] grass is worth something this year & I kept all the cattle of mine in the spring & pastuered them out. That

left me with a meadow as scarcely be found in the county.
If I can only get it all I intend to sell and kill all my stock
& sell my hay as it will not pay to winter them. If I can
rent the farm I shall sell everything of[f] except one cow
& come to Memphis or Chicago. I shall not rent the house
& garden [and] Rebecca will stay hare. You spoke of not
seeing many kirints [currants] and small fruit down south.
We wish you cold just get home a little wile. Now I think I
never saw larger an[d] finer kirints in my life then we have
this year & the bushes is so loaded that form a compleat
mat of fruit & guesbery the same bushels of them. Every
one that comes in the garden thinks it is the best garden
an[d] largest kirints tha ever saw. We thought of making
some wine this year but sugar is 35 cents per pound.[54]

Chilvers continued his farming advice to his uncle:

I am glad to find your crops are likely to be good. I wish I
could come home & help you to get your hay. If it is selling
as high as you say it is worth while to cut it. Do you think
it will command such prices all winter. You know the good
people of Ills. are apt to get excited about such things. I hear
cows are selling at fabulous prices up North. Some say they
are worth from $50 to $75 each but it hardly seems possible.
I don't think I should keep cows long if I could get such
prices, especially if I owed for the land I was living on as
many of the farmers do in Ills. If you could pay up your debt
or most of it by selling your stock I think there is no danger
but what you could make a liveing at something until times
was settled.[55]

George wrote about the difficult work that farming required:

I have no one to help me with my harvest only as Pat
Flanery and me changes work to stack.[56] I have finished
cutting my wheat & have it nearly all stacked but it rained
yesterday & today. So I have to weight till finer weather.
My wheat & Robinsons is abought all thare is round hare.
Some never cut any and others will not get half a crop. It
dose look horrible. No tame hay nor any straw for thare
cattle nor not much slue grass of account of thare poor cattle. In the spring as soon as the grass showed it self it was

nabed up. Then the dry weather set in & I tell you it looks like a slim chance for feed. Me & Robinson kept everything of ours & we never had as heavey grass before. I have got between 20 & 30 loads in the stack wich looks very nice. I tell you if you had done as you talked of we might have had more but we do not care much about it. We take it for granted that as Uncle Sam has fell short of his agreement.[57] You of cors will pay him with the same coin. Never the less we should very much like to see you on any other terms. I think I can cut about as much more hay as I have cut. It will be worth something this winter. I think of letting Flanery the land on shares next year. He offers me half of everything. I furnish half the seed, Rebecca would have the house & garden but I want him to fund his own seed & give me one third grain & half the hay in stack. That would give me a chance to sell all my seed & team & stock & hay & go quite a peace towards paying the mortgage of wich I would like to be done.[58]

Chilvers responded to his uncle in a letter dated August 21, 1864:

I suppose you are through with your harvest. Before this I should like to drop in & see how you get along. Wheat is selling pretty high according to the papers. There must be a change somewhere. I think green backs must take a fall & that very soon. The sooner you turn your stuff into money the better it will be for you.[59]

Chilvers restated his thoughts a few days later: "I think you have done well to rent your land for money rent. It is much the best way I think."[60]

Burnham stated a few weeks earlier:

We have trashed our little grain & sold it. I had 2 acres of wheat on the N. end of the bottom land & 6 on mine wich was both about equal average. I think about 11 bushels per acre. I have sold 75 bus. At 1.80 per bus 135.18. I had only 7 bus oats & 4 barley. Of your land not half anough to pay me for cutting them. I thought last spring I had sold my gun at a great price but like the plow that I traded the year before for seed the whole has been a total loss besides all my labour but we cannot help it now. The money that it would have bought a good fence round it but we must not give it up. When it gits well subdued it will grow something. You spoke of seeding it down well. It might do very well but we have all the grass thare is needed on 80 acres without it especially if you live so far from market, and to keep stock enough to use all of it. Thare would have to bee so many fences tha would cost more than the farm is worth. You can allways buy an improved farm for half what it cost maling them & you know I always looked at improvements as thow tha had ought to rise the farm in propotion to the post. I tell you will it may do well enough to go into great improvements but it ought to be whare it is likely to be worth something on a good prarie and near a citty. I think you & me had a very rough idea of stock raising or in other words in the grazing land slew land is poor grazing land and to lay apart of this little bit of slew land down would make it two small. The fact is we are in the rong place for such arrangements we want. If we want a farm at all to be on a road near some town ware we might do with out raising grain & put a small farm into a better use. Your idea of seeding the bottom land is very good so far as the land is concerned if it paid more a cutting. You know hay never fats a creature but it will sell if near a market in the spring for more than the creature is worth itself but a farmer cannot rais grain without stock. I never saw the advantages of living near a citty so much as I do this year. If a man cold rent a good farm near a citty ho cold better afford to give one third the crop than to have all the crop & pay taxes & keep up the fences besides all privelages but I must come back to my crops again. Well my wheat held out a 11 bus per acre 88 at a 180 - 158 – 40 barley on both lots 15 bus at 180 - 27. I have a few beans, buckwheat & corn & potatos. Just enough to keep me from going some ware to earn some money. Before I can take care of them the frost will come & it will be two late for the work in Chicago. I went to Mr. Toppings on Saturday & paid him 250 dollars. I wish I could have paid the whole. I have sold both Rebecca's cows & her colt & whatever stock I cold. I have only one old cow & one 2 years old. Both of them I shall butcher. I cannot sell the team yet as neather of them

is very saileble. I want to do a little fencing if I can. I am
alone to knight. Mrs. Bennet died this morning & Rebecca
is thare to set up. Last Friday we had an exhibition at the
church for the sick soldiers. got up by 3 of R. Sintons girls
& others tha done it first rate. I wish you cold have been
hare to have seen it. Thare was scors came that cold not get
in. I think tha got about $75. the girls intended it for the 95
if tha had staid at Memphis. I do not now whare tha will
send it now.[61]

At the end of August, George relayed to Will news about the marriage of
one of Will's former girlfriends, "Ester Ford was married last week to Mr.
Drake."[62] Chilvers responded, "I understand Ester Ford has married B. Drake
of the 4th Miss[ouri]. He used to be a member of co. A 95th [Illinois] but got
transferred at Natchez. I think she has done well. He is considered a good
fellow by all his acquaintances here. I am glad she has done so well. If you
should se[e] her [give her] my best wishes."[63]

In October, George wrote again about Ester Ford:

> We expect Ester & her man to visit tomorrow. You are mistaken
> abought her man. He has only one eye & never was in the army.
> He is from York state. I think he is as good as the family he
> has married in. I saw her today. I did not give her your com-
> plements as she never mentioned your name perhaps she
> may tomorrow. I expect tha will go out west in the spring.[64]

George recalled more information on the family farm in his letter dated October 1, 1864:

> We had Sam Parsons hare the other night. We had a debate
> on the scriptures until 1 or 2 o'clock in the morning without
> accomplishing much. He was to have started this morning
> for Ohio but got left. He had 3 pigs in a box & the train left
> him & his pigs behind. I sold him one 7 weeks old for 12
> dollars the handsomest [sic] I ever saw. I was loth to let it go
> but I had to let him have it. We sold it for 12 dollars. I offered
> him it for 6 but as it was all trade but 2 he sold the other
> 10 in order to make a big lick out of some of his friends in
> Mormondom. That is how Mormon preachers do things up.

Now I wil tell you my trade he relinquishes his rite of way across our land and a note of two dollars against Robinson. I consider it a grand strike. It will save a peace of fence. Wish we had it all fenced. It is a hard looking thing to see cattle every day eating up more corn but I cannot help it yet. I have paid 250 dollars this fall. Thare is left 130 wich I should like to pay by the 16 day of Jan if I can. I shall do all I possibly can for a 130 dollars will be very hard to pay when the war is over but we cannot tell when that will be.[65]

I have bought the lumber to fence the south 40 between me & Robinson. I should like to fence all round it. I saw Sarg Curtis last Saturday. Rebecca sent you a few dried straw-berries & black cirnts by him. I saw Cap Loope the same day pretty high in J seats. He had just returned from Atlanta. Fage is home yet Steave says he was working his tase [illeg-ible] out on the road & fel[l] sick just before his furlow run out & had to see the doctor & got his furlough extended.[66] James Manning brought the package all right. Your cusens likeness are both safe & the receipt for cream hear.[67]

Oct 2 our company has just left for home wich con-sisted of Ester & her man, the old lady, & Jane & children. Ester thinks she is abought match up with her 1000 dollar man. With what little I have seen of him today makes me think he is not as smart as I thought he was but I cannot tell. I do not think she has made a very great strike after all tha [sic] think of going out west. Thare is great excitement about the draft. Tha are round today trying to collect more money for vollenturs.[68]

Oct 4th on Monday morning I had to go abought 4 miles to a heffer and take his horne and kill her myself & take part of the beef to Harford. So being in such a hurry I forgot to take this letter & since then I have had no time to go to Chemung. I have had to husk my corn for the cattle is in every day. It is hard farming without a fence. I have as good as thar is in the county if I can save it but it rains every day or night so I am afraid I shall spoil what I do get. I wish I cold sell my team. I think tha will eate as much through the winter as tha will be worth in the spring but I cannot sell them yet. Will Stevenson is home on furlow & G. Robinson is home for good. He was offered 1500 dol-lars as a substitute for one year in Kanetucky but refused.[69]

Both Chilvers and his uncle were strong supporters of Gen. John Fremont for the election of 1864 and often discussed politics:

John Charles Fremont, the Pathfinder, led five expeditions to the American West in the 1840s, and became the first Republican Party candidate for president in 1856. Fremont was relieved of his command of the Department of the West by Abraham Lincoln for insubordination after announcing an edict to free slaves that were held in his Union held district.

> There is no excitement about the coming election down here. I don't suppose we will have anything to say eithert way. I think this regt. would go largely for Lincoln but Fremont has some very warm friends. Among the Fremont men of our co. is Ira D. Hill, & Paul Howstrawser, two of the most intelligent & patriotic men in the co. & they are always ready to give their reasons why they prefer the Pathfinder to the Slow Coach now at the head of the government.[70] It is the hardest thing in the world for any Lincoln man to give a good reason for keeping him in power another term except that they are afraid to divide the Union party & by the means to give us a copperhead president. For my part I had almost have Valandingham president as Abraham Lincoln. Though I had rather not se[e] either. Give me a man that will come out fair & square for or against us. This miserable sneeking half way policy will neither coax or whip them into the Union. The Union soldier is not as much respected as those that are trying to destroy the Union & the more a man tries to defraud the government the more he is respected but I hope it will soon end one way or another.[71]

Will thought that African Americans were misunderstood by the government as he wrote:

> We met a train of darkies yesterday bound north. They where halted & waited to se[e] how the comeing battle was desided before they whent any farther. It is all foolish to think they whant to come north if they could stay here. They are not people that like to leave there homes by any

means. They are perfectly satisfied to stay here if they can
& have there freedom.[72]

Earlier that summer, Chilvers advised his uncle on how he could avoid the
draft:

> Now if you was here as a British subject you could do well or if you
> was to join a militia company here you might get into some busi-
> ness. All able bodied men her has to join some militia co. without
> they are aliens. But it interferes but very little with their business
> for they have their regular days to drill which is once a week & all
> business is suspended during the hours of drill. So that those that
> are not in the companys has no advantage while they are drilling
> & I believe they are only enroll'd for the protection of the city. So
> as you se[e] it don't interfere with their business much after all.[73]

The draft remained a frequent topic of discussion between the two men
even into Fall 1864. Apparently, recruitment proved much more difficult in
Illinois despite much larger incentives. Burnham wrote:

> The draft wich is to com up next Monday is causing great
> excitement. Boone Co., has of $300, public subseriptions
> 50, government 100. making in all 450 for one year. It is
> quite a bate but thear great patriots are very shie. Belvidere
> has catched one man, Bonus & that is all I can hare of in
> the Co. up to last night. I was at a war meeting last night.
> Lawrence spoke to quite a crowd.[74] The 450 bait was
> throwd but not a fish caught. Thare was quite a job to even
> drag a sound out of them. A speaker calld for the song rally
> around the flag wich was only complied with after a very
> long pause was struck up by two or 3 of the ladies & a
> recruiting agent. This was at Capron & it is a fare sam-
> ple of the county. Lorance said he spoke in Belvidere the
> night previous and met with the same result. It is astinis-
> hon [astonishing] the difference thare is now. Them that is
> exempt dose all the blowing now & that only ware thare is
> no suns at home liable. So you see real Yankees patriotism
> amount to when tried but I need not tell you as you have
> had a better chance to see them tried then I.[75]

Chilvers responded to his uncle:

> I suppose you know by this time who was drafted & who is
> not. I hope you will escape but I am afraid not without you
> get[ting] British protection. I think you done wrong in not get-
> ting it before. For I tell you 16 dollars a month is nothing when
> you come to consider the price of everything. It is only eaquil
> [equal] to 7 or 8 dollars in gold. We cannot get a meal at the
> bluffs short of a dolla & 25 cents for a glass of lemonade. This
> paper costs 40 cents a quire & good paper is 50 to 60.[76]

In October, George continued his thoughts:

> I tell you their great patriots takes something [to] induce
> them. Boone town wants 4 more & thare is one thousand
> dollars bounty offord for them. I expect after the presidential
> election thare will be quite a draft. If the president had not
> reduced the 500,000 to 150,000 his chance would have been
> awful small for reelection. Let election get over [and] you
> will see he will call the balance out then tha must draft.[77]

By early October Mower's forces reached the "boot heel" of Missouri.[78]
Chilvers noted the event:

> Cape Girarideau, Oct 6th– We arrived here last night after
> a long march of 325 miles. We was about a week behind
> Price & had to come to this place for supplies. We trav-
> el'd through some rough country & awful bad roads. Our
> teams is about all used up battery horse as bad as the mule
> teams. The last 30 miles from Dallas to this place the road
> is McAdamized. The best I have seen in America. I have
> not been in town yet to get any news. This place is the
> nicest place I have seen since I left home. The people are
> all Union. The boys say we can buy things cheaper down
> town than we could at Chicago. I expect to go down this
> afternoon. We are estimating for clothing.[79]

By October, the Ninety-Fifth Illinois Infantry was transported by ship to
Missouri to be used to block the Confederate invasion of Missouri. Chilvers
explained the situation to his uncle:

William Starke Rosecrans was transferred to command the Department of Missouri following his loss at the Battle of Chickamauga in September 1863.

On Board the Omaha[80] We are now on our way to St. Louis but I don't think we will stay there any length of time. I think we will go to Jefferson City the capital of the state. We find it very cold here with our thin coverings. We will probably draw clothing at St. Louis for we are most naked a great many is bare footed. My shoes hold together yet. I had to use old rags for socks the most of the march but I managed to get along very well. I bought 2 pair of socks at the Cape for $1.00. The cheapest socks I ever had. We could buy everything we whanted to eat cheaper than you can at Belvidere. The inhabitants are mostly old country people. A great many are Swiss & strong Union. All the principal roads are McAdamized with toll gates & mile stones like the old country roads.[81] We have pass'd several nice settlements on the Ills. [Illinois] side of the river. We have just pass'd Liberty the people all appear to be loyal for they display'd loyal flags from their windows as we pass'd & hurra'd for Lincoln. The boatmen say we will be at St. Louis Sunday evening if we meet no accidents. How pleasant it would be to get on the cars at Illinois town Monday morning & surprise you in bed at 3 o'clock Tuesday morning. But I suppose we will be on our way up the Missouri by then & you will have to be contented with reading this scribble. I would like to hear from you once more now we have got so near home but I am afraid we will not stay long enough at one place to get any more mail. Old Price is cutting up dog in Mo. & I suppose he will run us all over the state this fall.[82] His head is too long for our shoulder straps.[83]

In a separate letter in the fall of 1864, Will wrote his uncle from Missouri:

In the reg there is another division (it is Rosecran's Division) comeing in and halted opposite us.[84] I don't know what division it is. The road is perfectly blockaded with trains & artillery moveing forward I suppose. We shall be into it soon. The sooner the better this marching tires the men before they commence fighting. For it is the most desolate country

I ever saw. The first day we marched [by] the fences & corn fields where we all on fire & we frequently had to leave the road. The fences are all rail & built so high they make quight a fire & so much smoke it would blind us but the boys did not complain much. They like to see the things burning up.[85]

Chilvers implied to his uncle that the officers were not concerned with the conditions of the troops as he wrote, "I suppose you know Sgt Anderson is dead.[86] He died at Chatanooga. Poor old man, he had right to be discharged a year ago but those men with shoulder straps will not discharge anyone if they can help it. They are afraid it will effect their promotion."[87]

As 1864 ended, the Ninety-Fifth Illinois was exhausted from heavy combat and miserable conditions. It is perceived that the war could not go on much longer as the Southern armies were further depleted. The North continued to eliminate the resources and manpower of the Southern armies.

CHAPTER 7

CARRYING THE COLORS

In the new year of 1865 the outcome of the American Civil War was within sight. The North continued to expand its path of invasion reducing the maneuverability of the Southern armies which had previously allowed them to avoid catastrophe and occasionally to earn victory. The last few months had seen multiple Union advances. The campaign of the March to the Sea had been crowned with the capture of Savannah on Christmas. John Bell Hood's army was crushed at Nashville. Finally, the Overland Campaign pinned Robert E. Lee's army to the trenches around Richmond and Petersburg. The Navy continued to prevent imports from reaching the South through its blockade and successful capture of most of the Confederate harbors. The successful attack on Fort Fisher in January 1865 closed the important port of Wilmington. This port furnished supplies to the forces of General Lee in Virginia and Gen. Joseph E. Johnston in North Carolina. The only Southern ports which remained were Mobile and Galveston.

Richard Scott Taylor was the only son of President Zachary Taylor, the Mexican War hero. Despite no formal military education he was responsible for commanding the successful Southern forces during the Red River Campaign.

The Ninety-Fifth Illinois Regiment divided, with some of its members following Sherman into Georgia and the Carolinas, while others went back to Tennessee before moving further west. Chilvers went with the forces who kept track of pesky Nathan Bedford Forest and Richard Taylor in the Trans-Mississippi Department. This department of the Confederacy controlled remnants of Arkansas, Louisiana, the Indian Territory, and an almost completely intact Texas.

Chilvers continued to live the life of a soldier as he traveled back to the relative boredom of Tennessee and Mississippi. The outcome of this part of the war had previously been decided through the Meridian Campaign, Price's Missouri Raid of 1864, and Nashville. The Ninety-Fifth had arrived shortly before the Battle of Nashville and were used as reserves. Chilvers wrote his uncle, "if you have got any of my letters you will learn that your fears about the affair at Nashville was all groundless as far as the 95th is concerned. We came out lucky indeed."[1] His service resumed with building structures such as fortifications, and repairing railroads interrupted with occasional skirmishes as he waited orders for more significant objectives such as movements into Texas or Mobile Bay.

Throughout Chilvers' letters he frequently mentioned their friend Pvt. Cordenio Bruce of Company K. Bruce went with the part of the Ninety-Fifth Illinois that travelled east with Sherman's forces following the Nashville Campaign. Chilvers was informed by his uncle of the unfortunate incident of Private Bruce.

Chemung Ill.[2]

Jan 4 /65

Dear nephew I again assume my pen to let you know we are both well as we hope this will find you enjoying good health. We think it so strange we do not hare from you. we have not haired from you since the 11th of Dec. wich does seem a long time & as we now thare has been so many hard battles to go through it makes us feel anxious to hare from you. we heard the other day of poor Cordena Bruce as he was not with you I will tell you all I know about him.[3] Gil Hammond told me in this way. Cordena & another had been in town which was some distance from camp. On returning they got off of the cars some little distance from camp & started on the track which was on along legnth of tressel work & another train came & caught them before they could get off killing the other & cutting off one leg & one arm of Cordena. He was at last account at Chatanooga. Timothy was to start the other day two him.[4] It is hard for him if he ever gits well again & for his family. I have not sent you the 5 dollars yet. I should have sent it the next day but it was riskey. The letter might fall into rebel hands but I will send it as soon as I hare from you. I have been a paid topping all the money & got the mortgage releast so the land is clear from all incumberance wich I think is a grand job done. I have the team and all my hay left yet. I hold Pats note of 100 for 90 & your 30 & 58. I had maid 178. So after all was paid it leaves me with 48 dollars on hand & my total paid 1015 [illegible] & we don't owe a dollar. So I think we are the best of[f] we ever have been since we have been in the country. We had Mathew & Mary over at Christmas & we went to their house at New Years. We all wished you cold have been with us. I sold my sled I spoke of last year for 14 dollars & got a mother abought half finished & sold that for a 11. so you see I have to keep at my trade yet.

But I must conclude for this time so no more at present from us both. We remain your ofectionat uncle & aunt George & Rebecca Burnham

George Burnham

Chilvers wrote back to his uncle later that month and mentioned that "Cordian is in the hospital at Nashville."[5] George Burnham kept William up to date with Private Bruce's progress: "I saw Ed Bruce the other day.[6] He says Cordena is a getting better.[7] Him is down at Nashville with him. I am glad to hear Cordien is getting better.[8] I hope he will soon be home discharged for Nashville is a miserable place for a soldier sick or well without he is with his regt."[9]

Chilvers often wrote his uncle about mutual friends who were in the army. He stated, "Wm. Stevenson is well.[10] Also H. Parsons Co. K joined us yesterday . . . I saw Mose Fitzer yesterday.[11] He came home with his brother. The poor fellow died on his way home. He was buried on Sunday. Mose is to leave home on the first of March."[12]

On January 3, 1864, Will wrote: "we have had another short march From Pulaski to this place but we took it easy from 10–15 miles a day.[13] The report is that we are a going to Eastport, Miss. About 45 miles up the river & about 20 miles east of Corinth. The same report has it that we are a going into winter quarters."[14]

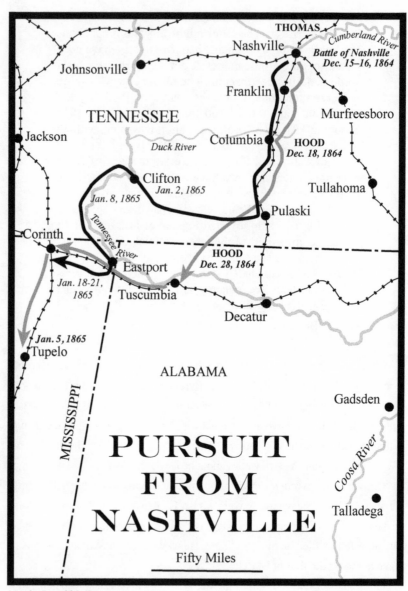

THOMAS

Cumberland River

Nashville

Battle of Nashville
Dec. 15–16, 1864

Johnsonville

Franklin

Murfreesboro

TENNESSEE

Jackson

Columbia

HOOD
Dec. 18, 1864

Duck River

Clifton
Jan. 2, 1865

Tullahoma

Jan. 8, 1865

Pulaski

Corinth

Tennessee River

Eastport

HOOD
Dec. 28, 1864

Jan. 18-21,
1865

Tuscumbia

Decatur

Jan. 5, 1865
Tupelo

ALABAMA

Gadsden

MISSISSIPPI

PURSUIT
FROM
NASHVILLE

Coosa River

Talladega

Fifty Miles

Map by Donald S. Frazier.

After chasing Hood's army from Nashville, the Ninety-Fifth Illinois arrived at Clifton, Tennessee, on January 2, 1865, where they stayed a few days. Adj. Wales Wood related, "This finally ended the severest campaign the Ninety-fifth was ever engaged. When the suffering in which prevailed in consequence of the extreme cold weather, and all the other circumstances are considered, it is believed there is no expedition in which the regiment participated during the service, which can compare with this one in point of suffering and fatigue."[15]

The Union forces camped at Clifton for several days and obtained extra rations from nearby farms. Chilvers wrote, "we made a Jayhawking tramp this morning & got some dried apples, potatoes, pork & molasses so we are living well at present."[16]

On January 8, the Ninety-Fifth was transported along with the Sixteenth Army Corps in a crammed steamer, the *Leni Leoti*.[17] They were taken to Eastport, Tennessee, where Gen. A. J. Smith's forces reported for winter quarters.[18] "We have orders to march tomorrow with 6 days rations on a reconnoitering expedition. I suppose towards Corinth. We expect to come back to our camp in a few days. We have been hard at work fixing up winter quarters but we have quit this afternoon to get ready."[19] The Ninety-Fifth Illinois left Eastport on January 18 to evaluate Confederate resistance around Corinth, Mississippi. Colonel Moore's division discovered no resistance except for a brief cavalry skirmish. Adj. Wales Wood noted that upon arrival at Corinth, they found that the enemy "had evacuated the place a few hours previously to our arrival, and had set fire to the 'Tishimingo House', which was filled with rebel commissary stores. The building was burning as we entered the town and could not be saved."[20] The men returned to Eastport after three days of scouting.

Despite the short stay that the Ninety-Fifth Illinois experienced in Corinth, Chilvers spoke to several citizens about the Southerners' future intentions. William wrote to Burnham:

Andrew Jackson "Whiskey" Smith was a successful Union commander who was involved in the Vicksburg and Red River Campaigns, and the Battles of Nashville and Tupelo. He was responsible for saving Banks' army during the Red River Campaign by launching a devastating counterattack at Pleasant Hill.

> but we have great peace rumors here but newspapers are very scarce. The citizens of Corinth says Texas has either join'd Maximillians government or are going

to right off.[21] The troops that has been station'd there are
Texans & they get their news from them. Most of the Rebs
think that the Confedracy is play'd out. The feeling in our
army here is that they can't make much of a stand anymore. In fact it looks brighter to us now than it has at any
other time since the war commenced but they may make a
greater stand than expected but I believe they must be in
great straights.[22]

George Burnham answered his nephew:

I think the war is not near over yet. You must not take much
notice of peace rumors. It is a bait for recruits. The South
will never except anything short of independence. Nothing
short of the bayonet will ever fetch them & you may expect
to find it about as you herd at Corinth concerning Mexico.[23]
I have allways looked at it so ever since the first expedition
left France for that part but time will tell.[24]

Chilvers commented to his uncle: "I think farming pays better than soldiering to say nothing about the hardships we have to endure. Most of the 9
hundred dollar recruits that come down to us last fall would give anything
to get out of the service. They don't find it as funny as they expected & they
have not seen the elephant yet."[25]

Chilvers commented on the proposed winter quarters in Eastport:

It looks rather rough to leave our comfortable quarters
after going to so much pain to fix them up. Otherwise I
have no particular desire to stay here for we have not had
the best rations for they have never pretended to issue
anything else but field rations (which consists of hard
tack, coffee, & sugar & nothing else except a little soap
occasionally) & part of the time we could not get that.[26]

We expect to go as far as Vicksburg, or Natchez, or possibly to Mobile, or Red River. We turn over all our camp &
garrison equipment tomorrow. The Capt. just told the co.
to be ready at 9-tomorrow morning to move. We will likely
have a long & tedious trip on the boats from one or two
weeks. You must excuse me for this time. I will write you
from Cairo if I can.[27]

The Ninety-Fifth moved frequently during the winter of 1865. On February 5 they left Eastport again and boarded the steamer *Adam Jacobs*.[28] The ship went down the Tennessee, Ohio, and Mississippi Rivers. They camped briefly at Memphis, and then were stationed at Vicksburg from February 12 to February 18. In Vicksburg, Chilvers wrote to Burnham: "we have very good times here. Our duty is light about once in ten days. We did have to drill 4 hours a day but we have not drilled any for over a week now. We have received lots of one year recruits in our regt. We have 112 men in our company and the regt numbers 1337 pretty full isn't it."[29]

The soldiers left Vicksburg on the same steamer and reached New Orleans on February 20, 1865.[30]

> I had no opportunity to write you from Memphis. I whent to the hospital to se[e] one of our boys & when I come back the boat had gone 2 miles up the river to coal & staid there all day.[31] We made a very quick trip from Memphis [to] here.[32] We left there yesterday morning at twenty minutes past 5 & landed here this morning at 9. The distance is 400 miles. We have landed to clean the boats & waite for the rest of the fleet. There is some talk of us staying here but I can't se[e] it.[33]

Pvt. John Fillingham wrote to Chilvers, his cousin, stating:

> Our Div is all the troops there is here now commanded by Brig Gen Hatch one of the best Cavalry Commanders in the Army.[34] The wether has been very wet here this spring and so they say it is up north. . . . We are all in a very pleas-ant camp 4 miles east of town. We have reviews most every day of late. Last night we was reviewed by General Carr.[35] We expect a division review in a few days.[36]

The draft was of major concern to the citizens of Illinois. This was partic-ularly so as the war dragged on, enthusiasm for the war effort waned, the list of casualties grew, and little interest was created by even progressively large bounties for enlistment. Burnham wrote his nephew, "I suppose thare will be another draft in a little while as thare is another call for 300,000 more. It is to take place on the 15th of Feb."[37] He continued his thoughts in a later note, "we hear a great many rumors about peace now again some say the Rebels are ready to make peace on almost any terms but nothing certain about it yet. I suppose they know the terms well enough and also what they have got to do to make peace when ever they are ready we are waiting. We are to have another draft here in about three weeks. I may have to come down there and do what I can to help you boys bury the rebellion. If it comes my turn I must not murmur but do what I have to do cheerfully."[38]

Burnham wrote that the draft was not well accepted in Boone County and many excuses were made by the citizens for not joining the army. He reported:

> I have no news except the draft to mention. Almost every man is either over age or lame or blind. I will mention our own. In the first place I am an [illegible] Silos Stevenson cannot . . . his two boys. Will Tailor is . . . Charles Millegon fanceys one of his legs is a little larger than the other. Barrows is a little deficient in his eyes. Pettit has a fork poked in his belly when a boy & the great patriot J. Sands says he is . . . and the balance cannot probably leave their busness.[39] So you see how the thing stands. There was never was such a sickly time in the United States before & all cause by the plag[ue] called [the] draft.[40]

George Burnham frequently expressed his thoughts on the draft with his nephew. Less than a month after his explanation about whom had developed what ailments, Burnham wrote:

> Our county has filled her coto again.[41] Our town bounty is 400 county 300 government 100 total 800 for one year . . . The new recruits started last Sunday from Meringo.[42] Thear ware 16 from out town most of them young boys. Amongst the crowd is John Ford.[43] I suppose you will wonder at that but I will tell you how it happened. A few weeks since he moved over the county line just in that little timber south of Al Bennots then started to meringo to get exempt. Old Coone the marshall snapt his name down for Dunham town.[44] Dunham would not vote any bounty until the last few days. Everyone said they must draft in that town. John got scared, came over to our town & enlisted & bought Stow's 50 acres & Stow takes his bounty. But I am

> afraid Stow will get the start of John. You see Stow was to
> get quick claim from Topping & I am certain that was due
> last fall but Stow never paid the 300.[45] Consequently he
> never got the deed. Now Stow sells it to John viz his claim
> or interest in the land. So it is doubtful if John ever gets
> much of a title to it. So that's about the hang of John's new
> arrangements.[46]

Chilvers wrote, "poor John Ford is trapped at last but I hope stow will not cheat him out of all his bounty."[47]

Chilvers wrote Burnham at the end of February 1865 that, "I suppose the excitement about the draft has subsided. I se[e] Matthews letter that the Woosters has swallowed the bounty but I guess all the good that their services will do to the government you can put in your eye."[48]

Pvt. John Fillingham wrote Chilvers about the horrid conditions of prison camps. The conditions tremendously worsened after the breakdown of the prisoner of war exchange and the worsening conditions in the South due to the effects of war and the blockade.[49] He wrote: "one of our neighbors, a member of co. K, 7th Cav who was taken prisoner at Colliersville about 18 months ago has got home he is a pityable sight almost starved to death.[50] He is lying sick with Typhoid fever, but I think he is getting better. Surely the men who does such deeds of barbarity will have a terrible reckoning to pay at last."[51]

Chilvers described to Burnham a mutual friend, Lawrence Fagan. Chilvers was worried about the poor health of this middle-aged man. He noted, "Fagan was left at Memphis.[52] He is trying hard to get a discharge. I think it is the only thing that will cure him."[53]

On February 27, 1865, Chilvers wrote:

> tomorrow is muster day. Uncle Sam will owe me (72) sev-
> enty two dollars but I don't know when we will get it. We
> expect to move towards Mobile as soon as we are mus-
> tered. I have not been to New Orleans yet & I don't think
> I shall go for I have no money to spend. We thought we
> discovered a sign of the near approach of the paymaster
> this morning in the shape of an express agent going around
> with bills advertising his business. But Curtis says he don't
> think we will be paid here.[54] The transports whent below

last evening. Some say there is a pass below here that leads into Lake Ponchartrain & that the boats are going into the lake.[55] It has rained all the time we have been here except yesterday. It is raining today.[56]

On March 22, the Ninety-Fifth Illinois boarded transports on Lake Pontchartrain. They arrived at Navy Cove, close to Fort Morgan, the next day.[57] Pvt. Henry Andrus of Company C wrote that they "had all the oysters that they wanted to eat right fresh from the shell."[58] Chilvers also wrote to his family from this location:

> I wrote you from Ceder Point but had no chance to mail it until yesterday when we was on the gunboat Rudolph.[59] We are now at a small landing on [the] Fish River on the opposite side of the bay from Ceder Point.[60] We left the point on the evening of the 22nd on a mosketoo gun boat & run across the bay to the mouth of the river & anchord until morning when we run up the river.[61] I don't know how large our force is here but I think about 20,000. Part 16th Corps & part 13th.[62] The balance of our regt. has not come up yet with the wagon train. We have nothing to draw our rations. We are bust building fortifications. Wm. Stevenson is on duty this morning throwing up breastworks.[63] It is very good diggin all sand with tall pines on, very good for reveting. Our camp is high, & dry, water good, plenty of wood, to cook rations & that is all we need wood for here. Without it is to smoke mosketoos with but we have got up too high for them this time. We was most cat-up with them at Ceder Point.[64]

On March 27 the Ninety-Fifth Illinois reached the defenses of Spanish Fort. This structure along with Fort Blakely composed the two major defensive keys to the city of Mobile. The Confederate fortifications were constructed under the command of Gen. Dabney H. Maury who was confident that the city could be defended.[65]

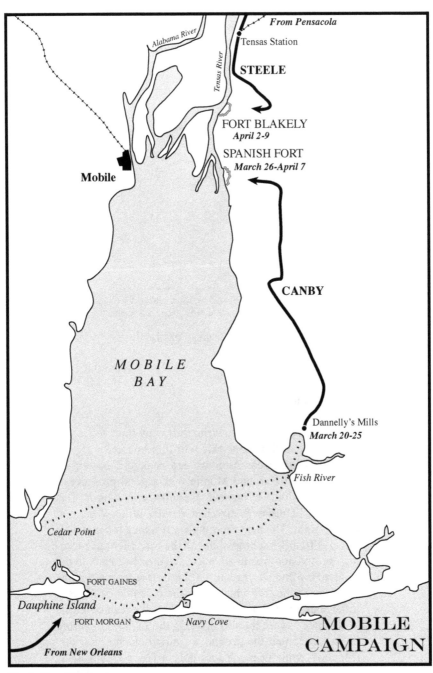

From Pensacola
Tensas Station
STEELE

Alabama River
Tensas River

FORT BLAKELY
April 2-9

SPANISH FORT
March 26-April 7

Mobile

CANBY

*M O B I L E
B A Y*

Dannelly's Mills
March 20-25

Fish River

Cedar Point

FORT GAINES

Dauphine Island

FORT MORGAN   Navy Cove

**MOBILE
CAMPAIGN**

From New Orleans

Map by Donald S. Frazier.

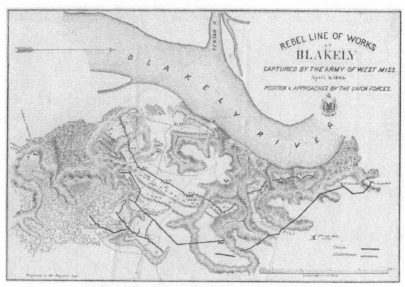

REBEL LINE OF WORKS
AT
BLAKELY
CAPTURED BY THE ARMY OF WEST MISS.
April 9, 1865.
POSITION & APPROACHES BY THE UNION FORCES.

Fort Blakely fell to Union forces on April 9, 1865, which resulted in the capture of Mobile, Alabama. This was the same day that Lee surrendered to Grant at Appomattox.

Chilvers wrote his aunt about the siege of Mobile:

Camp near Mobile[66]   Mar. 30th 1865

My dear Aunt,

I take this opportunity to write these few lines to let you know I am well & hope this will find you enjoying the same blessing. Dear Aunt we are engage'd in seiging one of the forts around Mobile with a good prospect of a steady business at present. We left the landing at Fish River last Saturday & marched about 7 miles & camp'd for the night. The next morning we resumed the march & travel'd 10 miles schirmishing all the way. Monday morning our division was in advance. We marched back to the camp of the 2nd Div. (about 1 1/2 miles) & march'd in the direction of the fort which is on the east side of the Bay (after marching about a mile & a half we formed a line to advance toward the fort driveing the Johneys in before us. We occupied the ground we now hold the first day (Monday) without much loss only a few slight wounds the next morning. A shell explode'd in Co A wounding 4, one mortally Wm. Wallace). The wounded in the regt. so far is Co A 8 & two more in the other right wing cos. Most of the wounds is slight, a great many have been hit by spent balls. The balls strike the lower limbs & glance. A gunboat just exploded a shell in the 33rd Wisconsin horribly mutilating 10 & slightly wounding 5 or 6 others. They are shelling us very bad today. They have splendid forts full of good guns & three very large water batteries with 3 or 4 heavy iron clad boats. The gun boats are doing us more damage than anything else. They have a clean sweep of our lines at easy range & our boats cannot get to them. Our division is on the estreem right of the line resting on the bay. Our Co. is in the works today, on reserve. We had quight a scare about 12 o'clock last night. We tumbled out of bed & run over one another for a few minutes quight lively but finally concluded. We was more scar'd then hurt & whent to bed again. I am haveing a easy time nothing to do but stay out of the way. I mean stay out of the way of bullet shells & co. which I have manage'd to do so far pretty well. They send two bullets through our tent yesterday. I don't stay in it much through the day. We get but very little news here. We had a mail yesterday but I got no letters. I hope you will write often for it is lonesome here & it does one good to get a letter occasionally from home. Remember me to all. No more at present from your affectionate nephew.

Wm. B. Chilvers

Maj. Gen. Gordon Granger commanded the Thirteenth Corps during the Mobile Campaign.

Capt. Cutbert Slocum commanded the Fifth Company of the Washington Artillery that was one of the premier units of the South.

Cousin John Fillingham wrote Chilvers of his experiences with the cavalry, under the command of Gen. James H. Wilson, who was riding through Alabama.[67]

If I had known you had been at Nashville when Old Hood was close there I would have come and seen you and I suppose you was at this place too when we was at the other side of the river and afterwards at Gravelly Springs Ala. As soon as you went down the river we came down and ocopied this place and have been here ever since . . . We got the news here yesterday that Richmond was taken and last night it was read to us on Dress parade. If they could not hold that place I would like to know what they can. I think this thing is about played out. I think we will end it in 65 yet if very thing works out as well as it has been. General Wilson left here about two weeks ago with 12000 Cav for some place near Mobile. I have not heard how he is getting along since he left. I must now close for this time.[68]

Burnham wrote on April 9, 1865, about the news he heard in Illinois about the progress of the war. He wrote:

Chemung Ill [69]   Apr 9 /5

Dear nephew I received yours dated Dauphin island March 17 & was glad to hare from you espeehely to hare you was well as I hope you was well as I hope this will find you still enjoying the same blessings. We expect before this reach you you will have had some hard marching & perhaps hard fighting to do but we can only hope for the best. If you come out of it at Mobeal I think all the hardest fighting is done as Richmond is taken & it was reported last evening Lee & all his army was captured. It is certain that thare will not be many escape so that it is a mare chance if the rebels can make much more of any stand for the men must be discouraged but they may hold out a little longer. I think the war will end before your time is out. Every kind of grain is lower. Oats has dropt to 20 cents & other grains in prepotion. You see the farmers suffers first then the machine laborer all before goods come down. There is nothing except common calaleos that has fill up if a man or woman goes to a store to get a dress thay will sell her it for from 15 to 25 cents & charge her 30 to 35 cents for a lining in it.[70] So you see the farmers & lower classes will have to pay for the war. I expect to start tomorrow for Chicago if the weather & all is well but in both cases it looks doughtfull for the last 4 days it has froze awful & now it snows & Rebecca has gone to bed sick. But if she is better in the morning I shall start. If I do I shall mail this in Chicago. I think you had better send your letters to Chemung again as Ankram Stevenson goes every week to Chemung & Rebecca can get them from thare. You must wright home as usual but you must not expect one every weeke from her as she will be tierd as night comes & perhaps will not feel much like wrighting but between the two of us we may manage one every week. Remember us to Will & the rest of the boys that we are acquanted with. We remain as ever your affectonat Uncle & Aunt

George & R. Burnham

In mid-April Burnham noted, "I saw several of the 95 in list already of kild & wounded at Mobeal I hope before this Mobeal has sorendeded."[71]

In a later April letter Burnham wrote, "our joyous victorys for the past days has been broken by the sad news of the death of the president.[72] Chicago is draped in mourning. It is a sad affair. Seward is not yet dead but his son is not expected. To lone over many howers they have not caught Booth the assasin."[73] Will wrote:

we have had some very good news of late from Virginia but the news of the death of Mr. Lincoln casts a gloom over all.[74] I don't see what benefit his death is a going to be for their cause. It only shows what a miserable bunch of cut throats they are.[75] We are in hopes the rebellion is about over. The Johnnies are continually comeing in. They are about as thoroughly whip'd as I ever saw anyone. They have gave up all hopes & only ask the privilege to go home to their families. But Sherman seems to be playing a strange part late. I can't make out what he means by granting them an armistice without he is going to surrender to Johnson.[76]

The Spanish Fort was besieged from March 27 to April 7 with the Confederates enduring artillery bombardment of an "estimated thirty to forty heavy guns and at least a dozen mortars. By April 7th the Federals had dug almost to the main Confederate works around Spanish Fort."[77] An effective water battery, Fort Eugee, was finally silenced when General Canby erected eight, sixty-four pounders against the position. On April 7 a general assault

Maj. Gen. Edward Richard Sprigg Canby commanded the Union forces during the Mobile Campaign. He accepted the surrender of Confederate forces under Richard Taylor on May 4, 1865, and those under Edmund Kirby Smith on May 26, 1865.

took Spanish Fort with the Ninety-Fifth being one of the advanced forces. Pvt. William B. Chilvers of Company B carried the colors over the parapet.[78]

Following the fall of Spanish Fort, Blakely was next assaulted. Carr's division was used as reserves for the Second Division of the Sixteenth Corps and the First Division of the Thirteenth Corps. A general assault carried Blakely on April 9, the same day Lee surrendered at Appomattox.[79] Three days later, Mobile was surrendered to the forces of Gen. Edward R. S. Canby.

Following the surrender of Mobile, General Maury withdrew his forces to Meridian, Mississippi, where he joined forces with Gen. Nathan Bedford Forrest. The department commander, Gen. Richard Taylor, arranged for a meeting with Union Gen. Edward R. S. Canby, commander of the Department of the Gulf. They met for a preliminary meeting at a place ten miles north of Mobile, and a temporary truce was established. A few days later at Citronville, Taylor surrendered his forces to Canby, and Commodore Farrand surrendered the ships in the Alabama River to Rear Adm. Thatcher.[80]

Following the capture of Blakely, the Ninety-Fifth Illinois Infantry as part of Steele's Sixteenth Army Corps, began a two-hundred-mile march to Montgomery, Alabama. Adjutant Wood noted that, "at almost every house a white flag appeared, which denoted submission and friendship on the part of the occupants, and claimed protection for their premises."[81]

The Union forces arrived in Montgomery on April 25, 1865, where they met no opposition. They learned of the surrender of Gen. Richard Taylor in early May which "closed out the Confederacy from the Atlantic Ocean to the Mississippi river."[82] After resting from their long march, the Ninety-Fifth Illinois took up light duty, and resumed battalion drills and dress parades. Maj. Gen. A. J. Smith witnessed the regiment on dress parade and "remarked he had never seen the Cadets at West Point excel this military performance."[83]

The Ninety-Fifth Illinois were ordered as part of Colonel Moore's brigade to the north-eastern part of Alabama on May 23 to perform garrison duty to preserve order and collect any remaining property of the Confederacy. The Thirty-Third Wisconsin and the Forty-Fourth Missouri were sent to Tuskegee, the Seventy-Second Illinois to Union Springs, and the Ninety-Fifth Illinois to Opelika. Wood wrote, "as the regiment marched through the village to its place of encampment, the houses w[e]re all kept closed; the fair occupants, incensed at our arrival, did not show themselves, and excepting a few Confederate paroled soldiers and citizens sitting around various rum-shops . . . the town appeared deserted and lifeless."[84]

With the exception of the remarkable battle victory at Palmetto Ranch, Texas, on May 13, 1865, the Trans-Mississippi Department deteriorated into desertions and riots. On June 2, 1865, generals Kirby Smith, commander of the Trans-Mississippi Department, and John Magruder, commander of the Department of Texas, "went aboard the Union steamer *Fort Jackson* off Galveston harbor and signed the articles of surrender." The last chapter of the Civil War had completed, and the war was over.[85]

The Ninety-Fifth Illinois was relieved from duty in late July by three companies of the Fifty-Second Indiana Infantry and left Opelika on July 18. They began their trip back home by traveling to Montgomery in part by train. On July 28 they were taken by the steamers *Red Chief* and *Coquette* down the Alabama River to Selma. The troops then were transported by rail through Demopolis and Meridian to Jackson, Mississippi. From there, the regiment then marched to Vicksburg. The rail from Jackson to Vicksburg had been thoroughly destroyed. On August 5 they were taken by the steamer *Mollie Able* to St. Louis which they reached on August 10. They were then taken by rail to Springfield, Illinois, and finally to "Camp Butler." On August 16, 1865, the Ninety-Fifth Illinois was formally mustered out of service of the United States Army by Capt. James A. Hall of the First U.S. Cavalry. On August 21 they received full and final payment. Honorable Allen C. Fuller met the troops in Chicago and escorted them back to Boone and McHenry counties, where patriotic ceremonies greeted the returning veterans.[86]

Adjutant Wood concluded: "Out of the aggregate nine hundred and eighty-three officers and enlisted men . . . only about half returned and mustered out

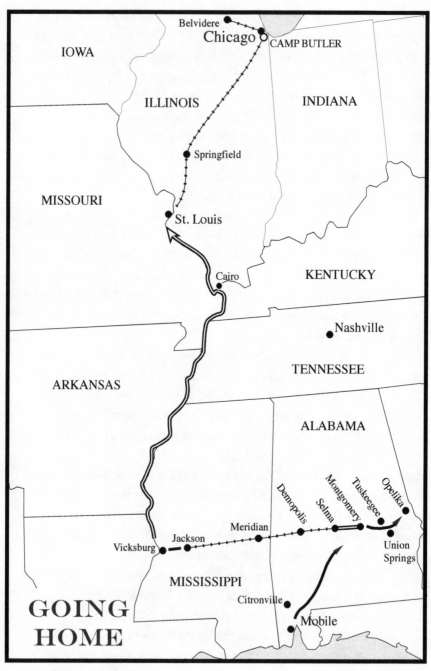

Map by Donald S. Frazier.

with the organization. One hundred and ninety men were discharged during the service . . . mostly for disabilities . . . eighty-three died of wounds in action . . . while one hundred and seventy-seven became the pitiful victims of disease."[87]

During the last year of the Civil War, life in northern Illinois improved for George and Rebecca Burnham. Burnham kept his nephew apprised of his efforts at farming:

> I have been a paid topping all the money & got the mortgage releast so the land is clear from all incumberance wich I think is a grand job done. I have the team and all my hay left yet. I hold Pats note of 100 for 90 & your 30 & 58. I had maid 178. So after all was paid it leaves me with 48 dollars on hand & my total paid 1015 [illegible] & we don't owe a dollar. So I think we are the best of[f] we ever have been since we have been in the country.[88]
>
> I will say I have been paid Topping all we owed him and have gotten the mortgage cancelled.[89] I sold Pat's note of $100 for $90 & your 30 & what I have payed it & left some to the good. I would like to get Stows 50 acres if we cold. I can get it for 850. If I cold see any chance to pay for it. I have about 60 dollars in cash & Will Taylor's note of $42.50 & very nearly all my hay yet & my taxis paid ($10.75) & what may seem strange to you we are out of debt for the first time for 9 or 10 years.[90]

George wrote Will about job prospects locally and outside of Boone County: "I think of coming to Nashville to work for the government. I think I cold pass of[f] well anough for a carpenter on bridges if not I could get 45 dollars a month. What do you think to it?"[91] Chilvers encouraged his uncle to look for jobs and leave Illinois:

> I suppose you are making calculations for next spring. I think Cairo will be a great place for work next summer.[92] I understand they are going to complete it to Kansas City.[93] You would have a fine opportunity to se[e] the country from Warrensburg west which I think is the best farming country I have seen in the United States.[94] I understand the price of grain is falling. It is my opinion that wheat won't be worth much if the war ends & some of the farmers that are

grumbling about the big bounty to soldiers will find themselves worse off when the war is over than they are now.[95]

Burnham wrote Chilvers about inflated prices for animals in Illinois:

> I would liked to be down at Cairo to have seen you when
> you came there. If I cold have sold my team I should have
> been down thare before this. But it seems impossible to sell
> them or my hay without an auction & at such places the
> men seems to bid as much for yearling colts as horses will
> be worth after the war is over. I was at an auction today &
> saw small last spring colts sold for 40-45 dollars yearlings
> & two year olds sell as high as 100 to 130. Thare will be
> an awful crash before long. I wrote you some time ago to
> know what you thought of I had better do if I had a chance
> to sell the land at 1200. if I keep it it must be fenced & the
> tax is very high. This last bounty alone will make a tax of
> 10 dollars a year for 5 years wich will make between 20 &
> 30 dollars a year taxes wich will come hard to pay of[f] this
> farm. I think the less property a man has the better. You see
> every thing we buy is taxed so awfull high. Everything is
> 4 times as high as it was before the war. Will grane is not
> more than one third higher. The farmer is imposed on more
> than any other men. You see thare will always be a tax on
> what we buy but for grain we shall have to sell it for what
> we can get for it. Wheat is only worth from 100 to 130.
> Oats 50- corn 75-. Compare that with tea 2.50 sugar 35 lb
> cotton cloth 55 cents & every other article in proportion.
> You see we pay a heavy tax on all we buy besides our land
> & war tax.[96]

Chilvers responded to Burnham's letters on farming and occupational
options:

> You whanted to know what I thought of your going to
> Nashville to work for the government.[97] Well I think you
> will find it the longest 6 months you ever saw. You had
> better work at Chicago for 25 cwnts if you whant to make
> money.[98] But I think you woud find no difficulty on getting
> 45 on the Pacific Rail Road or on any other RR.[99] Besides
> you would not be bound as the government employees

are. I know you would rue the day you had anything to
do with the government. If you whant to live on swill &
sleep in pens & get lousy go to Nashville. It will cost you
a good share of your 45 to buy something to eat for you
can't buy nick nacks at Nashville for nothing. You had
much better enlist in the Army of Tennessee but I don't
advise you to do either for you can do much better most
anywhere. You whanted to know what I thought of your
selling the land for $1200. I think I should hold onto it
without I could see a chance to better myself. At all event
you would whant at least 3 down & then you might stand
a chance to get the balance but if you sold on the long
time & the war ended (which would bring everything to a
specie basis) the purchaser may find it to his advantage to
let you have the land back. On the other hand if you had
money you might make use of it. You could pay it out to
good advantage in Mo. Or you might put it in some small
business but you must always remember $1200 is not as
good as 1200 in gold. I think you had better go at anything else than to work for the government. I have never
seen anyone yet that was satisfied with it. There are too
many blood suckers around you.[100]

Burnham wrote Chilvers in April 1865 that conditions were
difficult in Chicago, "I came in on 10 & came with Wi. Linton. It
is very dull now the prospects of peace has changed the appearance of things. Wages is low & board high. I will write more in
a few days."[101] Burnham continued his thoughts a few days later,
"Chicago has grown since I was here before. I am at work with W.
Linton driving but I shall not stay with him no longer than I can
better myself. Which I think will soon be but work has not hurt and
yet I get a chance to look at two or 3 papers daily."[102]

In May 1865 Burnham wrote his wife that he was having health
problems:

Dear Wife I take this opportunity to let you know my health
is good but my eyes has been so bad I thought I would
have had to leave my work. If I had been at home I should
not have thought of working but they feel some better this

morning. I have not been out in the evening only once this week and that was to Mr. Hansons & he urged me to stay till almost 10 o'clock. He fetched out a bottle of his wine & we drank almost all of it. We had quite a chat. He would like for us to go & live on his land. He says he will give us all we ask. That is to say in the priviledge of the land. He wishes to be remembered to you. he would like to see you any time you can make it convenient to come in. Dear wife you must not trouble about me for it is so rare that I can come home any time I like but if I keep well I stay hare as long can as it cost quite a little both ways. I have worked 3 1/2 days this week. It rained yesterday morning so we lost 1/2 day. I shall try and make all the time I can as my work is not very hard. The worst part of it is the smoke from the steamboats. It hurts my eye but I hope tha will get over that soon.[103]

Throughout the war Chilvers corresponded with his relatives in Illinois and England. Cousin James Fillingham wrote keeping his cousins informed of his life. "James Ewing & Elizabeth are living with us this winter but they have a place rented for to farm next summer.[104]

While George worked in Chicago, Rebecca managed their farm near Belvidere. Chilvers sent a note to his Aunt Rebecca:

Camp near Montgomery, Ala[105]   May 9th 1865

Dear Aunt

I take this opportunity to let you know I am well & I hope this will find you in good health & spirits. We get a mail last Sunday which was the first we had since we left Blakely but the letters were most a month old. The latest date was one from George dated 16th. We have had some very good news of late from Virginia but the news of the death of Mr. Lincoln casts a gloom over all. I don't se[e] what benefit his death is a going to be for their cause. It only shows what a miserable bunch of cut throats they are. We are in hopes the rebellion is about over. The Johnnies are continually comeing in. They are about as thoroughly whip'd as I ever saw anyone. They have gave up all hopes & only ask the privilege to go home to their families. But

Sherman seems to be playing a strange part late. I can't make out what he means by granting them an armistice without he is going to surrender to Johnson.

We are all in a very pleasant camp 4 miles east of town. We have reviews most every day of late. Last night we was reviewed by General Carr.[106] We expect a division review in a few days. I suppose you are busy in your garden. I wish I could come home to help you especially when the strawberries & currants are ripe but I'm afraid we won't get home before our time is out. I am afraid you will be lonesome this summer but hope this will be the last for I think George will be contented to stay at home after this summer. I hope you will write to me often for I should like to know how you get along alone. Remember me to the Sintens & Robinsons. Give my love to Uncle & Aunt Twelves & believe me ever your true friend & nephew.

Direct Wm. B. Chilvers   Co B 95th Ills. Inf. 1st Brig, 3rg Division,
16th Corps Via Cairo

CHAPTER 8

Back through Norfolk

William B. Chilvers lived a lifetime of suffering. He was born into a poor family in County Norfolk, England, where he was orphaned as a child. He came to America with the Burnhams as a teenager. Will worked briefly as a carpenter's assistant before he began farming with his uncle, George Burnham, in Northern Illinois, an area known for harsh winters. These difficult times were then followed by three years of arduous service in the Ninety-Fifth Illinois Infantry. He survived rugged weather, disease, exhaustion, and the horrors of battles at Vicksburg, Guntown, the pursuit during the Missouri Raid, Nashville, and Mobile. After discharge from the army, Chilvers' future opportunities included farming with the Burnhams, returning to England, or moving to the thriving city of Chicago. Chilvers matured into a resourceful, intelligent, ambitious, and independent young man, ready to build a new life.

Several factors prohibited Chilvers return to his native land. The massive expense to travel back to England made his return unattainable. Letters from his cousins made a return seem less appealing as well, as Chilvers' English family experienced a less thriving life than either the Burnhams, or even Chilvers. His English family continued to struggle economically, and like many families, deaths and squabbles disrupted its cohesiveness.[1]

Chicago became Chilvers' destination after his discharge in Illinois in August 1865. Will went to work as a carpenter improving on his skills he acquired as an assistant five years before. He was now living on his own and began to look to start his own family.

Uncle George and Aunt Rebecca Burnham somehow survived farming while Chilvers was off at war. In 1870 they paid off their debt and had some savings. That year, Stephen Stork, their close relative, wrote suggesting that the Burnhams and Chilvers join him homesteading in Nebraska.[2]

Chilvers took the opportunity and gave Stephen "Stork money to place a homestead stake for him . . . [and told Stork] he will come out this fall or early spring."[3]

Stephen Stork wrote George Burnham in an undated letter from the late 1860s or early 1870s:

Sunday   July 17[4]

Dear Friends

I now take the pleasure of writing to you to let you know something about Nebraska. Well George we got through first rate.[5] We came from Rockford to Fremont in twenty-one days and stayed there two days and came up to a little town called Evert Point and I left the family there, and Mr. Philips a man that came from Fremont the same time we did him and I got a buggy and came up here about 40 miles and took homesteads.[6] I have taken 160 acres and all it cost me was $150 and filed on one for Bill.[7] He says he will come out this fall or early in the spring. Hore Magoon and Henry Heywood came out with us and they have both taken homesteads here but they have gone back down to Fremont to work. Well George this is rather a wild looking country out here but it looks different than what it did when we came out here for it was nothing but a wild looking Please write soon as you can and let us know how you are faring but now I have got about 80 acres broke. There is a splendid looking meadow on my place. There is one house a quarter of a mile of ours and another about a mile both families came up at the same time we did. We have got a house but it is not very large for lumber is very dear and its a long way to haul it. I had to haul mine 40 miles. Our house is a side roof shingle and is 12 by 24. Well George there is plenty of government land out here [to] get for everybody that comes.[8] I like it first rate out here but I won't advise anybody to come or to stay away but I think the farm will be worth considerably in a few years. There is a town started about 7 miles from here. The railroad is coming through soon.[9] It is within 10 miles of Evert Point.[10] Now the people of Norfolk expect the railroad through there in less than a year's time.[11] There is a saw mill and a grist mill and a blacksmith shop and a hotel and two stores. John McClairie started his store this last week and there is a number of other buildings going up. Tell Bill Chilvers there is a good chance for carpenters out here and I think he would do first rate if he was out here.[12] Carpenters get from $5 to 8 ½ a day. Wood is scarce out here. What there is is most all owned by speculators. It is chiefly cotton wood but it don't cost us anything for firewood out here for we help ourselves to the speculators wood. Tell <u>Bill Chilvers</u> I wish he would use the wood for a scotch drag and send them out with Bill for timber is scarce to make them of out here. There is not any oak hardly out here and the cotton wood is of not much use for such. George if you could sell your farm and come out here I think you would like it first rate for there is plenty of chances for stores or eating houses or anything in Norfolk and I think it will be quite a town after the railroad comes through and if Bill was out here he could do well at his trade for there is a great call for carpenters here.[13] George I am sorry I sold my reaper. I sold it for $70 and it would have been worth 130 out here.

A new reaper and mower out here costs $190. I have got all my horses yet but I don't know but I shall trade one team off this week. <u>There is a river called the Elkhorn</u> about five miles from here north and a crick [*sic*] about five miles south called <u>Union Crick.</u>[14] George if you come out bring your gun out here for there is lots of deers and antellopes out here and there is lots of Indians out here.

There was about 500 comanches on the banks of the Elkhorn about 3 weeks ago but they have not troubled us yet. There is the Omahatribe, the Souix, the Winnebagoes, Pinnchaws.[15] Those three tribes went up to the Sioux reserve and had a fight with the Souix and killed a great many of both tribes. We are all well and hope this will find you all the same. I must close so no more at present. Write soon. I remain your friend as ever.
Stephen Stork
Direct to <u>Stephen Stork</u>   Mr. George Burnham
Norfolk
William Chilvers Madison Co   Neb

Map by Donald S. Frazier.

Letters to the Burnhams and Chilvers were written by other members of the Stork family. These letters encouraged the Burnhams and Chilvers to move to Nebraska due to its agricultural resources and tremendous economic potential for pioneers. William Stork, the brother of Stephen, wrote a convincing letter on November 15, 1870, to George Burnham:

> I am home in Nebraska . . . Well George you wanted me to let you know what I think about this part of the country . . . I like it better here than I did in Iowa. All I have against this country is its so windy and timber is so scarce. The soil is some sandy but I think it is pretty good for corn and small grain and I never saw any better meadows that we have here. The grass is up to a horse buggy this season and it has been very dry out here. George you had better come on to this part and see how you like it. There is some splendid valeys that is not taken up yet but no timber on it. The wood is on the streams. It is mostly oak & hard wood. There is some ark and live oak and willow.[16]

Rebecca Burnham's niece, Mate Stork, wrote her a delightful letter on November 15, 1870. She mentioned family and desired that the Burnhams move to Nebraska.[17]

Well Aunty I like our new home first rate. It is a great deal pleasanter than I thought it would be & I worked on it ten weeks this summer. I got three dollars a week. Beck is working up town now in the hotel.[18] . . . Aunty looks quite different out here to what it did when we come here for there was not a house within five miles when we came and now there is seven or eight within about two miles of here but there is not one young girl out here at all. Beck and I are the only American girls within ten miles.[19] Aunty I wish you and Uncle were out here and start a hotel at Norfolk. I think you could do pretty well for they charge five dollars a week for board.[20]

Ambrotype of William Chilvers after his return from the Civil War. [Photo from the Collection of C. Richard Chilvers.]

Stephen Stork wrote from Pleasant Valley, Nebraska, to William Chilvers on February 5, 1871. Apparently, after some deliberation, the Burnhams sold their farm in Illinois in late 1870, and set off for the treeless and gently rolling hills of the eastern part of Nebraska. This region had just pushed the Native Americans off the land, and was waiting for construction of the railroad. Stork wrote:

I received your letter. You menschen about railroad land and government land her[e] for homsteding but the sooner someone comes the better for they will have picked the best of it but it do not look so well now for it is very dry [and] burned all over. The speculators cannot cum in this country. Ther[e] is land for sale about 5 miles from us 300 and 40 acers sum wood and a crick runs thru it and I think it can be bart [bought] for 5 dolers per acer. It is a very nice piece as [nice] as I have seen. There is a good mill privede on it. There will be plenty of worke for carpenters next summer in Norfolk. The rarod [railroad] is cmen [coming] then. There will be a good open for a hotel and borden [boarding] house. Ther[e] is one now and it is doing good bisnes. The[y] do not sell any licer [liquor] ther[e]. Ther[e] is one licer store. He do not have any half the

Cousin Tom Chilvers moved from England to join Will Chilvers in Pierce, Nebraska, to explore opportunities in the new state of Nebraska. [Photo from the Collection of C. Richard Chilvers.]

time. Hurnren and John Barney have taken homesteads about 3 miles west from us and [illegible] Magrone he has a homested and Hank Harwood has one joining o[u]r Wills but he has not bene on it since he clame it.[21] There will be sumbody claim it if he do not come soon. The boys is goin to Fremont after corn. It is only 25 cents per bushel in the are [illegible]. You said in your leter that George had sold out his place.[22] I think he has dun well.

This is a good place for cows and stock. They have to hurd them. I do not want to persuade any one to cum but I think any one can do well here. They rase good crops and ease land to work. It is chief on sandy soil. It is a fine place for veitables.[23] We are haven the nises [nicest] winter we ever saw only for the wins [winds] but I suspect we feel it more because we are on the open prary. We have not had any snow here. We get or wood of[f] the specklaters. I have got big wo[o]d pile[d] up now and ceep going for more. I think horses will be here this spring. You can trade for catel [cattle] & stock any time you can get anuf [enough] money. Your buggy wad [would] sell here.

Wagins is here from a hundred and ten dolers. I think you wo[u]ld do well when you get acquainted. We have got quite a settlement in Pleasant Val[l]ey. When I came you could not see any w[h]eel tracks but there is plenty now. You can cum her[e] [on one of the] sides but the south is the nicest and then you have not to cross the river. There is no beige.[24] There is a bri[d]ge over Union Crick now that is about 6 miles from us southwest. Lumber is cheaper now than it was w[h]en I came. You can get anything for money except a woman. Ther[e] is plenty of pray here all over.[25] The pray is fech your gun. Plenty of deres and antlopes.[26] There is mor[e] in summer. Ther[e] is sum elke that ar[e] as big as a two ye[a]r old ste[e]re.[27]

Following his discharge from the service in 1865 Will Chilvers worked as a carpenter in Chicago. He kept up with events in Boone County which was within one hundred miles. During this period he met Nellie Pilcher.[28] Following the war, she moved with her family from Ohio to Boone County, Illinois. Nellie, her parents, and her sister Eliza lived in Bonus, which was close to Belvidere.

Chilvers followed George and Rebecca Burnham to Nebraska in the spring or summer of 1871. Apparently he continued to think of Nellie Pilcher despite her much younger age. He probably remembered Stork's previous note warning him of the difficulty on meeting women in the developing area of Nebraska. Chilvers wrote Nellie from the Norfolk House, Norfolk, Nebraska, on December 7, 1871, proposing marriage:

I wish I could spend a few minutes with you . . . What do you think about getting married in the spring it seems as if I could hardly waite until then but of course I must waite your pleasure although I hope you will not keep me waiteing too long now be a good girl & say you will be willing as soon as I can come which I hope will be in the spring. You know it is not as if we where only a mile or two apart one time would do most as well as another but you se[e] it is quite a journey & dont know when I can get away until my folks get out here. But I would like to have everything set[t]led so that if I could make arrangements to come for. So as to return with my Uncle, you would be willing to return with me for that is all I have to come for. We have had some very severe weather for this country yesterday & to day was very pleasant but the wind has got around to the North again & it is quight cold this evening I understand it has been cold in Ills.. We have had 8 or 10 days good sleighing the setlers says there has not been so much in 5 years before. I am at work at the hotel now . . . The weather has been too cold to do much out of doors. I am doing laboring work generally this winter . . .

Union Veteran Organization Grand Army of the Republic Reunion Ribbon of Will Chilvers in Pierce, Nebraska. [Photo from the Collection of C. Richard Chilvers.]

one day I am making sleighs & the next tables, cupboards
or something else I expect to have some considerable work
next summer if everything turns out right & if I have a little
wife to go home too Saturday evenings I don't see why I
can't get along . . . Give my respects to all enquiring friends
& particular to Eliza.[29] Tell her to be a good little girl. But
I supose she begins to think she is some by this time if not
more. Tell her if she is a good girl I will bring her a beaux
from Neb. When I come. That is if I can . . . But then I don't
supose she knows how to darn a stocking yet, or bake a pra-
tee [illegible] Hoping to hear from you soon.[30]

Nellie accepted his proposal but noted that her parents were cautious
regarding the specifics of their arrangement. Chilvers wrote Nellie from
Norfolk, Nebraska, on February 11, 1872, offering to return to Illinois, work
in Chicago and marry her.

After he completed the construction of the Hetzel Hotel, Will Chilvers
moved back to Illinois in the summer of 1872.[31] He married Nellie Pilcher
on October 6, 1872, in Sharon, Wisconsin, and the couple lived in Chicago.
The newlyweds rented a house with another family. Chilvers wrote Nellie on
September 17, 1872, from Chicago:

I am trying to rent a place to move into I thought I had a place
Al Thornton & I was going to rent a small house between us
we would have had a square room bed room & pantry each
for $6 a month but the man has concluded not to rent it if we
had got it Thornton was going home on Saturday to fetch
his family & I should have got furniture & then come for
you. How would an arrangement of that kind suit you[?] I
thought it would be so nice to go home when I get through
work in the evening & if we get married right off we must
have some place to live in until spring & we could make a
start here as well as anywhere write me what you think of
it I think you would like it better here then anywhere else
after you got used to it for everyone attends to their own
business here & don't bother themselves about other people.
Mrs. Thornton & you would be company for each other. I
sup[p]ose you are not acquainted with her she is Wm. Frys
daughter & he is cousin to Thomas Thornton that used to

live between Geo. Aecks & the Widow Fryr I shall be back
on Bonus next week I cant come very well before. I have not
heard from Neb.[32] Yet I have been expecting my tool chest
but have not heard from it yet . . . Give my love to Eliza.[33] I
am sorry my letter should make you uneasy & cause you to
take such a long journey[34]

The couple lived in Chicago in 1873. George Burnham wrote Chilvers
to inform him of developments and urging him to return to Nebraska. The
Burnhams had moved from Pierce to Roseville which was about fifteen miles
away.[35] On January 22, 1873, George wrote his nephew and niece:

> I cannot think what use thare is staying in Chicago this
> winter except you intend to stay thare this next summer I
> think Chicago [is] a poor place in the winter your rent &
> fire must cost you so much as would keep you out thare . . .
> I think thare will be several new settlers in the spring thare
> is great talk of the Suyz City & Columbus road going by
> Stanton Craton has had several settlers this fall send me
> word what you think of doing if you could furnish me the
> wire & me the poasts & make a god pasture field I have got
> some two or three hundred poasts.[36]

On December 29, 1873, George Burnham wrote his nephew a letter
of frustration at their lack of communication and that the Chilvers had not
returned to Nebraska. George has obtained some influence in the region and
has been elected a county commissioner. George Burnham wrote:

> it is a long time since I heard from you your letters are few & far
> between you can not take much intrest in the west you want me
> to send you all the particulars of the settlement I notice you do
> not send me much of anything . . . Do you think of coming out
> hare soon or not as thare is two or three mall jobs you could do
> if you was hare Wagner wants you & Lucas is a going to bould
> a peace more on the end of his house & thare is to be another
> schoolhouse near P. Shonecies & another in the Buckley settle-
> ment & I think we shall bould another bridge over the Norfolk
> . . . & move one the bridge boulders has just got thare pay for
> the 2 bridges 2700. Tha have made a big thing out of them I
> objected to pay them & condemn the bridge & it did not fill

the contract & was very poor work on them but the other two
commissioners paid them . . . I am afraid we shall catch some
hard weather in the spring. I quite expected to get a letter from
you this mail but failed I mailed one for you on 11 at Norfolk to
Capron as I expected you would be thare[37]

Apparently, Chilvers responded to Burnham's letter. Will had successful
business activities with W. W. Cones, a banker and developer that his uncle
apparently did not approve. On January 28, 1874, George wrote:

I rec. yours of 14 a few days ago you astonish me in the
way and tone you write you are oulde to know what to do &
also what this country is & you can also can see how much
you have made over a living in Illinois if you have not got
considerable push by you you cannot have made much ove a
living you could have done that hare & improved your property wich of corse will not improve without you if you do
not intend coming out hare make your mind up & stay ware
you are & buy something that you can be improving on or
go in with Cones as I think he could loan you something[.][38]
[Y]ou are his last resource thare is no othert man west of
Chicago he could hier to go in with him if he had any money
but that is not the case he has none but he thinks you have
a few dollars & might stand a chance to get a few little out
hare & he takes that plan to try to get you into it[.][39] [T]he
fact is he cannot get anything in this state let alone Stanton
or Pierce neither can you or any other man if [he] comes in
plaid out but for your self I shall not trouble my self anymore
abought the matter I will say this much I am sure you had
better stay ware you are than to come out hare if you cannot
come without hanging on Cones coat tail[40]

George continued to be suspicious of Cones and frustrated with Chilvers
not moving to Nebraska. In a letter to his nephew dated February 19, 1874,
Burnham wrote:

Roseville   Pierce[41]   Feb 19/ 74

Dear Nephew & Niece yours of the 3 came to hand on the
16th you seem to think the tax in our county rather high

you think Cones may well complain of the county tax you don't know Cones as well as we do[.][42] [I]t was Cones that caused such a tax in our settlement our school tax alone for the district was 23 mills on the dollar and he thought by telling them to go on with the schoolhouse that tha would vote for him & his party & so tha did in James Goulds district all but James. Cones would support any tax only let him have the contract or be a party in it he even tould the school board to go on and bould the school on government land without any deed wich the law strictly for bids he allso took 50 dollars out of supervisor Brier for one days work on the road he told brier it as worth 50 dollars to fill up the ends of the Norfolk bridge he gave him the contract he done it in one day and thought it was all right I gave him the job to hall [haul] 640 ft pine from Wisner to his house at Pierce[.] [H]e charged 12 dollars that's W. W. Cones is economy for the county. Principally all our tax has been caused by such a heavy school tax all the bigges [bridges] has been nothing but what was needed. We are to have an a lection to see wither the county is to vote & give $ 10,000 to some party to bould a grist mill at Pierce[.] [T]hare seems to bee quite a number [that] wants it[.] [W]e shall give notic[e] to the voters on the second of March it will probably be abought the first of April the election if you are a comming out you aught to be hare by that time if you ar[e] not comming I would like to know[.] [W]e want a platform & desk & several other little jobs doing at the co[u]rthouse van has been thare most of this winter a trying to put up the bannersters such another job you never saw if you do not come out I shall try & git All [illegible] Burnham to finish it & do what county woork I can get him if we vote the mill bonds I shall bee some little interested in it so much that it will be left to us to let some man or company have rhe bonds to bould the mill & run it. Tha will have to bould a mill when in running order worth double the amount of bonds. The bonds will run ten years & in that time Pierce County will have ten times the popelation in so the princable will not be much left. We are having a splendid winter so far you was a speaking of Mr. Barr he may do buseness yet but he has to do it intierly by his pen [as] he has lost his speech. I am afraid thare sections will not come back yet[.] Mr.

Wellch the Norfolk land recorder & receiver says he is a of them coming again for another levey tha clame tha have not got all grand yet but I hoope tha have you spoke of not knowing anything of Pierce Co. without I could send you some papers some advertisements something to puff the county up I did not think you needed any at all events wishing you was hare you could talk it up pretty fare when I was at Capron & spoke of staying you said I must come to Neb you would not lose your chance for a 1000 dollars. I think that was considerable puff abought that if you do the same now I think you might sell once in a while for 4 to six dollars per acre I can buy from 3 1/2 to 5 all I want if you couldn't sell & find a good small farm for trade mine of[f]. I will give a deed for the whole of mine 2500 with all the improvements on wich aught to be worth 1000 of[f] it[.] I think of planting out eighteen on my homestead or on a timber clear 10 acres this summer if you start befor[e] spring opens make arrangements for Mr Pilcher to send out a bag of kerints [currants] cherries & other stuff &n if you stay you can send them but let me know by return of mail.[43]
Me & Rebecca is both a little under the weather for the last few days[.] Ellen & family is well as I hoope this will find you injoying the same blessings
I remain as ever yours truly George Burnham
Roseville   Pierce   Nebraska

Nellie and Will Chilvers moved to Nebraska in the spring or summer of 1874. Eliza wrote them in Nebraska in September 1874.[44] He homesteaded near Plainview where he had filed on a timber claim.[45] Chilvers got involved in local politics and had business and political associations with W. W. Cones.[46] William Burnham Chilvers became successful in construction, farming, and as a landowner. He built the first store building for Herman Mewis in 1874.[47] Will Chilvers served as president of the village board at Pierce, a member of the school board, a charter member of the Pierce Post of the G.A.R., and of the Masonic lodges of both Norfolk and Pierce. He put up the first frame house in this part of the state and served Plainview as its first postmaster, county clerk and recorder. In 1900, Chilvers was elected as the clerk of the District Court where he served for twelve years.

Will was honored with a street named for him in Pierce, and later the city park in Plainview.

Nellie and Will's first daughter, Eliza Mae, was the first child of European ancestry born in the Plainview settlement.[48] The couple had six more children: John P., Alfred W., George W., Frances, Nellie, Charles H., and Anna. Surprisingly, only Charles Henry Chilvers (1891–1983) had children.[49] Charles was a successful banker and abstract title officer. He had three sons with Mary Genevieve Bechter (1897–1981). All three sons served in the military during World War II: Bob (1923–1995), William Bechter (1921–2011), and Tom (1925). Tom lives close to his grandfather's three-story house in Pierce, Nebraska.[50]

William Burnham Chilvers died on December 16, 1914, "due to heart failure occasioned by kidney disease and dropsy . . . his mind was still as vigorous as youth, and not withstanding his extreme age he still took great interest in public affairs and had the entire supervision of his large business interests, both on the farm and in the office. . . . One of the earliest pioneers he probably contributed more to the upbuilding and development of this part of the state than any other individual. Many today can point their success to their first start in life—to the sound advice of 'Uncle Bill' Chilvers. He was held in highest esteem by all."[51]

Notes

Chapter 1

1. See for example, the Poor Law Act of August 14, 1834, *An Act for the Amendment and better Administration of the Laws relating to the Poor in England and Wales* [4 & 5 Will. IV c.76]. The act was created to reduce the number of people listed on the poor rolls, but not to help them. The poor were considered criminals and could be sent to debtors' prisons. The Factory Act of 1833 [3 & 4, Will. IV c. 103], *British Parliamentary Papers* (1836) No 356. Slavery Abolition Act 1833 [3 & 4 Will. IV c. 73]. *Representation of the People Act of 1832*, commonly known as the Reform Act of 1832. Act of Parliament [2 & 3 Will. IV c. 45].

2. Obituary of William Burnham Chilvers, *Pierce County* [Nebraska] *Call*, December 24, 1914.

3. Clayton Roberts, David Roberts and Douglas R. Bisson, *A History of England*, Volume II: 1688 to the Present, 5th Edition (Upper Saddle River, NJ: Prentice Hall, 2002), 253. The Earl of Norfolk was an active leader in the Tudor Period under King Henry VIII.

4. H. S. Tanner, *The New Universal Atlas of the World* (Philadelphia: H. S. Tanner Publishers, 1836), 37.

5. "Normal for Norfolk," is an example of British medical slang. See Adam T. Fox, Michael Fertleman, Pauline Cahill, and Roger D. Palmer, "Medical Slang in British Hospitals," *Ethics and Behaviour* 13, no. 2 (2003), 173–89.

6. Chilvers Family Papers [Manuscript], in the collection of C. Richard Chilvers of Shreveport, Louisiana. The majority of the information in the manuscript consisted of letters and excerpts from letters between William Burnham Chilvers and his aunt and uncle, Rebecca and George Burnham. The manuscript also contains a few letters from other family members in America and Great Britain.

7. Ibid.

8. Ibid.

9. Ibid. Belvidere, Illinois, is the county seat of Boone County.

10. Chilvers Family Papers; U.S. Department of Commerce, Eighth Decennial Census (1860), Boone County, Illinois. Unpublished tabulations in the National Archives and Records Administration, Washington, D.C.

11. Wales Wood, *History of the Ninety-Fifth Regiment Illinois Infantry Volunteers* (Belvidere, IL: Boone County Historical Society, 1993), 14–16. The troops mustered in as Ninety-Fifth Illinois Volunteer Infantry Regiment by Lt. J. W. Tibbatts, of the regular army with Fields and Staff, Col. Lawrence S. Church; Lt. Col. Thomas W. Humphrey; Maj. Leander Blanden; Adj. Wales Wood; Company B, Capt. Charles B. Loop; 1st Lt. Milton E. Keeler; 2nd Lt. Aaron F. Randall.

12. National Archives, *Report of the Adjutant General of Illinois*, Vol. 4 (Springfield, IL: State of Illinois, 1863).

13. Ezra Warner, *Generals in Blue* (Baton Rouge: Louisiana State University Press, 1964), 244–45.

14. Walt Whitman, "A Terrible Shock," Washington, D.C., July 1861, found in: Brooks D. Simpson, Stephen W. Sears, and Aaron Sheehan-Dean, eds., *The Civil War: The First Year Told by Those Who Lived It* (New York: Penguin, 2011), 500–503.

15. Clement Laird Vallandigham (1820–1871) was a Congressman from Ohio who was arrested by Union authorities for treasonable utterance and banished to the Confederacy. See Frank L. Klement, *The Limits of Dissent: Clement L. Vallandigham and the Civil War* (New York: J. Walter & Co., 1864; Reprint, Lexington: University Press of Kentucky, 1970), 191.

16. Interestingly Governor Yates gave Ulysses S. Grant his first job in his service to the United States in the Civil War. Grant had applied to the governor for a commission and was declined as there was no vacancy at the time. Yates was having a very difficult time in implementing a program to raise troops from Illinois to reach the quota required. The Governor, "did not know the minutiae of regimental organization, how many men composed a company, or how many subordinate officers there should be in a regiment. In his distress, he asked the Representative of the plain little man to who he had been introduced, if he knew any of these matters. The Representative replied by bringing Grant into the presence of the Governor. 'Do you understand the organization of troops?' the governor asked Grant. 'I do, Sir.' 'Will you accept a desk in my office for that purpose?' 'Anything to serve my country,' was Grant's reply." Frazier Kirkland, *The Book of Anecdotes of the War of the Rebellion* (Hartford, CT: Hartford Publishing Company, 1866), 405.

17. Ibid., 15.

18. Wood, *History of the Ninety-Fifth Regiment*, 211, 213.

19. Kirkland, *The Book of Anecdotes*, 18.

20. Ibid., 19.

21. Chilvers Family Papers, Letter from William B. Chilvers to George and Rebecca Burnham, written at Jackson, Tennessee, November 9, 1862. Jackson, Tennessee, is about eighty miles due east of Memphis and is located on the Forked Deer River and at the intersection of the Memphis & Ohio Railroad and the Mobile & Ohio Railroad. Wood, *History of the Ninety-Fifth Regiment*, 7–29, 32, 36.

22. Woodstock is in McHenry County, Illinois, and is the hometown of Colonel Church. The Ninety-Fifth boarded the Northwest Rail Road at Woodstock taking them to Chicago. Wood, *History of the Ninety-Fifth Regiment*, 14.

23. Maj. Leander Blanden of Harvard, McHenry County, Illinois. Blanden was a thirty-two-year-old single, grain dealer. He was promoted to lieutenant colonel on January 24, 1863, colonel June 12, 1864, and brevet general on March 26, 1865. He died in Fort Dodge, Iowa, on April 21, 1904. Adjutant General Record [Illinois], Muster Rolls for Illinois Regiments in the Civil War, Roll #47, 15; Roger Hunt and Jack R. Brown, *Brevet Generals in Blue* (Palmira, VA: Olde Soldiers Books, 1990), 61. "We got into Chicago in the dark of the day here the major got his horse off the car and then mounted him when a dray backed up against him and scared him so that he backed up against an engine that was passing on another tack sloly [slowly] and run over his leg and broke it. So Orrion Barnes (Pvt. Orrion Barne, Company G, Ninety-Fifth Illinois Infantry) shot him. The Major was slightly hurt but came along with us. He is a good officer so the boys threw in a little to get him another." Franklin R. Crawford, ed., *My Dear Wife: The Civil War Letters of*

Private Samuel Pepper. Company G – 95th Illinois Infantry 1862–1865 (Caledonia, IL: The Muffled Drum, 2003), 12.

24. Dr. Jacques Lisfranc de St. Martin described a fracture dislocation of the mid-foot in which one or more metatarsals being dislocated from the tarsal bones occurring in several French soldiers in the Napoleonic Wars when a wagon wheel rolled over their foot. Kevin Burroughs, Curtis Reimer, Karl B. Fields, "Lisfranc Injury of the Foot: a Commonly Missed Diagnosis," *American Family Physician Journal* (July 1998), 1:58(n1), 118–24.

25. The Central Illinois Railroad transported the Ninety-Fifth Illinois Infantry from Chicago to Cairo. Wood, *History of the Ninety-Fifth Regiment*, 26, 27.

26. Kankakee is located on the Iroquois River at the point that it flows into the Kankakee River in Northern Illinois. Kankakee County borders Indiana.

27. One of the many advantages the North had was a much more developed railroad system which provided for easier troop transport. The North had more than ninety percent of the track miles at the initiation of the war.

28. Centralia, Illinois, is located in Marion County about sixty miles east of St. Louis. This southern Illinois town is located where two branches of the Illinois Central Railroad converge.

29. "Secesh" was a term used for Confederate citizens and troops. Phillip Van Doren Stern, ed., *Soldier Life in the Union and Confederate Armies* (New York: Bonanza, 1961), 174.

30. Cairo is located at a strategic location in the southern tip of Illinois where the Ohio River flows into the Mississippi River. It served as a major U.S. Navy repair and supply station. Wood, *History of the Ninety-Fifth Regiment*, 26–28, 81, 121, 128, 131, 132, 158; Often misspelled "Dacotah," the vessel was the sternwheeler *Decotah*, laid down at Belle Vernon, Pennsylvania, in 1858. The vessel displaced 230 tons. It ran the Pittsburgh-Cincinnati packet trade. At the time Chilvers was aboard, it was owned by Johnson & Heydock of Cairo. She was burned during a Confederate raid at Paducah, Kentucky, on March 25, 1864. See Frederick Way, Jr., *Way's Packet Directory, 1848–1994: Passenger Steamboats of the Mississippi River System Since the Advent of Photography in Mid-Continent America* (Athens, OH: Ohio University Press, 1994), 122. All *Way's Packet Directory* listings are given a number by which they are identified. The *Decotah*'s Registry number is (1480). All subsequent entries in *Way's Packet Directory* will include the unique number for the vessel being cited. Wood, *History of the Ninety-Fifth Regiment*, 27.

31. The sidewheeler timberclad gunboat U.S.S. *Tyler*, built at Cincinnati, Ohio, in 1857 and converted as one of the first three U.S. Navy warships in 1861. She had a length of 180 feet, a beam of 45.3 feet and a draft of 7.7 feet. Way, *Way's Packet Directory*, 461, Way's Registry (5481); See also Gary D. Joiner, *Mr. Lincoln's Brown Water Navy: The Mississippi Squadron* (New York: Scholarly Resources, 2007), 23–24, 36–39, 49–51; and Paul H. Silverstone, *Warships of the Civil War Navies* (Annapolis, MD: Naval Institute Press, 1989), 158–60; The sidewheeler packet *De Soto*, built at New Albany, Indiana, in 1860. She had a length of 180 feet, a beam of thirty-five feet and a draft of seven feet. The vessel was acquired by the U.S. Army Quartermaster Corps (QMC) in 1861. The *De Soto* was well known for transporting Commodore Andrew H. Foote, after the Battle of Shiloh, up the Ohio River, before his death at Cleveland. The *De Soto* was captured from the Confederates at the Battle of Island No. 10. Way, *Way's Packet Registry*, 126, Way's Registry (1517). The sidewheeler *Memphis* was built in Jeffersonville, Indiana, by Howard shipbuilders in 1860. She displaced 645 tons, was 263 feet in length, had a beam of thirty-

eight feet, and a draft of seven feet. The *Memphis* was intermittently in the U.S. QMC service during the war. It carried the Sixty-Sixth Illinois Infantry Regiment from St. Louis to Fort Henry in April 1862, where they occupied the abandoned fort. Way, *Way's Packet Registry*, 319, Way's Registry (3897).

32. Columbus, Kentucky, is located on the Mississippi River across from Belmont, Missouri. It was heavily fortified by the Confederates under Maj. Gen. Leonidas Polk who crossed from Tennessee to Kentucky on September 3, 1861, strengthening the left flank of the Southern defenses at that time. His move was "militarily important . . . but politically unfortunate" as the first to invade a neutral state alienated many Kentuckians. O. E. Cunningham, *Shiloh and the Western Campaign of 1862*, Gary D. Joiner and Timothy Smith, eds. (New York: Savas Beattie, 2007), 6.

33. Ulysses S. Grant led the Union forces at the Battle of Belmont, Missouri, on November 6, 1861.

34. Jackson, Missouri, is the county seat for Cape Girardeau County.

35. Col. Lawrence Church.

36. Chilvers Family Papers, Letter from William B. Chilvers to George and Rebecca Burnham, December 24, 1862.

37. Corinth, Mississippi, was a strategically located town at the intersection of the Memphis & Charleston Railroad and the Memphis & Mobile Railroad. It served as a staging area for the Confederates before the Battle of Shiloh. The Confederates attempted to retake the position under Gen. Earl Van Dorn, which resulted in the Battle of Corinth fought October 3–4, 1862. Wood, *History of the Ninety-Fifth Regiment*, 151, 152; Salem, Mississippi, is located in Walthall County in the northern part of the state on the Mississippi Central Railroad. Wood, *History of the Ninety-Fifth Regiment*, 48–50, 110, 113.

38. Gen. Earl Van Dorn was a lieutenant in the Second U.S Cavalry prior to the war. He was commander of the Army of Mississippi and was unsuccessful at the Battles of Corinth and Elkhorn Tavern (Pea Ridge, March 7–8, 1862) but led a well-executed raid of the Union base at Holly Springs on December 20, 1862. He was killed by a jealous husband, Dr. Peters, who thought the general had made unacceptable advances on his wife Jessie. John S. Bowen, *Who Was Who in the Civil War* (East Bridgewater, MA: World Publications Group, 2011), 210.

39. In this instance, the term "butternut" was an African American and not a Confederate soldier.

40. Col. Lawrence Church was a judge in Woodstock, McHenry County, Illinois, prior to the war. In the fall of 1862, he became commander of the Camp Fuller Post and was in charge of the Ninety-Second, Ninety-Fifth, and Ninety-Sixth Illinois Infantry Regiments. While at Camp Fuller, his "health was very feeble" but despite his illness "his ardent patriotism, and an overwhelming desire to be with his men all the time, determined him to remain with them, though already prostrated with illness." Initial orders to leave Camp Fuller were received on September 29 but were promptly rescinded. On October 30 orders were sent from Adj. Gen. Alan C. Fuller from Springfield, Illinois, to move the command to Columbus, Kentucky. The Ninety-Fifth Illinois Infantry was to report to Maj. Gen. Ulysses S. Grant, commanding the Department and Army of the Tennessee. Upon receiving further orders, the troops were shipped by train to Cairo, Illinois, shipped upon the "Dacotah" to Columbus, Kentucky, and then by rail to Jackson, Tennessee. Col. L. S. Church, "was

wearied and broken down still more by the long journey," and "was obliged to leave the command and return to his home" in Columbus, Ohio. Wood, *History of the Ninety-Fifth Regiment*, 14, 18–19, 24–27.

41. Ripley, Mississippi, is the county seat of Tippah County. Wood, *History of the Ninety-Fifth Regiment*, 110.

Chapter 2

1. Shelby Foote, *The Civil War: A Narrative* (Alexandria, VA: Time-Life Books, 1998), 2:257.

2. Chilvers Family Papers, Letter from William B. Chilvers to Aunt Rebecca, January 3, 1864.

3. Chilvers Family Papers, Letter from William B. Chilvers to George Burnham, January 3, 1863.

4. Ibid.

5. Holly Springs, Mississippi.

6 Chilvers Family Papers, Letter from William B. Chilvers to George and Rebecca Burnham, Written at Memphis, Tennessee, January 14, 1863.

7. *The Belvidere Standard* was founded in 1851 in this northern Illinois community close to the Wisconsin border.

8. Chilvers Family Papers. John Fillingham was Chilvers' cousin and a member of Company K, Seventh Illinois Cavalry Regiment who lived in Canton, Illinois. Frederick A. Dyer, *A Compendium of the War of the Rebellion* (Des Moines, IA: The Dyer Publishing Co., 1908), 1,025.

9. There are multiple John Galbraiths named in the *Dyer's Compendium* from Illinois. They are mentioned in the Fifteenth, Seventeenth, Forty-First, and Eighty-Fifth, and as unassigned soldiers.

10. Capt. Charles W. Cringle was a quartermaster with the Sixty-Ninth Illinois Infantry Regiment. *Dyer's Compendium*, 1,076–1,077.

11. The governor of Illinois in 1863 was Richard Yates. Governor Yates accepted the regiment, and directed the companies to meet at "Camp Fuller," Rockford, Illinois, to muster into United States service. The Ninety-Fifth Illinois Infantry was ordered, by Governor Yates, to leave the training camp and proceed to Columbus, Kentucky, to soldier under the command of Maj. Gen. U. S. Grant's Department and Army of the Tennessee on October 30, 1862. Wales Wood, *History of the Ninety-Fifth Regiment Illinois Infantry Volunteers* (Belvidere, IL: Boone County Historical Society, 1993), 15, 24; the Chicago and Galena Railroad was built in Northern Illinois.

12. The Northern Doughfaces were anti-war democrats.

13. Amanda Foreman, *A World on Fire: Britain's Crucial Role in the American Civil War* (New York: Random House, 2010), 172. *Casus belli* is defined as an event or act to justify a war.

14. War speculators

15. Confederate raids occurred into Arkansas in January 1863, under the command of Missourian Gen. John S. Marmaduke. Shelby Foote, *The Beleaguered City: The Vicksburg Campaign* (New York: the Modern Library, 1995), 304.

16. Chilvers Family Papers. Mary was married to Rebecca Burnham's brother, George Woodward, who was about to lose his job as a blacksmith near Sheffield, England. At the time, they had a nine-month-old son named George William. They asked the Burnhams to send them money to pay for the trip to America. See letter dated January 4, 1863.

17. Capt. Charles B. Loop, Company B, Ninety-Fifth Illinois Infantry. Wood, *History of the Ninety-Fifth Regiment*, 83, 91, 131–33, 202, 205. Franklin R. Crawford, ed., *My Dear Wife: The Civil War Letters of Private Samuel Pepper. Company G – 95th Illinois Infantry 1862–1865.* (Caledonia, IL: The Muffled Drum, 2003), 108.

18. 2nd Lt. Aaron F. Randall, Company B, Ninety-Fifth Illinois Infantry, was mustered in September 4, 1862, and resigned January 16, 1863. Wood, *History of the Ninety-Fifth Regiment*, 213; Chilvers Family Papers, Letter to William Burnham Chilvers, July 13, 1863.

19. Pvt. Isaac Conner, Company B, Ninety-Fifth Illinois Infantry, was discharged prior to the end of the war. Wood, *History of the Ninety-Fifth Regiment*, 219.

20. Pvt. George H. Griffin, Company B, Ninety-Fifth Illinois Infantry, was discharged prior to the end of the war. Ibid.

21. Pvt. Pete Cramer, Company B, Ninety-Fifth Illinois Infantry, was discharged prior to the end of the war. Ibid.

22. Pvt. Edward Barker and Pvt. Osborn Allen, both from Company B, Ninety-Fifth Illinois Infantry, were discharged prior to the end of the war. Pvt. Walter Harder, Company B, Ninety-Fifth Illinois Infantry was mustered out with the regiment August 21, 1865. Ibid.

23. Pvt. George Marvin and Pvt. Hiram Draper were both in Company B, Ninety-Fifth Illinois Infantry, and were discharged from the service prior to the end of the war. Ibid.

24. Cpl. William R. Stevenson, Company B, Ninety-Fifth Illinois Infantry. Ibid., 218, 233.

25. Chilvers Family Papers. Houghman was a merchant in Boone County, Illinois.

26. Brooks D. Simpson, Stephen W. Sears, and Aaron Sheehan-Dean, eds., *The Civil War: The First Year Told by Those Who Lived It* (New York: Penguin, 2011), 39.

27. Chilvers Family Papers, Letter from William L. Chilvers to George Burnham, January 21, 1863.

28. Newly freed African Americans became refugees and fled to Union army camps in the west. Cyrus Boyd wrote, "they fly for their freedom to the union army and we are not able to do much for them as it is all we can do to take care of ourselves." Boyd's fellow Northern soldiers expressed their overt racism by greeting these newly freed black people with "cries of 'kill him' 'drown him.'" "The prejudice against the race seems stronger than ever." Mildred Throne, *The Civil War Diary of Cyrus F. Boyd, Fifteenth Iowa Infantry 1861–1863* (Baton Rouge: LSU Press, 1998), 118–19; Special Field orders No. 2, HQ, Department of the Tennessee, February 12, 1863, U.S. War Department, *War of the Rebellion: The Official Records of the Union and Confederate Armies* (Washington, D.C.: United States Government Printing Office, 1890–1901), 128 vols., 24 pt. 3:46–47, Hereinafter cited as *OR*. Earl Hess, *The Civil War in the West: Victory and Defeat from*

the *Appalachians to the Mississippi* (Chapel Hill, NC: University of North Carolina Press, 2012), 143.

29. The large group of vessels was Adm. David Porter's Mississippi squadron. Gary D. Joiner, *Mr. Lincoln's Brownwater Navy* (Lanham, MD: Rowman & Littlefield Publishers, Inc., 2007), 90, 92, 94.

30. Dewett Abbey was a friend or fellow soldier of Chilvers. Perhaps this is Lt. John Abbe, Company K, Ninety-Fifth Illinois. Abbe was promoted to second lieutenant on May 22, 1863, as a result of promotions regarding the death of Capt. Gabriel Cornwell. Abbe resigned his commission on September 19, 1864. Wood, *History of the Ninety-Fifth Regiment*, 216; NARA, Adjutant Records, Muster Rolls for Illinois Regiments in Civil War, Roll #47, 15.

31. Capt. Charles Loop, Company B, Ninety-Fifth Illinois Infantry. He was a twenty-six-year-old man with two children when he was mustered in on September 4, 1862. Loop was unanimously elected captain and promoted to major in command of the men of the Ninety-Fifth Illinois who were attached to Gen. William T. Sherman's march on Atlanta. These men were reattached to the Ninety-Fifth in time to participate in the Battle of Nashville on December 15, 1864. Loop mustered out with his men on August 17, 1865. Wood, *History of the Ninety-Fifth Regiment*, 83, 91, 131–33, 202, 205; Crawford, *My Dear Wife*, 108; Adjutant General Records, Muster Rolls for Illinois Regiments in Civil War, Roll #47, 15; and Charles Loop, service and pension records, RG 94, National Archives.

32. A surveying rod was historically a linear measure equal to five and one-half yards (sixteen and one-half feet) in length.

33. Graybacks or lice was a major problem for armies in close quarters as they were easily transmitted. They were a major cause of itching as well as Rickettsial disorders such as Typhus, Rickettsial pox, and Rocky Mountain Spotted Fever. One soldier noted, "every soldier had a brigade of lice on him." H. H. Cunningham, *Doctors in Gray: The Confederate Medical Service* (Gloucester, MA: Peter Smith, 1970), 170.

34. Aaron Randall was the second lieutenant of Company B of the Ninety-Fifth Illinois Infantry and resigned from duty on January 16, 1863. He apparently was a friend of William B. Chilvers. Wood, *History of the Ninety-Fifth Regiment*, 213.

35. Pvt. Pete Cramer, Company B, Ninety-Fifth Illinois Infantry. The thumb was essential in operating a rifle and precluded a soldier from duty; and a self-induced injury would be an effective way to be discharged from the army. Alfred Jay Bollet, *Civil War Medicine: Challenges and Triumphs* (Tucson, AZ: Gallen Press, 2002), 263–64; Cunningham, *Doctors in Gray*, 164.

36. Chilvers Family Papers, Letter from William L. Chilvers to George Burnham, March 3, 1863.

37. Illinois House of Representatives, January 5, 1863.

38. Funk's speech was reprinted in a New York pamphlet titled "Copperheads under the Heel of an Illinois Farmer." Simpson, *The Civil War: the Third Year*, 39.

39. Lt. Col. Thomas Humphrey, Ninety-Fifth Illinois Infantry. Wood, *History of the Ninety-Fifth Regiment*, 14, 19, 22, 23, 29, 33, 37, 70, 75, 76, 78, 79, 89, 98, 103, 110, 111, 113, 115. Fred Shannon, ed., *The Civil War Letters of Sergeant Onley Andrus* (Urbana, IL: University of Illinois Press, 1947), 19, 20, 41, 52–53, 70–71, 55, 61, 62, 72.

40. Copperheads, or Peace Democrats, "thought that the war, from its inception, was really about emancipation. Already Maj. Gen. John C. Fremont had unilaterally freed all slaves belonging to Confederates or Confederate sympathizers, only to have his orders countermanded by Lincoln, who feared that Fremont's measure would drive the border states from the Union." The *Chicago Times* in an editorial published that "if white men could not save their own government, it was better to let it go." Weber, *Copperheads*, 38–39; The *Woodstock Sentinel* and the *Belvidere Standard* (founded in 1851) were the local newspapers in these northern Illinois communities close to the Wisconsin border.

41. Chilvers Family Papers, Letter from William L. Chilvers to George Burnham, March 16, 1863.

42. Capt. Charles Loop was born in Avoca, Stephen County, New York, and moved to Boone County to farm. For more information on Captain Loop, see note 31.

43. Chilvers Family Papers, Letter from William B. Chilvers to George Burnham, February 23, 1863.

44. The brigade commander was Col. George W. Dietzler. On January 26, 1863, Dietzler's Brigade, consisting of the First Kansas, the Sixteenth Wisconsin, and Ninety-Fifth Illinois Infantry Regiments, reached Milliken's Bend, which was fifteen miles upstream from Vicksburg and across the river. Then they went to Young's Point where one of Grant's canals was being dug. According to Wood, the Ninety-Fifth Illinois was not there long, being "at the head of the brigade, if not the division, in reputation of good order and discipline." They were transferred to Lake Providence on February 3. Wood claimed the First Kansas Infantry, which Dietzler first commanded, taught the Ninety-Fifth Illinois Infantry the art of foraging. They acquired a "reputation of appropriating things to their own use . . . learning the skillful modus operandi of bringing eatables into camp . . . with jay-hawking propensities." Wood, *History of the Ninety-Fifth Regiment*, 39, 49–50. Ezra Warner, *Generals in Blue* (Baton Rouge: Louisiana State University Press, 1964), 116–17.

45. Col. Thomas Humphrey was promoted to colonel on January 24, 1863, while the Ninety-Fifth was at Lake Providence. He had taken over command after Col. Lawrence Church had left the regiment due to poor health at Columbus, Kentucky. In April 1863, Colonel Dietzler's brigade was left to garrison Lake Providence while the rest of General McArthur's division was sent sixty miles down the Mississippi River to Milliken's Bend, Mississippi. Warner, *Generals in Blue*, 288; Wood, *History of the Ninety-Fifth Regiment*, 53–54, 70–71.

46. Col. Robert C. Murphy was the Union commander of the supply depot at Holly Springs during the raid on December 20, 1862, led by Confederate Gen. Earl Van Dorn. Murphy was found under his bed by the raiders during the dawn attack and presented still in his nightclothes to Van Dorn. Murphy was quoted as saying, "my fate is most mortifying. I have wished a hundred times that I had been killed." Grant was furious and uncharacteristically dismissed Murphy without a hearing. The *Richmond Dispatch* dated January 15, 1863, listed 1,500 men including 150 commissioned officers were captured, along with 1,809,000 ordinance stores including 5,000 rifles and 2,000 revolvers; also destroyed were 100,000 suits of clothing, 5,000 barrels of flour; $1,000,000 of medical stores; and $600,000 worth of sutlers stores. Interestingly, earlier that fall, Murphy had appeared before a court-martial board headed by Gen. John McArthur. The board exonerated the colonel for his actions at Iuka, Mississippi. That board found Murphy not guilty of both the charge of "misbehaving in the face of the enemy," and that of "shamefully abandoning a post which he had been commanded to defend." Thomas P.

Lowry, *Tarnished Eagles: the Court-Martial of Fifty Union Colonels and Lieutenant Colonels* (Mechanicsburg, PA: Stackpole Books, 1997), 176–81; Holly Springs, Mississippi, was on the road taken by General Grant's army in Northern Mississippi which led further south into the towns of Abbeville and Oxford. Holly Springs served as a depot for the Union army in the fall of 1862, and was successfully raided by the bold and unexpected actions of the Confederates under Gen. Earl Van Dorn in December 1862. Wood, *History of the Ninety-Fifth Regiment*, 40, 42, 45, 47–49, 51. Samuel Pepper wrote, "Saturday the 20th the rebels under Van Dorn made a dash into Holy Springs and 7 or 8 thousand mounted men and captured the place and held it long enough to capture a large mail that belonged to our Army and destroy'd a great am[oun]t of army stores ammunition cotton and set fire to the depot engine house and the best part of the city." Crawford, *My Dear Wife*, 25–26; Chilvers Family Papers, Letter of William B. Chilvers to George Burnham March 15, 1863.

47. Chilvers Family Papers, Letter from William B. Chilvers to George Burnham, January 25, 1863.

48. Bell Irvin Wiley, *The Life of Billy Yank: the Common Soldier of the Union* (Garden City, NY: Doubleday and Company, 1971), 37–41.

49. "It seems doubtful that one soldier in ten at any time during the conflict had any real interest in emancipation per se." Wiley, *Life of Billy Yank*, 40.

50. Sgt. Onley Andrus, Company D, Ninety-Fifth Illinois Infantry noted, "keep the Niggers where they belong. Which is in Slavery and the more I see of them the more I think so, for this reason. Take a look at the costs of freeing the Black Devils. No less than 300,000 of our own free white citizens have already been sacrificed to free the small mite that have got their freedom . . . I consider my life & the Happiness of my family of more value than any Nigger." Throughout Andrus' letters, the sergeant "became almost violent in his disgust because the conflict had turned into a war to free the slaves. Like a good portion of other Northerners, including a large share of the soldiers, he was for saving the Union, but he had the irrational notion that free Negroes would have a more depressing effect on the labor of white men than would slaves." Shannon, *The Civil War Letters of Sergeant Onley Andrus*, 15–16, 28–29.

51. Chilvers Family Papers, Letter from William B. Chilvers to George Burnham, February 9, 1863.

52. Bayou Macon, Louisiana; Chilvers Family Papers, Letter from William B. Chilvers to George Burnham, March 5, 1863.

53. Secretary of War Edwin M. Stanton was a former U.S attorney general who replaced Simon Cameron as the secretary of war in January 1862. He ensured that the Union armies were well fed and supplied, enforced strict compliance with conscription laws, restricted the press, pushed for the Emancipation Proclamation and the employment of black troops. "Lincoln set policy and handled political matters, and Stanton managed overall military operations and day-to-day war business." Margaret E. Wagner, Gary W. Gallagher, and Paul Finkelman, eds., *The Library of Congress Civil War Desk Reference* (New York: Grand Central Press Book, 2002), 175–76; Doris Kearns Goodwin, *Team of Rivals* (New York: Simon and Schuster, 2005), 404–405; Goodwin, *Team of Rivals*, 404; Warner, *Generals in Blue*, 502–503.

54. Chilvers Family Papers, Letter from William B. Chilvers to George Burnham, March 20, 1863.

55. Pvt. John Martin, Company B, Ninety-Fifth Illinois Infantry Regiment. He mustered out with the company. Wood, *History of the Ninety-Fifth Regiment*, 219.

56. By mid-April Thomas had authorized ten regiments, of about one thousand men each, and appointed white officers from veteran units in the region. By the end of the war Thomas had enrolled more than 76,000 men. There were three regiments of black troops at the Battle of Milliken's Bend on June 7, 1863, the Ninth and Eleventh Louisiana and the First Mississippi Volunteers of African Descent. According to Assistant Secretary of War Charles A. Dana, "the bravery of the blacks at the battle of Milliken's Bend completely revolutionized the sentiment of the army with regard to the employment of negro troops." John David Smith, *Black Soldiers in Blue* (Chapel Hill, NC: University of North Carolina Press, 2002), 55, 10; Wood, *History of the Ninety-Fifth Regiment*, 69–70.

57. Lt. Milton Keeler, Company B, Ninety-Fifth Illinois Infantry was a married grocer from Belvidere when he enlisted on September 4, 1862. He was elected as the company's first lieutenant. He was born in Truxton, Courtland County, New York. He resigned his commission on April 1, 1864. Adjutant General Records, Muster Rolls for Illinois in Civil War, Roll #47, 15.

58. There is no Lieutenant Pells associated with the U.S. Colored Troops. *Dyer's Compendium.*

59. Chilvers Family Papers, Letter from William B. Chilvers to George Burnham, April 10, 1863.

60. Chilvers Family Papers, Letter from William B. Chilvers to George Burnham, April 1863. The specific date of the month is not noted.

61. Piles is an antiquated term for hemorrhoids. Harold Webster Jones, Norman L. Hoerr, Arthur Osol, eds., *Blakiston's New Gould Medical Dictionary* (New York: Blakiston Company, 1949), 455.

62. Capt. Charles Loop, Company B, Ninety-Fifth Illinois Infantry. He was promoted to major before the end of the war. In November 1863 Loop was detailed to proceed north to obtain recruits. Captain Loop was detailed as an engineer officer for the Third Division Seventeenth Army Corps on June 14, 1864. Wood, *History of the Ninety-Fifth Regiment*, 83, 91, 131–33, 202, 205.

63. Lt. Milton E. Keeler, Company B, Ninety-Fifth Illinois Infantry. Wood, *History of the Ninety-Fifth Regiment*, 213.

64. The First Kansas Infantry Regiment was commanded by George Washington Dietzler, who was born on November 30, 1826, in Pine Grove, Pennsylvania. He moved to Lawrence, Kansas, in 1855 where he became involved in the Free State movement, an organization that worked to prevent slavery in Kansas. He actively participated in the Free State movement, serving on committees and writing for newspapers. With the onset of the Civil War, he was appointed as colonel of the First Kansas Infantry. He was severely wounded at the Battle of Wilson's Creek on August 10, 1861. Colonel Dietzler was promoted to a brigade commander during the Vicksburg Campaign of 1863. He was promoted to brigadier general on April 4, 1863. He resigned his commission on August 27, 1863, but was called back to command the Kansas militia during Confederate Gen. Sterling Price's Raid through Missouri in the fall of 1864. He moved to Emporia, Kansas, after the war. He and his family moved to San Francisco in 1872 where they lived until 1884. While visiting Tucson, Arizona, he was thrown out of a buggy he was driving and was instantly killed.

He was buried in Lawrence, Kansas, at the Oak Hill Cemetery. Warner, *Generals in Blue*, 116–17.

65. First Kansas Infantry was organized at Camp Lincoln, Fort Leavenworth, on May 20–June 3, 1861. They were attached to Dietzler's Brigade where they were involved in the Battle of Wilson's Creek, Grant's Central Mississippi Campaign, and the Vicksburg Campaign. They were mustered out of the service on June 19, 1864. The regiment lost seven officers and 120 men who were killed and mortally wounded, and three officers and 122 who died of disease. The total loss was 252. *Dyer's Compendium.*

66. In 1861, the Federal government issued a call for soldiers and finances for the war. "On April 14th, President Lincoln issued his call for 75,000 volunteers; early in May more than 200,000 had been called for; and immediately after the battle of Bull Run in Virginia, congress ordered a call for 500,000 more. At the same time, Congress made an appropriation of $500,000,000 to meet the expense of the Army and Navy." John H. Brinton, *Personal Memoirs of John H. Brinton: Civil War Surgeon, 1861–1865* (Carbondale, IL: University of Southern Illinois Press, 1996), 21.

67. Pvt. John N. Mouton, Thirty-Fourth Iowa Infantry, wrote his sister about Grant's failed strategy during six weeks of heavy rain, which transformed the low-lying country into mud, disease, and a shortage of rations. On February 1, 1863, he wrote his sister "the canal is a failure, the men all dying off pretty fast if you call 47 days anything out of one regiment. The 34th Iowa lost that amount . . . I am lonesome and down hearted in Spite of my Self. I am tired of Blood Shed and Saw enough of it." Wiley, *Life of Billy Yank,* 278–80.

68. On March 3, 1863, Lincoln signed "An act for enrolling and calling out the National Forces, and for other purposes" which was the first effective Federal conscription law. Wagner, et al., eds., *Civil War Desk Reference*, 27.

69. Chilvers Family Papers, Letter from William B. Chilvers to George Burnham, 1863 (specific date not noted).

70. Jones, et al., eds., *New Gould Medical Dictionary*, 455.

71. Chilvers Family Papers, Letter from William B. Chilvers to George and Rebecca Burnham, 1863. The specific month and day was not written.

72. Wiley, *Life of Billy Yank*, 278; John N. Tallman to his brother, March 3, 1863, manuscript, Chicago Historical Society; Diary of John H. Williams, December 9, 1862, typescript translation from the Welsh, Vermont Historical Society; Samuel Storrow to his parents, December 23, 1862, manuscript, Massachusetts Historical Society; C. W. Bardeen, *A Little Fifer's War Diary* (Syracuse, NY: C. W. Bardeen, 1910), passim.

73. Richmond, the capitol of the Confederacy, was not taken until April 1865. Wagner, et al., eds., *Civil War Desk Reference*, 159; Vicksburg was surrendered by Gen. John C. Pemberton to Gen. Ulysses S. Grant on July 4, 1863. Wagner, et al., eds., *Civil War Desk Reference*, 280–81; The last battle of the Civil War was fought at Palmito Ranch, Texas, on May 12–13, 1865. Wagner, et al., eds., *Civil War Desk Reference*, 328–29. Philip Thomas Tucker, *The Final Fury: Palmito Ranch, the Last Battle of the Civil War* (Mechanicsburg, PA: Stackpole Books, 2001), vii.

74. Chilvers Family Papers, Letter from William B. Chilvers to George Burnham, January 3, 1863.

75. Pvt. Cordenio Bruce, Company K, Ninety-Fifth Illinois Infantry. Wood, *History of the Ninety-Fifth Regiment*, 230, 236; the term *rheumatism* derived from the Greek *rheumatismos*: a flux. The first use of this term was attributed to Galen, to describe inflammation or degenerative diseases of the joints, bones, muscles, or bursae. James T. Cassidy, Ross E. Petty, Ronald M. Laxer, and Carol B. Lindsley, *Textbook of Pediatric Rheumatology* (Philadelphia, PA: Elsevier Saunders, 2005), 2.

76. Cpl. William R. Stevenson, Company B, Ninety-Fifth Illinois Infantry. Wood, *History of the Ninety-Fifth Regiment*, 218, 233.

77. Chilvers Family Papers, Letter of William B. Chilvers to George Burnham, March 1, 1863.

78. Col. Robert C. Murphy, Eighth Wisconsin Volunteer Infantry, was promptly court-martialed for his performance at Holly Springs. On January 8, 1863, Gen. Ulysses S. Grant wrote General Orders No. 4, Headquarters, Department of the Tennessee: "Colonel Robert C. Murphy of the Eighth Regiment Wisconsin Infantry Volunteers, having, while in command of the post of Holly Springs, Mississippi, neglected and failed to exercise the usual and ordinary precautions to guard and protect the same, having after repeated and timely warning of the approach of the enemy, failed to make any preparations or defense, or show any disposition to do so, and having with a force amply sufficient to have repulsed the enemy and protected the public stores entrusted to his care, disgracefully permitted him to capture the post and destroy the stores – and the movement of troops in the face of the enemy rendering it impractical to convene a court martial for his trial, is therefore dismissed [from] the service of the United States to take effect from the 20th day of December, 1862, the date of his cowardly and disgraceful conduct." Thomas P. Lowry, *Tarnished Eagles: the Courts-Martial of Fifty Colonels and Lieutenant Colonels* (Mechanicsburg, PA: Stackpole Books, 1997), 176–81.

79. Gen. Earl Van Dorn of Mississippi led the raid. It was his most successful battle of the war. This action temporarily disrupted Grant's projected operations against Vicksburg. Van Dorn was assassinated by a Dr. Peters, who claimed the general had "violated the sanctity of his home." Warner, *Generals in Blue*, 314–15.

80. The six companies of the Second Illinois Cavalry who were stationed at the fairgrounds "made a spirited defense" according to Colonel Brown of Confederate leader General Van Dorn's staff. A Confederate soldier, Private Deupree, noted "the First Mississippi met a foe worthy of their steel in the Second Illinois." Three other companies of the Second Illinois also fought well. To the north was Capt. Benjamin Marsh of Company G, to the south Maj. Daniel B. Bush, and finally Maj. John J. Bush on the west. Captain Marsh successfully led Company G in a headlong saber charge to the north and cut their way out of the southern line. This inspired Bush and Mudd who broke out of the Confederate cordon. About seventy men rode off to the safety of Memphis and the majority rode north and joined the Ninetieth Illinois Infantry. Thomas E. Parson, "Thwarting Grant's First Drive on Vicksburg: Van Dorn's Holly Springs Raid" *Blue and Gray,* XXVII, no. 3, (2010), 23–24.

81. Chilvers Family Papers. Dr. Jones was probably a physician who was not officially a member of the army. He is not mentioned by Wood as a member of the Ninety-Fifth Illinois Infantry.

82. Chilvers Family Papers, Letter from William B. Chilvers to George Burnham, January 3, 1863.

83. The Ninety-Fifth arrived at Milliken's Bend, Louisiana, which was about fifteen miles upstream from Vicksburg. They were a little upriver from Young's Point, which was where

one of Grant's canals was being dug. They were sent to dig but not long as they had been commended by brigade commander, George W. Deitzler, as standing at the head of the last of the brigade, if not the division, in point of good order and discipline, and so good of a regiment was needed elsewhere. On February 2, 1863, they were moved upriver to Lake Providence. Shannon, *The Civil War Letters of Sergeant Onley Andrus,* 39.

84. "Mounted infantry" was used in the Civil War. The most famous of these troops was Col. John Thomas Wilder's Seventeenth Indiana Infantry, who were armed with repeating rifles and known as the "Lightning Brigade." They were particularly effective in the Chattanooga Campaign of 1864. Wiley, *Life of Billy Yank,* 342; Roger D. Hunt and Jack R. Brown, *Brevet Generals in Blue* (Palmyra, VA: Olde Soldiers Books, 1990), 672; The Third Illinois Cavalry, was an unattached unit involved in Sherman's Yazoo expedition. They were involved in skirmishes at Milliken's Bend on January 21, and at Richmond, Louisiana, on January 29, 1863. *Dyer's Compendium.*

85. Paroling.

86. Chilvers Family Papers, Letter from William B. Chilvers to George Burnham, February 1, 1863.

87. Ibid., Letter from William B. Chilvers to George Burnham, March 31, 1863.

88. Ibid., The Storks were close friends from England, or possibly relatives, who had moved to Boone County, Illinois, with the Burnhams and Will.

89. Ibid. The neighbors' son, Pvt. George Robinson, Forty-Fifth Illinois Infantry.

90. Pvt. Cordenio Bruce, Company K, Ninety-Fifth Illinois Infantry, and Pvt. John Butler, Company B, Ninety-Fifth Illinois Infantry. Wood, *History of the Ninety-Fifth Regiment,* 219, 230, 236.

91. Chilvers Family Papers, Letter from William B. Chilvers to George Burnham, January 3, 1863.

92. Ibid., Letter from William B. Chilvers to George Burnham, undated.

93. Chilvers Family Papers. Hattie Sinten was probably a teenage girl whose family was friends of the Burnhams and Chilvers.

94. Ibid. Ester Ford was a girlfriend of Will Chilvers in Boone County, Illinois; Letter from William B. Chilvers to George Burnham, February 1, 1863.

95. Ibid. Probably this is the close family friend Silos Stevenson, who is the father of Cpl. William R. Stevenson, Company B, Ninety-Fifth Illinois Infantry. Wood, *History of the Ninety-Fifth Regiment*; Chilvers Family Papers, Letter from William B. Chilvers to George Burnham, February 11, 1863.

Chapter 3

1. Third Louisiana Redan was part of the well-designed Confederate defenses at Vicksburg which were built by engineer Maj. Samuel Lockett. William L. Shea and Terrence J. Winschel, *Vicksburg is the Key: The Struggle for the Mississippi River* (Lincoln, NE: University of Nebraska Press, 2003), 37. Samuel H. Lockett, "The Defense of Vicksburg" in Robert Underwood Johnson and Clarence Clough Buel, *Battles and Leaders of the Civil War* (New York: Thomas Yoseloff, Inc., 1956), 3:482–92.

2. Grant crossed the Mississippi River from Hard Times Landing, Louisiana, to Grand Gulf, Mississippi. Grand Gulf served as a strong position and had been taken by the Union army on May 12, 1863. Wales Wood, *History of the Ninety-Fifth Regiment Illinois Infantry Volunteers* (Belvidere, IL: Boone County Historical Society, 1993), 70, 72.

3. The Battle of Raymond was fought on May 12, 1863, when Confederate Gen. John Gregg's brigade attacked Union Gen. James McPherson's Seventeenth Corps. The Confederates were able to hold McPherson back for three hours but it cost him a large number of casualties and prevented him from joining Pemberton in the defenses of Vicksburg. "Grant's tactic of separating his corps in order to feel out the enemy to his front reaped great benefits at Raymond." Michael B. Ballard, *The Civil War in Mississippi: Major Campaigns and Battles* (Jackson, MS: University of Mississippi Press, 2011), 154–58; The capture of Jackson was important, as the transportation center of the state as well as Vicksburg was lost to the South, and "more important was the scattering of Joe Johnston's small army (which after the battle became known as the Army of Relief)." Timothy B. Smith, *Champion Hill: Decisive Battle for Vicksburg* (New York: Savas Beattie, 2004), 102.

4. Gen. Joseph Eggleston Johnston had been appointed commander of the Department of the West by Jefferson Davis in November 1862. In this capacity, Johnston served in supervision of both the Department of Mississippi and East Louisiana (under Lieutenant General Pemberton) and Gen. Braxton Bragg's Army of Tennessee. He was in the "anomalous position of attempting to relieve the situation in Vicksburg" in which Pemberton was receiving conflicting orders from Richmond. Ezra Warner, *Generals in Blue* (Baton Rouge, LA: Louisiana State University Press, 1964), 161–62.

5. Champion Hill was fought on May 16, 1863. "Perhaps more significant than any larger or bloodier action of the Civil War, the decisive action of the campaign for Vicksburg, led directly to the fall of the Confederate bastion on the Mississippi River and, truly, sealed the fate of Richmond." Smith, *Champion Hill*, x. "Whatever chance Pemberton had of joining Johnston disappeared, for the Confederate army was in disarray as it fell back to defensive works east of the Big Black along either side of the railroad crossing." The Battle of Big Black River Bridge was a disastrous loss of "defenses and more than 1,750 soldiers convincing Pemberton his effort to connect with Loring had gone badly awry." Smith, *Champion Hill*, 391–95; Ballard, *The Civil War in Mississippi*, 160–63.

6. Lt. Gen. John Clifford Pemberton was born in Philadelphia and graduated from West Point in 1837. He won two brevets in the War with Mexico. In 1848 he married a Virginian, Martha Thompson, which led to his decision to join the Confederacy. He was promoted to lieutenant general on October 10, 1862, as commander of Mississippi and East Louisiana including Vicksburg. His command was complicated by conflicting orders given simultaneously by Johnston and Jefferson Davis. He led a stubborn defense but eventually was compelled to capitulate on July 4, 1863. Warner, *Generals in Blue*, 232–33; Davis respected those who shared his devotion to the Confederate cause. He admired the Pennsylvanian Confederate who turned his back on his siblings and a large fortune to fight on the side of his wife's family. Also, both men were highly principled, states-rights men, and were amazed at Grant's brilliance in the Vicksburg Campaign. Steven E. Woodworth, *Jefferson Davis and His Generals: The Failure of Confederate Command in the West* (Lawrence, KS: University of Kansas Press, 1990), 218–20; "By the time the Vicksburg campaign was well underway, Johnston and Davis were barely on speaking terms." Smith, *Champion Hill*, 93. "Despite the general's unattractive behavior, however, the president deserves the most blame over Vicksburg" according to government insider Robert Garlick Hill Kean, as Davis "delegated responsibility without delegating authority and then

refused to exercise the authority he withheld from the responsible commander." Gary W. Gallagher and Joseph T. Glatthar, eds., *Leaders of the Lost Cause: New Perspectives on the Confederate High Command* (Mechanicsburg, PN: Stackpole Books, 2004), 188–89.

7. Grant told Surgeon John Brinton that "the art of war is simple enough; find out where your enemy is, get at him as soon as you can, and keep moving on." John H. Brinton, *Personal Memoirs of John H. Brinton*, John S. Haller, ed. (Carbondale, IL: Southern Illinois Press, 1996), xiv; the May 19 attack was joined by the Ninety-Fifth Illinois Infantry and "led forward by its gallant colonel, advancing under a galling fire to a ridge within one hundred yards of the rebel works, and held this position the remainder of the day." The Ninety-Fifth was part of Brig. Gen. T. E. G. Ransom's brigade (composed of the Eleventh, Seventy-Second, Ninety-Fifth, the Fourteenth and Seventeenth Wisconsin, and Battery F, Second Illinois Artillery) of the Sixth Division, Seventeenth Army Corps (McPherson's Army of the Tennessee). McPherson held the center while General Sherman's Fifteenth Army Corps was on the right, and the Thirteenth Corps under Gen. John McClernand was on the left. Colonel Humphrey received the following note from General Ransom: "Col. - You have done well, nobly. I desire that you hold your position. Do not expose your men or waste ammunition. I occupy the rear of the ridge back of you. Will move forward as soon as we are supported on the right and left. I expect to hear from General McPherson. T. E. G. Ransom, Brig. Gen'l." Casualties of the Ninetly-Fifth Illinois Infantry included seven men and fifty-four wounded including Col. Tom Humphrey, who had been shot in the foot. Wood, *History of the Ninety-Fifth Regiment*, 72–75.

8. Chilvers Family Papers, Letter from William B. Chilvers to Aunt and Uncle, written from Vicksburg, May 27, 1863.

9. The Ninety-Fifth Infantry was involved in the attack on the Stockade Redan on May 22, 1863. The Ninety-Fifth Illinois Infantry was under Brigadier General Ransom's Brigade of Gen. John McArthur's Sixth Division of Gen. James B. McPherson's Nineteenth Corps (Third Division John Logan Seventh Division Isaac Quinby, and Francis Herron's Division) of the Army of Tennessee (other corps present were John G. Parke's Ninth, John McClernand/Edward Ord's Thirteenth, William T. Sherman's Fifteenth, and Cadwallader Washburn's Sixteenth. Ransom's charge on May 22, 1863, occurred against the south part of Stockade Redan under the Confederate command of Gen. Francis Cockrell. In the May 22 attack, Ransom led his brigade as a column through enfilading fire from the Southerners. When the attack seemed to waiver, T. E. G. Ransom grabbed the regimental flag, ran to the front and shouted, "Forward, men! We must and will go into that fort, who will follow me?" The men rallied and captured one of the outside trenches. However, the strength of the defenders was determined by Ransom to be too strong for his efforts to be successful and in a loud clear voice he addressed his troop. Ransom shouted, "men of the second brigade we cannot maintain this position. You must retire to the cover of that ravine, one regiment at a time." He then commanded the order of their rearward movement and announced that, "the first man who runs or goes beyond that ravine, shall be shot." Under fire Ransom then sat on a stump where he could watch his troop proceed with his orders. Linus Pierpoint Brockett, *The Camp, the Battlefield, and the Hospital: or Lights and Shadows of the Great Rebellion* (Philadelphia, PA: National Publishing Company, 1866), 511–12. Gen. William T. Sherman once stated, "I saw Ransom during the assault of the 22nd of May 1863 . . . I then marked him as of the kind of whom heroes are made." "The Vermont Boy Who Volunteered in 1861, Served Bravely, was Wounded Grievously, and Died for the Union," Eulogy of General T. E. G. Ransom given before Ransom Post No. 131, Grand Army of the Republic (GAR), St. Louis, Missouri, June 20, 1884, *Washington National Tribune*, June 1884.

10. Pvt. Job H. Westbury, Company B, Ninety-Fifth Illinois Infantry was killed at Vicksburg on May 22, 1863. Wood, *History of the Ninety-Fifth Regiment*, 220, 237.

11. Cpl. William R. Stevenson, Company B, Ninety-Fifth Illinois Infantry, of Bonus, Illinois, was wounded at Vicksburg, May 19 or 22, 1863. Cpl. John Horan, Company B, Ninety-Fifth Illinois Infantry was wounded at Vicksburg on May 22, 1863, and died on June 12 at Memphis. Pvt. Orlando Loper, Company B, Ninety-Fifth Illinois Infantry, of Belvidere, was wounded at Vicksburg and was discharged at another location than with the regiment. Pvt. David Cox, Company B, Ninety-Fifth Illinois Infantry. He was born in Burnham, Essex County, England. He lived at Belvidere, Illinois, at the date of his enlistment. A shot took his "finger off" during the May 22, 1863, attack on the Confederate defenses at Vicksburg and discharged prior to the regiment being mustered out on May 5, 1865. Pvt. John Sexton, Company B, Ninety-Fifth Illinois Infantry, wounded in skirmish near Lake Providence, Louisiana, on February 10, 1863. He died in the service. Pvt. Alexander S. Cummings, Company B, Ninety-Fifth Illinois Infantry, was wounded at Vicksburg on May 19 and 22, 1863. Pvt. John Martin, Company B, Ninety-Fifth Illinois Infantry as wounded at Vicksburg on May 22, 1863. Pvt. James R. Manning, Company B, Ninety-Fifth Illinois Infantry was wounded badly in the shoulder in the May 22 attack on Vicksburg. The single farmer was twenty-three when he entered the army on August 14, 1862, and discharged on September 18, 1864. Manning was born in London, Ontario. M539 roll 19, Adjutant General Records, Muster Rolls for Illinois Regiments in the Civil War, Roll #47, 15. Pvt. Benjamin Easton, Company B, Ninety-Fifth Illinois Infantry died of wounds on June 19, 1863. Pvt. Alfred M. Horton, musician, Company B, Ninety-Fifth Illinois Infantry, wounded at Vicksburg. Wood, *History of the Ninety-Fifth Regiment*, xxxiv (photo of John Horan), 218, 219, 220, 233.

12. Pvt. Walter Harder, Company B, Ninety-Fifth Illinois Infantry. He is buried in the Andrus Cemetery, Bonus Township, Boone County, Illinois. Wood, *History of the Ninety-Fifth Regiment*, 219. The description of his foot being run over by a wagon wheel is similar to the injury described by Dr. Lis Franc in the Napoleonic Wars in which a fracture and dislocation occurs between the tarsal and metatarsals in the mid foot. M. Goossens, and N. DeStoop, "LisFranc's Fracture-Dislocations: Etiology, Radiology, and Reviews of Treatment: a Review of 20 Cases," Clinics in Orthopedics and Related Research, June 1983, Vol. 176, 154–62.

13. Pvt. Elias Shockley, Company B, Ninety-Fifth Illinois Infantry. Wood, *History of the Ninety-Fifth Regiment*, 219.

14. Pvt. Cordenio Bruce, Company K, Ninety-Fifth Illinois Infantry of Belvidere, Illinois, was wounded slightly in right shoulder at Vicksburg. He was mustered out somewhere different than with his regiment. Wood, *History of the Ninety-Fifth Regiment*, 230, 236.

15. Pvt. William Bassett, Company E, Ninety-Fifth Illinois Infantry of Bonus, Illinois, was killed at Vicksburg on May 17, 1863. Wood, *History of the Ninety-Fifth Regiment*, 224.

16. Capt. Gabriel E. Cornwell, Company K, Ninety-Fifth Illinois Infantry was killed at Vicksburg on May 22, 1863. Wood, *History of the Ninety-Fifth Regiment*, xxxiii, 239.

17. Capt. Jason Manzer, Company C, Ninety-Fifth Illinois Infantry of Harvard, Illinois, was killed at Vicksburg on May 22, 1863. Wood, *History of the Ninety-Fifth Regiment*, xxvi, 237.

18. Capt. Edward Cook, Company D, Ninety-Fifth Illinois Infantry was wounded at Vicksburg on May 22, 1863. He died on June 11, 1863. Wood, *History of the Ninety-Fifth Regiment*, xxvii, 234.

19. Col. Thomas Humphrey of the Ninety-Fifth Illinois Regiment was severely wounded in the left foot at Vicksburg in May 1863 and killed-in-action at the Battle of Guntown, June 10, 1864. Wood, *History of the Ninety-Fifth Regiment*, 232, 237.

20. Pvt. Schuyler Wakefield, Company K, Ninety-Fifth Illinois Infantry was wounded in the left leg at Vicksburg. His leg was amputated. He was discharged prior to the end of the war. Wood, *History of the Ninety-Fifth Regiment*, 231, 236–37. He was born in 1841 and died in Omaha, Nebraska, on April 10, 1891, where he is buried at Forest Lawn Memorial Park, plot 3. He was a member of GAR post 7.

21. "After the first year, the medical teams of both the North and the South delivered care and produced survival rates for diseases and injuries far better than either the civilian physicians of the time or European practitioners in subsequent wars." Despite widespread and inaccurate reports "anesthesia was used almost universally from the beginning of the Civil War." Jay Bollet, *Civil War Medicine: Challenges and Triumphs* (Tucson, AZ: Galen Press 2002), 78.

22. Women played a tremendous part in the care of the sick and wounded on both sides during the Civil War. Prominent hospital administers included Phoebe Pember, and Capt. Rose Greenhow of the Chimborazo and Robertson Hospitals in Richmond. Famous nurses include Clara Barton (of New Jersey), Harriet Becher Stowe, Elizabeth Cady Stanton, Kate Cummings (of Mobile), and Dorothea Dix was appointed superintendent of Union Nurses. Dr. Mary Waker won the Congressional Medal of Honor for her bravery under fire while saving the lives of hundreds of troopers. Nina Silber, *Daughters of the Union: Northern Women Fight the Civil War* (Cambridge, MA: Harvard University Press, 2005); Bell Irvin Wiley, *Confederate Women* (Westport, CT: Greenwood Press, 1975); Frank Moore, *Women of the War: their Heroism and Sacrifice* (Hartford, CT: SS Scranton, 1867), passim.

23. Harvard is a town located in McHenry County, Illinois. Wood, *History of the Ninety-Fifth Regiment*, 14.

24. Chilvers Family Papers, Letter from William B. Chilvers to George Burnham, June 13, 1863.

25. The Siege of Vicksburg began on May 18 and lasted until General Pemberton's surrender on July 4, 1863. Ballard, *The Civil War in Mississippi*, 139–71.

26. Chilvers Family Papers, Letter from William B. Chilvers to George Burnham, June 27, 1863.

27. Chilvers Family Papers, Letter from William B. Chilvers to George Burnham, June 5, 1863. This letter was written after the Union assaults of May 19 and 22 on the Confederate lines.

28. Chilvers Family Papers. The Robinsons are neighbors of Chilvers, and his aunt and uncle, the Burnhams. Their son George W. Robinson married Sarah Adelia Hill on January 30, 1867. Pvt. George W. Robinson was probably a member of Company B, Forty-Fifth Illinois Infantry. Frederick A. Dyer, *A Compendium of the War of the Rebellion* (Des Moines, IA: The Dyer Publishing Co., 1908).

29. Cpl. William R. Stevenson, Company B, Ninety-Fifth Illinois Infantry was wounded at Vicksburg. Wood, *History of the Ninety-Fifth Regiment*, 218, 233.

30. Cpl. Smith T. Marvin, Company B, Ninety-Fifth Illinois Infantry of Bonus was promoted to corporal before the end of the war. Wood, *History of the Ninety-Fifth Regiment*, 219.

31. Pioneer Corps acted as engineers for Grant's army. They constructed a pontoon bridge over the Big Black River in Mississippi on May 18, 1863. Smith, *Champion Hill*, 395.

32. Pvt. Henry J. Munzer, Company B, Ninety-Fifth Illinois Infantry of Bonus, Illinois. Wood, *History of the Ninety-Fifth Regiment*, 219.

33. Gen. T. E. G. Ransom, during the Battle of Vicksburg, commanded the Second Illinois Artillery to dismantle two twelve-pound cannons, and soldiers from his brigade dragged them to an earthwork position within 100 yards of the Confederates. The artillery supported Ransom's attack of the Stockade Redan on May 22, 1863. Jim Miles, *A River Unvexed* (Nashville, TN: Rutledge Hill Press, 1994), 491.

34. Eighth Missouri Infantry Regiment. Sherman's Corp was the Fifteenth Corps at Vicksburg. McPherson's Corp was the Seventeenth Corps at Vicksburg. They composed the assault on Stockade Redan on May 22. McClernand's Corps was the Thirteenth Corps at Vicksburg where they were involved in the May 19 attack. *Dyer's Compendium*.

35. Gen. John McArthur was born on November 17, 1826, in Scotland where he became a blacksmith. He immigrated to Chicago where he established the Excelsior Iron Works. He was the captain of a militia, the "Chicago Highland Guards," becoming colonel of the Twelfth Illinois Infantry. He was promoted to brigadier general and took over the command of W. H. L. Wallace, who was killed at Shiloh. He served at Vicksburg, Chattanooga, Nashville, and Selma. He was brevetted major general. He died in Chicago on May 15, 1906, where he is buried. Warner, *Generals in Blue*, 288; Gen. Frances Preston Blair, Jr., was from a very powerful political family who owned a house across from the White House in Washington, D.C. He was born in Lexington, Kentucky, and moved to St. Louis. He was elected to Congress on the "Free-oil ticket" in 1856. He fought to prevent the extension of slavery despite being a slave-holder himself. He organized the "Wide Awakes" and "Home Guard" to counter the secessionist activities of Missouri Gov. Claiborne Jackson. He was a major force in preventing Missouri from seceding. He enlisted seven regiments for the Union. He served as a brigade general during the Yazoo Expedition against Vicksburg and subsequently commanded the Fifteenth and Seventeenth Corps through Georgia and the March to the Sea. He was praised for his leadership by Gen. U. S. Grant and his close friend Gen. William T. Sherman. He served as a U.S. Senator from Missouri in the 1870s. He died in St. Louis on July 8, 1875, and was buried in Bellefontaine Cemetery. Warner, *Generals in Blue*, 35–36.

36. Vicinity.

37. "Old Tom" was Col. Thomas Humphrey. Wood, *History of the Ninety-Fifth Regiment*, 211.

38. Chilvers Family Papers. Pvt. George Robinson, Fifteenth Illinois Infantry, was the son of the Burnham's neighbors in Boone County, Illinois. *Dyer's Compendium*.

39. Chilvers Family Papers. Edmund Emery was Chilvers' cousin who lived in Canton, Illinois.

40. Fits is a nineteenth century term for seizures. There was no treatment for seizures until the development of anticonvulsants in the twentieth century.

41. Interspersed.

42. Cpl. Smith T. Marvin, Company B, and Pvt. Henry J. Munzer, Company B, Ninety-Fifth Illinois Infantry. Wood, *History of the Ninety-Fifth Regiment*, 219.

43. Wisconsin troops at Vicksburg, especially the Fourth and Eighth regiments, were despised by the Confederates. Capt. Joseph Bailey, Company D, Fourth Wisconsin.

44. Chilvers Family Papers, Letter from William B. Chilvers to George Burnham, June 10, 1863.

45. "The nightly trickle of hungry deserters had recently turned into a flood" as the siege progressed to early June. Shea, *Vicksburg is the Key*, 175.

46. The Peace Democrats were branded as "Copperheads" by the Ohio Republicans in 1861. Their motto was, "the Union as it was, the Constitution as it is." They frequently attacked the war policies of the Lincoln administration. By 1864 most Northerners thought they were traitors to the cause of the Union. Jennifer L. Weber, *Copperheads: the Rise and Fall of Lincoln's Opponents in the North* (Oxford: Oxford University Press, 2006), ix, 1.

47. "Now a to these riots in different Citys I think when a person takes poison they must take enough to kill or they will have to have a spasm and the effects of the spasm will learn the person better than to do it again. So the minds of the Peace Democrats have been poisoned with the doctrins of disloyalty and treason by the speaches of Vallandingham & Fernando Wood and this class of peace politicians and now the spasm as come in the shape of a Riot to resist the conscription   But after its effect is over they will learn by sad experience that Military Law is not to be sneezed at and wht words od advice fails to do for to set the peoples minds right. If ever the army and navy was manaced & insulted by any one it is by the Copperheads of the Northern states but let them take a timely warning for the Soldiers Sware that if they continue to do so after they get home they are all of them dead men." Franklin R. Crawford, ed., *My Dear Wife: The Civil War Letters of Private Samuel Pepper, Company G – 95th Illinois Infantry 1862–1865* (Caledonia, IL: The Muffled Drum, 2003), 68. Chilvers Family Papers, Letter from William B. Chilvers to George Burnham, June 11, 1863.

48. John C. Pemberton, "The Terms of Surrender," in Robert Underwood Johnson and Clarence Clough Buel, *Battles and Leaders of the Civil War* (New York: Thomas Yoseloff, Inc., 1956), 3:543–45; Fred Shannon, ed., *The Civil War Letters of Sergeant Onley Andrus* (Urbana, IL: University of Illinois Press, 1947), 15–16, 27–29, 58, 63–64, 75; "Yesterday, the glorious Fourth of July was made doubly so, by the surrender, and occupation of this, the strongest position in their Confederacy," William Henry Harrison Clayton to Amos and Grace Clayton, July 5, 1863, found in Brooks D. Simpson, ed., *The Civil War: The Third Year Told by Those Who Lived It* (New York: Penguin, 2013), 348–51. The term "Bloodless Ninety-Fifth" comes from Wales Wood in his history of the Ninety-Fifth Illinois.

49. Chilvers Family Papers, Letter of William B. Chilvers to George Burnham, July 1863. The Confederates surrendered to Grant's Union troops on July 4, 1863.

50. Chilvers Family Papers. Richard Sinten was a friend of the Burnhams in Boone County, Illinois and father of Hattie, who was a girlfriend of Chilvers.

51. different

52. Pvt. Israel Wood, Company E, Ninety-Fifth Illinois Infantry was transferred to the Forty-Seventh Illinois Infantry, Company E, on February 2, 1864, and was mustered out on August 17, 1865. Wood, *History of the Ninety-Fifth Regiment*, 224. According to the 1860 Census, Israel Wood was born in Canada about 1842 and was a tanner. He lived in Dunham, McHenry County, Illinois, with a post office in Chemung. His household members included: H. A. C. Griffin, aged fifty-eight; Sarah Griffin, aged forty-seven; John Griffin, aged twenty-five; James Griffin, aged twenty-four; Amelia Griffin, aged nineteen; Christopher Griffin,

aged eighteen; Emma Griffin, aged thirteen; [illegible]Edson Griffin, aged five; J. A. Wood, aged forty-three (blacksmith); Sarah Wood, aged forty-three; Israel Wood, aged eighteen (tanner); Harriet Wood, aged seventeen; Thomas Wood, aged sixteen; Sanford Wood, aged twelve; James Wood, aged eight; Thomas Wood, aged eighty-seven (tailor); and David Beck, aged sixteen. The 1880 Census listed an Israel Wood born in Canada and married to Rosella Wood of Illinois living in Jackson County, Gentry, Missouri. Chilvers Family Papers. Hattie Sinten is the daughter of Richard Sinten who was a girlfriend of Chilvers.

53. Chilvers Family Papers, Letter from William B. Chilvers to George Burnham, May 29, 1863.

54. Ibid. Canton, Illinois, was the town where Chilvers' cousins, the Fillinghams, lived.

55. Pvt. John F. Fillingham, Company K, Seventh Illinois Cavalry Regiment, Canton, Illinois, mustered in September 13, 1861. He re-enlisted on March 30, 1864, and mustered out as a first sergeant on November 4, 1865.

56. Chilvers Family Papers, Letter from William B. Chilvers to George Burnham, May 29, 1863.

57. Ibid. "Grandfather" was William Burnham of Lynn, Norfolk County, England. William Spooner was a close relative of Chilvers who lived in England.

58. Ibid. Maria Burnham was the daughter of the Burnhams who apparently stayed in England with her grandparents Burnham.

59. Ibid. Susan (possibly Chilvers) Watson was the aunt of Will Chilvers.

60. Ibid. Thomas Chilvers was William Burnham Chilvers' uncle. He had a son that he named Thomas Chilvers, Jr., who eventually moved to Nebraska to live close to Will.

61. Ibid. Cousin Lidda.

62. Ibid. William Spooner. James and Esther probably Spooner.

63. Ibid., Letter from William B. Chilvers to George Burnham, June 10, 1863.

64. Ibid. Uncle Mathew Twelves had a drinking problem.

65. Ibid., Letter from William B. Chilvers from George Burnham, August 16, 1863.

66. Wood, *History of the Ninety-Fifth Regiment*, 81–86, 88–90.

67. Twenty Confederate officers and soldiers were captured while attempting to escape. They had been led by Col. John L. Logan who commanded the post. Wood, *History of the Ninety-Fifth Regiment*, 82.

68. 2nd Lt. Aaron Randall, Company B, Ninety-Fifth Illinois Infantry was mustered into the army on September 4, 1862, and resigned January 16, 1863. Wood, *History of the Ninety-Fifth Regiment*, 213.

69. Chilvers Family Papers, Letter of William B. Chilvers to George Burnham, July 12, 1863. The Battle of Helena, Arkansas, was fought on July 4, 1863, and was a Union victory. Theophilus Holmes' three pronged attack was defeated by the strong fortifications of the Union garrison. Mark K. Christ, *Civil War Arkansas 1863: The Battle for the State* (Norman, OK: University of Oklahoma Press, 2010), 116–44.

70. The Provost Marshall of the Second Congressional Office of Illinois was Lt. Col. James Oakes. U.S. War Department Provost Marshall General's Bureau Illinois Records, 1861–1865.

71. Vicksburg surrendered on July 4, 1863. The Battle of Gettysburg was fought on July 1-3, 1863. Battle of Helena, Arkansas, was fought in July 1863 and was a Union victory.

72. Casualties of the May 22 attack at Vicksburg in Company B include: Sgt. Charles Anderson, Cpl. John Horan (died of wounds), Pvt. Benjamin Easton (died of wounds), Pvt. Thomas Moore, Pvt. John Martin, Pvt. Alfred M. Horton, Pvt. David Cox, Pvt. Alex S. Cummings, Pvt. Orlando Loper, Pvt. James R. Manning, Pvt. William R. Stevenson, Pvt. John Sexton, and Pvt. Job H. Westbury (died of wounds). Pvt. David F. Studley, wounded June 10, 1863, at Vicksburg, later died of these wounds. Wood, *History of the Ninety-Fifth Regiment*, 233.

73. Cpl. John Horan, Company B, Ninety-Fifth Illinois Infantry died of wounds received at Vicksburg, May 1863. Pvt. Benjamin Easton, Company B, Ninety-Fifth Illinois Infantry died of wounds inflicted at Vicksburg, May 1863. Wood, *History of the Ninety-Fifth Regiment*, 233.

74. Pvt. David F. Studley, Company B, Ninety-Fifth Illinois Infantry was wounded on June 10, 1863, at Vicksburg. He died of these wounds. Wood, *History of the Ninety-Fifth Regiment*, 233.

75. 2nd Lt. Aaron Randall's health apparently caused him to resign on January 16, 1863. Wood, *History of the Ninety-Fifth Regiment*, 213.

76. Quartermaster Gardner S. Southworth was promoted from first lieutenant, Company I, on May 14, 1863. Marengo, Illinois, was where the Ninety-Fifth Illinois staff and field officers met for the first time on August 16, 1862. Wood, *History of the Ninety-Fifth Regiment*, xxxii, 14, 211.

77. Maj. William A. Avery was promoted from captain, Company A, to major on May 21, 1863. He was promoted to lieutenant colonel on November 21, 1863. Wood, *History of the Ninety-Fifth Regiment*, 211.

78. Dr. Mimm was a local doctor in Boone County, Illinois.

79. Addie Little was a mutual friend of Chilvers and Randall in Belvidere. Chilvers Family Letters.

80. Charles Curtis was an eighteen-year-old single farmer living in Spring Township, Boone County, when he joined Company B, Ninety-Fifth Illinois Infantry on August 5, 1862. He was born in the state of New York. He was promoted to sergeant major on July 7, 1864, and was wounded slightly at Spanish Fort on March 30, 1865, and mustered out with the regiment on August 17, 1865. Adjutant General Record, Muster Rolls for Illinois Regiments in the Civil War, Roll #47, 15.

81. The Colt Navy revolver featured an octagonal barrel. It was a six-shot, .44 caliber, was thirteen inches long, weighed 2.63 pounds, and had a muzzle velocity of seven-hundred-sixty feet per second. Francis A. Lord, *Civil War Collector's Encyclopedia: Arms, Uniforms, and Equipment of the Union and Confederacy* (Harrisburg, PA: The Stackpole Company, 1963), 206.

82. "Grant dispatched a force under Brigadier General Thomas E. G. Ransom to Natchez, seventy miles south of Vicksburg, after receiving a report that the Confederates were crossing cattle from the Trans-Mississippi. Reaching Natchez on July 13, Ransom captured five thousand Texas beef cattle; he sent nearly half of them to Banks at Port Hudson and the rest to Vicksburg. Upon discovering that 150 wagons filled with ordnance were in

the process of crossing to the west bank, he managed to seize three hundred muskets and two hundred thousand rounds of ammunition before the column moved out of reach." Earl Hess, *The Civil War in the West: Victory and Defeat from the Appalachians to the Mississippi* (Chapel Hill, NC: University of North Carolina Press, 2012), 161–62.

83. Chilvers Family Papers, Letter from William B. Chilvers to George Burnham, August 12, 1863.

84. Forty-Fifth Illinois Infantry Regiment. Boone County Illinois supplied troops for the Ninth Illinois Cavalry and the Fifteenth, Thirty-Seventh, Forty-Fifth, Sixty-Fifth, and Ninety-Fifth (Companies B, G, and K), 142nd (Company C), and the 153rd (Companies A and B) Illinois Infantry Regiments. *Dyer's Compendium.*

85. Pvt. James Stevenson, Company E, Ninety-Fifth Illinois Infantry was wounded by a shell at Vicksburg in May 1863. Wood, *History of the Ninety-Fifth Regiment*, 234.

86. Shannon, *The Civil War Letters of Sergeant Onley Andrus*, 15–16, 27, 28–29, 58, 63–64, 75.

87. "Slavery Abolishment Act of 1833; Section XII," August 28, 1833.

88. Sgt. Onley Andrus, "simply could not stand Negroes; he did not like them, and he made no effort to conceal his feelings about them. Sometimes he became almost violent in his disgust because the conflict had turned into a war to free the slaves. Like a good portion of other Northerners, including a large share of the soldiers, he was all for saving the Union, but he had the irrational notion that free Negroes would have a more depressing effect on the labor of free white men than would slaves. He could even become angry enough to express the hope that Confederate raiders would wreck their destruction on his own smug community in Illinois." Shannon, *The Civil War Letters of Sergeant Onley Andrus*, 15–16, 27, 28–29, 58, 63–64, 75, 87.

89. Newly emancipated African Americans soon began to flock into Natchez, and Ransom had to feed about five hundred refugees. He sent some of them to Vicksburg. Ransom wrote to headquarters that, "they are anxious to go" even though "they do not know what for." Through the "Conscription Act" many of the men were placed as soldiers for the North. Hess, *The Civil War in the West*, 162.

90. Chilvers Family Papers, Letter from William B. Chilvers to George Burnham, August 16, 1863.

91. The Marine Hospital was located in Vicksburg next to the railroad. Many soldiers were then moved to larger hospitals up the rail lines. Pvt. Samuel Pepper, Company G, Ninety-Fifth Illinois Infantry was ill and hospitalized at the Benton Barracks in St. Louis he wrote his wife on July 11, 1863, "We have had arrivals from Vicksburg and Memphis Hospitals this week and last. Sick and wounded several with their arms and some with fingers off and others wounded in their bodies legs or feet throat or head eye or face but these are nothing compared to many at Memphis & below the paper has a list of new arrivals many from the Ninety-Fifth as you will observe by consulting the list." Crawford, *My Dear Wife*, 65.

92. Capt. Charles B. Loop, Company B, Ninety-Fifth Illinois Infantry. Wood, *History of the Ninety-Fifth Regiment*, 211; Chilvers Family Papers, Letter from William B. Chilvers to George Burnham, June 5, 1863.

93. Camp Fuller, in Rockford, Illinois, was where the Ninety-Fifth Illinois Infantry completed its training in the fall of 1862. Wood, *History of the Ninety-Fifth Regiment*, 15, 9, 20, 24, 30, 39.

94. Chilvers Family Papers, Letter from William B. Chilvers to George Burnham, August 20, 1863.

95. "The first draft lottery conducted in New York City under the 1863 conscription act was held on July 11. Two days later a mob attacked the draft office at Third Avenue and 46th Street, beginning five days of violence in which at least 105 people were killed. The riots were eventually suppressed by several regiments of Union troops, some of which had fought at Gettysburg." George Templeton Strong, *George Templeton Strong Diary*, edited by Allan Nevins and Milton Halsey Thomas (Seattle: University of Washington Press, 1988), July 13–17, 1863; Leslie M. Harris, *The Draft Riots: New York, July 1863* (Chicago: University of Chicago Press, 2003); Brooks D. Simpson, ed., *The Civil War: The Third Year By Those Who Lived It* (New York: Penguin, 2013), 382–89.

96. Chilvers Family Papers.

Chapter 4

1. Maj. Gen. Richard Taylor was commander of the Western District of Louisiana. Gary Dillard Joiner, *One Damn Blunder From Beginning to End: The Red River Campaign of 1864* (Wilmington, DE: Scholarly Resources Books, 2003), 19; Lt. Gen. Nathan Bedford Forrest was a brilliant leader of Southern forces. In a letter to Secretary of War Edwin Stanton, William T. Sherman wrote on June 5, 1864, there will never be peace in Tennessee till [Gen. Nathan Bedford] Forrest is dead." John D. Wright, ed., *The Oxford Dictionary of Civil War Quotations* (Oxford: Oxford University Press, 2006), 367.

2. Following his victory at Vicksburg, Grant believed "momentum ought to be used, and he had plans for following up the conquest of the Mississippi Valley with a campaign against the important Confederate port of Mobile, Alabama. Halleck and Lincoln saw matters in a different light. The general-in-chief had never understood the concept of momentum in war, and the president was preoccupied with the French presence in Mexico. Over the next nine months, they diverted various elements of the Army of the Tennessee to several ill-conceived schemes aimed at securing territory west of the Mississippi and showing the United States flag in Texas as a political statement to the French." Steven E. Woodworth, *Nothing But Victory: The Army of the Tennessee 1861–1865* (New York: Alfred A. Knopf, 2005), 459. Sam Houston proposed that if Texas chose to leave the Union in 1861, that they should return to becoming an independent country and not join the Confederate States. The secession of Texas would have been legal by the terms of the republic's entry into the United States in 1845. Texas Gov. Edward Clark wrote to Jefferson Davis that he suspected "an effort will be made soon by the submissive parts of the state, with General Houston as its head to convert Texas into an independent republic." John Hoyt Williams, *Sam Houston: The Life and Times of the Liberator of Texas an Authentic American Hero* (New York: Promontory Press, 1993), 357. John Ehle, *Trail of Tears: The Rise and Fall of the Cherokee Nation* (New York: Anchor, 1988), 388–89.

3. Parts of Texas were thriving during the Civil War through a trade of Texas-grown products. Cotton and cattle were sent to the South, and also were exported to Europe through Mexico. "The rebel victory at Manassas put New England in a bad position economically, it's main employer was the textile industry and, in 1861, textiles could not be produced without cotton. By the fall of 1861, Northern cotton reserves were nearly exhausted, with no hope of renewal, unless a Southern cotton-growing region could be seized." By July

1862, at least 80 percent of all Northern cotton mills had closed down. Unemployment was rampant. Samuel W. Mitcham, Jr., *Richard Taylor and the Red River Campaign of 1864* (Gretna, LA: Pelican Publishing Company, 2012), 9–10. A. Sellew Roberts, "The Federal Government and Confederate Cotton," *American Historical Review* 32 (January 1927): 262–75.

4. Through the Confiscation Act, newly freed slaves joined freemen of color as soldiers of the Union. Almost 179,000 black men served in these units. Black soldiers performed heroically at the Battle of Milliken's Bend on June 7, 1863. Assistant Secretary of War Charles Dana noted, "the bravery of blacks in the Battle of Milliken's Bend completely revolutionized the sentiment of the army with regard to the employment of negro troops." John David Smith, ed., *Black Soldiers in Blue: African American Troops in the Civil War Era* (Chapel Hill, NC: University of North Carolina Press, 2002), 55.

5. Chilvers Family Papers, Letter from William B. Chilvers to Burnhams, August 17, 1863.

6. Ibid. Letter from William B. Chilvers to the Burnhams, written from Vicksburg, October 23, 1863.

7. Ibid. Natchez, October 3, 1863.

8. Ibid.

9. Ibid. October 9, 1863.

10. McPherson's Seventeenth Corps was composed of four divisions: John A. Logan's Third Division, John McArthur's Sixth Division, Isaac F. Quinby's Seventh Division, and Francis J. Herron's Division.

11. The incidence of measles was much higher in black than white troops with a ratio of 2-0 black/white cases. The number of cases per year, per 1,000 black troops was sixty-five compared to thirty-two in whites. Jay Bollet, *Civil War Medicine: Challenges and Triumphs* (Tucson, AZ: Galen Press 2002), 328, 331. Author Joseph T. Glatthaar wrote, "as a result of such woeful and discriminatory medical care, nine times as many black troops died from disease as on the battlefield, and compare to white volunteers, two and one-half times as many black soldiers per one thousand died of disease. Over twenty-nine thousand died from illness, with pneumonia, dysentery, typhoid fever, and malaria taking he heaviest tolls on the black ranks. Within specific commands, the number of deaths was sometimes staggering. A black heavy artillery regiment lost over eight hundred men, and one infantry regiment, in service less than one year, had 524 deaths, nearly 50 percent of its strength. A lieutenant in Louisiana wrote, 'the mortality in our Regt. beats anything I ever saw . . . They frequently drop dead in the streets, and in two or three incidences have been found laying dead in the weeds some distance from camp' . . . He had just ordered his men to build one dozen coffins and pondered in disillusionment, 'how long do you suppose they will last the old Dr.?'" Joseph T. Glatthaar, *Forged in Battle: The Civil War Alliance of Black Soldiers and White Officers* (Baton Rouge, LA: Louisiana State University Press, 1990), 195.

12. The name of the pen that black soldiers and their families were placed into was called the "Devil's Punchbowl." Estimates of those that died in this horrific condition number as high as 20,000 according to some sources. Jeff Brown is not listed as a soldier in the Ninety-Fifth Illinois Infantry. Frederick A. Dyer, *A Compendium of the War of the Rebellion* (Des Moines, IA: The Dyer Publishing Co., 1908).

13. Chilvers Family Papers. J. Robinson, the Burnhams' neighbor, owned three groups of land in the 1858 Boone county census: Section 1 of 78 acres, Section 6 of 80 acres, and Section 7 of 80 acres.

14. The Sixth Mississippi Regiment (African Descent), also known as the Fifty-Eighth U.S. Colored Infantry Regiment, was organized on March 11, 1864. It was attached to the Port of Natchez, Department of Vicksburg, where it provided guard and garrison duty during the entire term. They were sent on an expedition from Natchez to Gillespie's Plantation from August 4–6, 1864. They were mustered out April 30, 1866. *Dyers Compendium.*

15. Chilvers Family Papers, Letter from William B. Chilvers to the Burnhams, September 19, 1863.

16. St. Louis was the location of the Department of the Missouri, which since the fall of 1863 was commanded by Gen. William Rosecrans. The Medical Department was commanded by Dr. Madison Mills, and many hospitals were located in St. Louis. John H. Brinton, *Personal Memoirs of John H. Brinton Civil War Surgeon, 1861–1865* (Carbondale, IL: Southern Illinois University Press, 1996), 315.

17. Chilvers Family Papers, Letter from William B. Chilvers to the Burnhams, written from Natchez, September 28, 1863.

18. Ibid., September 1, 1863.

19. Chilvers Family Papers, Letter from William B. Chilvers to the Burnhams, written from Natchez, October 27, 1863. Bloody gilux is dysentery and these water-borne illnesses were a leading cause of death in the Civil War. "Typhoid is an intestinal infection spread by ingesting food or water contaminated by the fecal bacteria *Salmonella typhi.*" Louisa Mae Alcott said of the Union Hotel Hospital, "for a more perfect pestilence-box than this house I never saw—cold, damp, dirty, full of vile odors from wounds, kitchens, wash-rooms, and stables." Ira M. Rutkow, *Bleeding Blue and Gray: Civil War Surgery and the Evolution of American Medicine* (New York: Random House, 2005), 226–27.

20. Cpl. Harvey Smith, Company B, Ninety-Fifth Illinois Infantry. Wales Wood, *History of the Ninety-Fifth Regiment Illinois Infantry Volunteers* (Belvidere, IL: Boone County Historical Society, 1993), 219.

21. Chilvers Family Papers, Letter from William B. Chilvers to the Burnhams, written from Natchez, November 28, 1863. Pvt. John J. Merrill, Company B, Ninety-Fifth Illinois Infantry; Cpl. Robert Horan, Company G, Ninety-Fifth Illinois Infantry mustered out with his regiment; Pvt. Oscar F. Herrin, Company B, Ninety-Fifth Illinois Infantry. Wood, *History of the Ninety-Fifth Regiment*, 219, 226.

22 With the fall of Vicksburg, the North captured large supplies of arms, munitions, supplies and the South suffered 32,363 casualties including 29,491 men surrendered. Paul Mathless, ed., *Vicksburg: War, Terrible War had Come to our very Hearthstone* (Richmond, VA: Time-Life, 1997), 131.

23. Chilvers Family Papers, Letter from W. R. Stevenson to William B. Chilvers, written from St. Louis, Missouri, August 17, 1863.

24. Fort Sumter and Fort Wagner were part of the defenses of Charleston. Robert N. Rosen, *Confederate Charleston: An Illustrated History of the City and the People During the Civil War* (Columbia, SC: University of South Carolina Press, 1996), 158; Chilvers Family Papers, Stevenson letter, September 1, 1863.

25. Chilvers Family Papers, Letter from William B. Chilvers to the Burnhams, written from Natchez, October 3, 1863.

26. Ibid., September 6, 1863.

27. Rodney, Mississippi, was located about twenty miles south of Vicksburg and a crossing point on the massive river. George W. Fly, "Feminine Fortitude in War Times," *Confederate Veteran*, Volume XI (1903), 278.

28. Chilvers Family Papers, Letter from William B. Chilvers to the Burnhams, October 9, 1863.

29. Ibid.

30. The textile mills in New England were devastated by the unavailability of Southern-grown cotton and their production was reduced by 80 percent. Mitcham, *Richard Taylor*, 9–10.

31. Chilvers Family Papers, Letter from William B. Chilvers to the Burnhams, written from Vicksburg, October 16, 1863.

32. Ibid.

33. Fort Hill, Mississippi, was occupied by the Third Louisiana Infantry and was thought to be "the most dangerous post" along the defenses of Vicksburg, which had been designed by Confederate engineer Samuel Luckett. During most of the siege, the Third Louisiana was commanded by Maj. David Pierson. "The regiment's trenches were twice undermined and exploded by massive charges of black powder laid by federal sappers, first on June 25 and then on July 1, 1863." Thomas Cutrer and T. Michael Parrish, eds., *Brothers in Gray: The Civil War Letters of the Pierson Family* (Baton Rouge, LA: Louisiana State University Press, 1997), 7.

34. The Battle of Colliersville, Tennessee, occurred on November 3, 1863, when Confederate Brig. Gen. James Chalmer led a division from Mississippi to attempt to destroy part of the Charleston & Memphis Rail Road that lay behind Sherman's Fifteen Corps. Union Col. Edward Hatch expectantly attacked Chalmers flank and the Southerners thought they were outnumbered and retreated.

35. Chilvers Family Papers, Letter from William B. Chilvers to the Burnhams, written from Vicksburg, October 22, 1863.

36. Second Iowa Cavalry. *Dyer's Compendium.*

37. Gen. James Ronald Chalmers led the Confederate forces at the Battle of Colliersville. The general was born in Virginia on January 11, 1831, and graduated from South Carolina College. Prior to the war, Chalmers had been an attorney in Holly Springs, Mississippi. He fought at Shiloh, Perryville, and Murfreesboro, and led a division under Gen. Nathan Bedford Forrest. He served in Congress for three terms after the war. Ezra Warner, *Generals in Blue* (Baton Rouge, LA: Louisiana State University Press, 1964), 46–47.

38. Chilvers Family Papers, Letter from James and Lavinia Fillingham to William B. Chilvers, written from Banner, Illinois, November 23, 1863.

39. Gen. Ambrose Burnside became head of the Department of the Ohio in the summer of 1863. He led the invasion of the eastern part of Tennessee with its predominant loyalist population. Gen. William Rosecrans was replaced as commander of the Army of the Cumberland by Gen. George Thomas in mid-October 1863 when Ulysses S. Grant became

the commander of the newly created Military Division of the Mississippi. Earl J. Hess, *The Civil War in the West: Victory and Defeat from the Appalachians to the Mississippi* (Chapel Hill, NC: University of North Carolina Press, 2012), 187, 194. Surgeon John H. Brinton wrote in his memoirs about his meeting with General Rosecrans in October 1864 and an unusual conversation that occurred: "The General was very nice and gave me a warm welcome. Somehow or other, I said something about soap, I believe in this way. A fire had been built in front of our tents, as evening closed in. The wind was high, and the smoke drifted in our faces, and some allusion was made to the cleaning powers of soap. The General addressed his conversation chiefly to me, and I listened well. He had been much interested in the manufacture of soap before entering the army (he was a West Point graduate), and once on his favorite topic he talked, and talked. The men of the staff dropped off to their tents and sleep, but still he talked, and still I listened." Brinton, *Personal Memoirs*, 319.

40. Gen. Stephen A. Hurlbut was commander of the Sixteenth Corps which occupied western Tennessee and northern Mississippi, and was based in Memphis in 1863. Woodworth, *Nothing But Victory*, 479. Chattanooga was captured by Rosecrans in September 1863, aided by Illinois troops to "relieve the beleaguered union army there and to establish federal control in that region" following the setback at the Battle of Chickamauga. "Over seventy regiments then came to the immediate command of General Grant." These troops were then transferred to General Sherman "when Grant was called to Washington to assume, under the title of lieutenant general, the command of all the armies of the United States." Arthur Charles Cole, *The Centennial History of Illinois, Volume 3: The Era of the Civil War, 1848–1870* (Chicago, IL: A. C. McClurg & Co., 1922), 288.

41. Gen. Elias Smith Dennis was a U.S. Marshall and Illinois politician prior to the Civil War. Dennis was mustered into the service in August 1861 as lieutenant colonel of the Thirtieth Illinois Infantry. He served at Fort Donelson, Vicksburg, and Mobile, and was promoted to brigadier general in November 1862. Jack D. Welsh, *Medical Histories of Union Generals* (Kent, OH: Kent State University Press, 1996), 95.

42. Chilvers Family Papers, Letter from William B. Chilvers to the Burnhams, written from Vicksburg, October 27, 1863.

43. Pvt. Cordean Bruce, Company K, Ninety-Fifth Illinois Infantry, was Chilvers' good friend from Belvidere. He was wounded in the shoulder at Vicksburg in May 1863. He was mustered out at a different location than his regiment. Wood, *History of the Ninety-Fifth Regiment*, 230, 236.

44. Capt. Charles B. Loop, Company B, Ninety-Fifth Illinois Infantry. Ibid., 211.

45. Bounty was money used as an enticement for men to join the army. Chilvers Family Papers, Letter from William B. Chilvers to the Burnhams, written from Vicksburg, December 7, 1863.

46. Ibid., November 16, 1863.

47. Battle of Moscow, Tennessee, located on the Wolf River. Wood, *History of the Ninety-Fifth Regiment*, 51. Maj. Gen. Stephen A. Hurlbut complemented the troops participating in the conflict of December 4, 1863. On December 6, 1863, he wrote a general order to commend specifically the Second Regiment West Tennessee Infantry of African Descent, stating: "the recent affair at Moscow, Tennessee [December 4] has demonstrated the fact that colored troops properly disciplined, and commanded can and will fight well." Maj. Gen. Stephen A. Hurlbut, Memphis, Tennessee, December 5, 1863, *O.R.*, Ser. I, vol. 31, pt. I, 577.

Both commanders, Col. Frank Kempson and Lt. Col. George W. Trafton, wrote a detailed summary of the battle. Frank A. Kempson, Colonel, Second Regiment Western Tennessee Infantry, acting commander, *O.R.*, Ser. I, Vol., 31, pt. I, 583–86. Report of George W. Trafton, Lieutenant Colonel, Seventh Illinois Cavalry, headquarters LaGrange, Tennessee, December 9, 1863, *O.R.*, Ser. I, vol. 31, pt. I, 586–87.

48. Chilvers Family Papers, Letter from John Fillingham to William Chilvers near LaGrange, Tennessee, December 16, 1863. Col. Edward Hatch, Second Iowa Cavalry, commanded the brigade in which Fillingham belonged. He was wounded at the Battle of Moscow in December 1863. *O.R.*, Ser. I, vol. 31, pt. I, 586–87.

49. Chilvers Family Papers, Letter from William B. Chilvers to the Burnhams, written from Vicksburg, October 22, 1863. Col. Leander Blanden, Ninety-Fifth Illinois Infantry, was born in Burlington, Otsego County, New York, on October 19, 1830. He was a farmer and capitalist who was appointed major with the formation of the regiment on August 22, 1862. He was promoted to lieutenant colonel on May 21, 1863, to rank from January 24, 1863. On October 13, 1864, he was promoted to colonel to rank from September 1, 1864. He was breveted brigadier general, U.S.V., March 26, 1865, for faithful and meritorious services during the campaign against the city of Mobile and its defenses. Wood, *History of the Ninety-Fifth Regiment*, 211; Roger D. Hunt and Jack R. Brown, *Brevet Generals in Blue* (Gaithersburg, MD: Olde Soldiers Books, 1990), 61.

50. Thomas William Humphrey was born on April 4, 1835, in Danville, Knox County, Ohio. He attended Beloit College in Wisconsin and served as clerk in the DeKalb County, Illinois, Recorder's office. He was killed in action on June 10 at Guntown, Mississippi. He was honored as brevet brigadier general, U.S.V., June 10, 1864, for gallant and distinguished conduct in the battle near Guntown, Mississippi. Hunt, *Brevet Generals in Blue*, 303.

51. Chilvers Family Papers, Letter from William B. Chilvers to the Burnhams, written from Vicksburg, October 22, 1863.

52. Ibid., November 3, 1863.

53. Frederick Augustus Staring was born May 24, 1834, in Buffalo, New York, and graduated from Harvard Law School in 1866. He was a civil engineer, lawyer, and diplomat. He served as a major in the Forty-Sixth Illinois Infantry, a major in the Second Light Artillery, a colonel in the Seventy-Second Illinois Infantry, and a provost marshall general in the Department of the Gulf. He was awarded brevet brigadier general, U.S.V., March 13, 1865, for faithful, efficient and valuable services. Hunt, *Brevet Generals in Blue*, 582. *See also* note 169.

54. Chilvers Family Papers, Chilvers letter dated November 3, 1863.

55. Chilvers Family Papers, Letter from William B. Chilvers to the Burnhams, written from Vicksburg, November 3, 1863. By Christmas 1863, Colonel Humphrey had become very popular with the Ninety-Fifth Illinois Infantry. He was credited by taking better care of the troops. Sgt. Onley L. Andrus comments on a Christmas spree in 1863, writing: "Col. Tom turned out 15 galls of Rotgut & several of the boys got Happy, and some pugilistic, and as a consequence some had Eyes Red & some Black and all felt as though they had been poorly staid at best." Fred Shannon, ed., *The Civil War Letters of Sergeant Onley Andrus* (Urbana, IL: University of Illinois Press, 1947), 72.

56. Chilvers Family Papers, Letter from William B. Chilvers to the Burnhams, October 22, 1863.

57. Ibid., November 10, 1863.

58. Ibid., Letter from James and Lavinia Fillingham to William B. Chilvers, written from Banner, Illinois, November 23, 1863.

59. Ibid.

60. Ibid., Letter from William B. Chilvers to the Burnhams, Undated.

61. Ibid., Letter from William B. Chilvers to the Burnhams, written from Vicksburg, October 16, 1863.

62. Ibid., Letter from William B. Chilvers to the Burnhams, written from Vicksburg, November 3, 1863.

63. Ibid., September 26, 1863

64. Ibid., November 3, 1863.

65. Ibid., Letter from George Burnham to William Chilvers, January 3, 1864.

66. Ibid., Letters from William B. Chilvers to the Burnhams, written from Vicksburg, October 27, 1863, and November 10, 1863.

67. Ibid., Letter from William Chilvers to George and Rebecca Burnham, December 24, 1863.

68. Ibid., Letter from William Chilvers to George Burnham, December 24, 1863.

69. Ibid., Letter from William B. Chilvers to the Burnhams, written from Vicksburg, December 24, 1863.

70. Ibid., written from Natchez, September 28, 1863.

71. Ibid. Young Thomas Chilvers was born in 1860, and eventually moved to Pierce, Nebraska, to live close to his uncle Will.

72. Ibid., Letter from John Fillingham to William B. Chilvers, written from LaGrange, Tennessee, November 26, 1863.

73. Ibid., December 16, 1863.

74. Ibid., [Additional address] Company K, Seventh Illinois Cavalry, November 26, 1863.

75. Ibid., December 16, 1863.

76. Ibid., Letter from James and Lavinia Fillingham to William Chilvers, written from Banner, Illinois, November 23, 1863.

77. Ibid., Letter from William B. Chilvers to the Burnhams, written from Natchez, September 28, 1863.

78. Ibid., written from Vicksburg, November 28, 1863.

79. Ibid., December 24, 1863.

80. Ibid., December 7, 1863.

Chapter 5

1. Chilvers Family Papers, Letter from George Burnham to William B. Chilvers, written from Belvedere, Illinois, January 3, 1864.

2. Ibid., Letter from William B. Chilvers to George Burnham, January 12, 1864. Company B, Ninety-Fifth Illinois Infantry, consisted of soldiers from Boone County, Illinois. William R. Stevenson of Bonus mustered in on September 4, 1862, and was mustered out on August 17, 1865. He was promoted to corporal and was listed as being wounded. Alvin M. Smith of Belvidere mustered in September 12, 1864 (according to records – which is not consistent with Chilvers entry), and out on August 17, 1865. Harvey Smith of Belvidere mustered in September 4, 1862, and out on August 17, 1865, as a corporal. John Johnson of Bonus was mustered in January 18, 1864 (again not consistent with Chilvers letter), and transferred to Company B, Forty-Seventh Illinois Infantry Regiment. Tim Sergeant of Flora was mustered in November 28, 1863, and transferred to Company B, Forty-Seventh Illinois Infantry. Wales Wood, *History of the Ninety-Fifth Regiment Illinois Infantry Volunteers* (Belvidere, IL: Boone County Historical Society, 1993), 219. A shebang is a hut, shed: one's dwelling or quarters "Shebang," *Oxford English Dictionary Online*, http://www.oed.com/

3. Chilvers Family Papers, Letter from William B. Chilvers to George Burnham, February 11, 1864. The 1864 presidential election was a landslide victory of Abraham Lincoln over Peace Democrat and former Union Gen. George B. McClelland with an electoral landslide of 223 to twenty-one. McClellan won only the states of New Jersey, Delaware, and Kentucky. William Marvel, *Tarnished Victory: Finishing Lincoln's War* (New York: Houghton Mifflin Harcourt Publishing, 2011), 224.

4. Chilvers Family Papers, Letter from William B. Chilvers to George and Rebecca Burnham, January 9, 1864. Maj. David Hunter was a controversial man who was best known for burning the Shenandoah Valley including Virginia Military Institute in 1864. He presided over the court martial of Gen. John Fitz-Porter as well as the Lincoln Conspirators Trial. Gen. James Birdseye McPherson was a highly respected Western commander by both Grant and Sherman. A native of Clyde, Ohio, he graduated first in the West Point class of 1853. He served as the Seventeenth Corps commander at Vicksburg and through the western campaign until he was killed in action at Atlanta on July 22, 1864. Gen. Michael Kelly Lawler was born in County Kildare, Ireland, and immigrated with his family to Gallatin County, Illinois. He served as brigade and division commander. He was known for enforcing discipline with his fists, feeding emetics to drunks, and threatening both his men and officers. His most stellar event in the war was his assault at Vicksburg where more than eleven hundred Confederates were captured by his command. Gen. Elias Smith Dennis was born in Newburgh, New York, and moved to Illinois. He was mustered into the Thirtieth Illinois Infantry as lieutenant colonel and promoted to colonel in May 1862 after being commended for his efforts at Fort Donelson and in Tennessee, and then to brigadier general in November 1862. He commanded forces of Logan's Division of McPherson's Seventeenth Corps at Vicksburg. He was brevetted major general for meritorious services following the capture of Mobile. He served briefly as military governor of Shreveport. Gen. Andrew Jackson "Whiskey" Smith was born in Bern, Switzerland, and eventually settled in Galena, Illinois, where he recruited and organized the Forty-Fifth Illinois Infantry Regiment. He was promoted to brigadier general in November 1862 and commanded a brigade of Logan's Division of McPherson's Seventeenth Corps at Vicksburg. He subsequently was involved in Sherman's "March to the Sea." During the Mobile Campaign he commanded the reorganized Sixteenth Corps of two divisions. Smith was "one of the

most competent division and corps commanders in the service." He served as postmaster and city auditor of St. Louis after the war. He died in St. Louis, Missouri, on January 30, 1897, where he is buried in Bellefontaine Cemetery. Ezra Warner, *Generals in Blue* (Baton Rouge, LA: Louisiana State University Press, 1964), 118–19, 243–44, 306–308, 454–55.

5. Rock Island is a government-owned island of three miles long by one-half mile wide that is between Davenport, Iowa, and Moline, Illinois. It was first opened as a prisoner-of-war compound on December 3, 1863, when 5,592 Confederate prisoners arrived on a day when the temperature was thirty-two degrees below zero and the compound was covered by two feet of snow. Tragically, ninety-four of the captured soldiers were discovered to have small pox. The supervisory officer, Col. William H. Hoffman, "neglected to include any plans for a hospital in his new prison camp. Consequently, the sick had to be left in the barracks along with the healthy. By the end of the month, 245 prisoners were sick from smallpox and pneumonia, and ninety-four had died. Before long, there would be an average of 250 deaths a month in the prison's first four months of operation." The Northern Newspaper, the *Rock Island Argus*, called it the "Andersonville of the North" and "many have taken 'the oath,' any oath to save themselves from actual starvation." Lonnie R. Speer, *Portals to Hell: Military Prisons of the Civil War* (Mechanicsburg, PA: Stackpole Books, 1997), 154–55.

6. Brevetted Maj. Gen. Arthur McArthur was born in Scotland and immigrated to Chicago. He began the war in 1861 as captain of the "Chicago Highland Guards" and rapidly was promoted, first as colonel of the Twelfth Illinois Infantry, and before the end of the year to command the First Brigade of the Second Division of the District of Cairo under Ulysses S. Grant. He became division leader at Shiloh after the mortal wounding of W. H. L. Wallace. He led divisions under Edward Ord at Iuka and Corinth, James McPherson's Seventeenth Corps at Vicksburg, and George Thomas' Sixteenth Corps at Nashville. He received the Congressional Medal of Honor as did his son Gen. Douglas McArthur. Warner, *Generals in Blue*, 288. Thomas Humphrey was a very successful farmer in Franklin Township of DeKalb County, Illinois, where he was married and father of two girls. He was born in Danville, Ohio, and graduated from Beloit College in Wisconsin. He was elected as lieutenant colonel of the Ninety-Fifth Illinois Infantry. He was instrumental in the regiment's formation. When illness forced the resignation of Col. Lawrence Church, Humphrey was promoted to the position on January 20, 1863. He was slightly wounded in the left foot at the Siege of Vicksburg. He was killed at the Battle of Brice's Crossroads (Guntown) on June 10, 1864. Lt. Wales Wood noted that Humphrey "exerted himself energetically and constantly to promote the welfare and efficiently of the command, and give it as thorough preparation as possible for the field." His remains were buried at the Charter Oaks Cemetery in DeKalb County. Wood, *History of the Ninety-Fifth Regiment*, 19; Adjutant General Records for Illinois Regiments in the Civil War, Roll #47-15; and *Belvidere Daily Standard*, June 29, 1864. "Our Colo has the name here of a brave soldier & he will never stop short of one star on his shoulder strap instead of an eagle." Pvt. Samuel Pepper, Company G, Ninety-Fifth Illinois Infantry, letter to his wife. Franklin R. Crawford, ed., *My Dear Wife: The Civil War Letters of Private Samuel Pepper. Company G – 95th Illinois Infantry 1862–1865* (Caledonia, IL: The Muffled Drum, 2003), 123. "He is so anxious for Stars that he pays no attention to the wants of the men under him, only to keep them doing duty, & for featr that the Regt will get the name of being the smallest Regt in the Brig (as it is), he wont allow the Surgeon to excuse any one from duty who is able to stand up & eat his rations . . . Old Tom (gd Dn him) is so afraid that he will fail in obtaining Stars that he would willingly Sacrifice evetry man in the Brig, if he had the honor to obtain that one thing, the idol of his mind, the Pearl of great price, a Star." Fred Shannon, ed., *The Civil War Letters of Sergeant Onley Andrus* (Urbana, IL: University of Illinois Press, 1947), 71.

7. Gen. John Alexander Logan was a very successful civilian Western commander from Jackson County in Southern Illinois. Due to his black hair and eyes he was known as "Black Jack." He was in command of the Third Division of McPherson's Seventeenth Corps at Vicksburg and led the Fifteenth Corps during the Atlanta Campaign. He temporarily became the commander of the Army of Tennessee following the death of James B. McPherson at Atlanta. He was the unsuccessful Republican Vice-Presidential nominee in the election of 1884. Warner, *Generals in Blue*, 281–83.

8. Chilvers Family Papers, Letter from William B. Chilvers to George Burnham, January 9, 1864.

9. No Leacherson is noted on the rolls of the Ninety-Fifth Illinois. Similar names include Chester C. Leach (Belvidere mustered in November 26, 1863), Elisha J. Leach (Belvidere mustered in September 4, 1862), and Kittle Mikkleson (Bonus mustered in January 5, 1864, and died in Memphis on July 14, 1864). No Sergeant from Caledonia is noted on the roster of Company B. Chilvers friend, Timothy Sergeant, who was previously noted came from Flora. He mustered in November 28, 1863, and transferred to Company B, Forty-Seventh Illinois Infantry. The only soldier noted from Caledonia was David A. Moore who mustered in September 3, 1864. *Dyer's Compendium.*

10. Three Wakefields (Abner, Leonard, and Schuyler) from Belvidere were mustered into Company K, Ninety-Fifth Illinois Infantry on September 4, 1862, and mustered out August 17, 1865. Daniel Wakefield mustered in December 4, 1863, and was discharged on June 10, 1865. *Dyer's Compendium*; Wood, *History of the Ninety-Fifth Regiment*, 231; Chilvers Family Papers, Letter of William Chilvers to George Burnham, January 13, 1864.

11. Lincoln had drafted 300,000 men in the fall of 1863. A new draft would be particularly unpopular following the horrific battles of Vicksburg, Chancellorsville, Gettysburg, and Chickamauga, and the New York City Draft Riots of 1863. From July 13–17, 1863, "armed mobs interrupted enforcement of the first federal conscription and struggled with authorities for sway over the nation's manufacturing and commercial capital . . . The draft riots gave sudden focus to . . . national issues included the fate of federal conscription, the authority of the new Republican government in Washington, and the future of post-Emancipation Proclamation war effort." Five Union army regiments were ordered back from Gettysburg to suppress the riots in which the rioters turned their wrath against the black community. At least "105 people were killed, making the draft riots the most violent insurrection in American history." Iver Bernstein, *The New York City Draft Riots: Their Significance for American Society and Politics in the Age of the Civil War* (Oxford: Oxford University Press, 1990), 3; There were four drafts held in the North. James M. Greiner, Janet L. Coryell, and James R. Smither, eds., *A Surgeon's Civil War: The Letters and Diary of Daniel M. Holt, M.D.* (Kent, OH: Kent State University Press, 1994), 114.

12. Chilvers Family Papers, Letter from George Burnham to William B. Chilvers, January 19, 1864.

13. The Seventeenth Wisconsin Infantry Regiment. *Dyer's Compendium.*

14. Chilvers Family Papers, Letter from William B. Chilvers to George Burnham, February 4, 1864.

15. Ibid., February 11, 1864. Col. Thomas W. Humphrey, Ninety-Fifth Illinois Infantry. Wood, *History of the Ninety-Fifth Regiment*, 211.

16 Manassas was the location of two Confederate victories in the American Civil War: July 21, 1861, and August 29–30, 1862. Burnham's reference was to the Seven Days Campaign

series of battles around Richmond in June 1862. Confederate forces under newly appointed Gen. Robert E. Lee defeated George "Little Mac" McClelland reversing the war in the East. The two battles of Fredericksburg occurred on December 13, 1862, and on May 4, 1863.

17. Chilvers Family Papers, Letter from George Burnham to William B. Chilvers, March 28, 1864.

18. Chilvers Family Papers, Letter from William Chilvers to George Burnham, January 3, 1864.

19. Infectious diseases are a major problem for any army. In the American Civil War two-thirds of the deaths of soldiers are attributed to infectious diseases such as typhoid, pneumonia, dysentery, diarrhea, and measles. *See* Robert E. Denney, *Civil War Medicine: Care and Comfort of the Wounded* (New York: Sterling Publishing, 1994).

20. Pvt. Cordenio Bruce, Company K, Ninety-Fifth Illinois Infantry. Wood, *History of the Ninety-Fifth Regiment*, 230.

21. Rock Island, Illinois, was the site of a notorious prisoner-of-war camp where more than 2,000 Confederates were buried. Speer, *Portals to Hell*, 154. See note 11.

22. Col. Thomas W. Humphrey, Ninety-Fifth Illinois was liked by Chilvers, and often by Pvt. Samuel Pepper, Company G, but not by Sergeant Andrus, Company D. Pepper and Andrus both thought Humphrey was trying to become a general, "looking for stars," instead of taking care of the men. Crawford, *My Dear Wife*, 123; Shannon, *The Civil War Letters of Sergeant Onley Andrus*, 53.

23. John Heenan and Tom King were engaged in a boxing match on December 10, 1863.

24. One of the world's first boxing matches was held on December 10, 1863, at the Cocksmount Farm near Wadhurst, East Sussex, England. The fight was between the defending champion, John C. "Benica Boy" Heenan, and challenger Tom "Fighting Sailor" King. King, the Englishman, won in the twenty-fifth round over the American. Heenan's strategy was reported to come "close and put the hug on to crush his antagonist by once by dashing him violently to the ground." Controversy surrounded the event when King was given longer than the rules for recovering from an eighteen-round knockdown. King "knocked the boy clear off his pins" in the twenty-fifth round, but Heenan later declared his collapse occurred because he was drugged. "John C. Heenan vs. Tom King – The Great Prize Fight in England," *Philadelphia Enquirer*, December 24, 1863.

25. Chilvers Family Papers, Letter from William B. Chilvers to George Burnham, January 9, 1864.

26. Jay Monahan, *Abraham Lincoln Deals With Foreign Affairs: A Diplomat in Carpet Slippers* (New York: Bobbs-Merrill Company, 1945), ix, xiv.

27. For more information on the international scene at the time, see Howard Jones, *Blue and Gray Diplomacy: A History of Union and Confederate Foreign Relations* (Chapel Hill, NC: University of North Carolina Press, 2010), 276–77; Amanda Foreman, *A World at War: Britain's Crucial Role in the American Civil War* (New York: Random House, 2010), 192, 326, 328–30, 667. "The dominant culture of the peoples of the United States has been English . . . Suspicion, fear, religious bigotry, and hatred of Catholicism when intertwined with rivalry, distrust, dislike, and the strangeness of the great masses of foreigners," many from Germany and Ireland gave rise to the formation of the American Party in 1854. The

expressions of anti-foreignism and anti-Catholicism, or nativism, were features of this group. "All members professed ignorance of the party and were instructed to reply "I don't know" to all questions, thus gaining the name "Know-Nothing" for the party. W. Darrell Overdyke, *The Know-Nothing Party in the South* (Baton Rouge, LA: Louisiana State University, 1950), 1, 2, 40.

28. Chilvers Family Papers, Letter from George Burnham to William B. Burnham, March 4, 1864.

29. Dysentery or "bloody diarrhea" is due to pathogens such as salmonella, shigella, and campylobacter. It was a major cause of morbidity and mortality during these pre-antibiotic, pre-intravenous fluid days of the Civil War. Denney, *Civil War Medicine*, 9, 41, 65–66, 174, 229, 328.

30. The treatment of dysentery was often ineffective. Agents used included opium, camphor, and calomel (mercurial based which if overdosed would leave a patient "mad as a hatter" due to the cerebral toxic effects of this heavy metal). The narcotic laudanum was used to treat pain, agitation, and dysentery. Greiner, et al., *A Surgeon's Civil War*, 243; Ronald L. Numbers and Todd L. Savitt, *Science and Medicine in the Old South* (Baton Rouge, LA: Louisiana State University Press, 1989), 287, 288; Pvt. Samuel Pepper, Company G, Ninety-Fifth Illinois Infantry had several remedies for this ailment. In one episode, Pepper noted using dew berries and a dozen blue pills (probably calomel, which contained mercury). When he experienced another episode he told his wife he had, "pain before his passages" and requested that she send him some cayenne pepper. Crawford, *My Dear Wife*, 184, 189.

31. Chilvers Family Papers, Letter from William B. Chilvers to George Burnham, January 9, 1864.

32. Ibid., Letter from William B. Chilvers to George Burnham, January 24, 1864.

33. Ibid., Letter from William B. Chilvers to George Burnham, March 4, 1864.

34. Seventeenth Wisconsin Regiment, like the Ninety-Fifth Illinois, was part of Brig. Gen. John McArthur's Division in 1862, and both were assigned to Brig. Gen. T. E. G. Ransom's brigade, Sixth Division, Seventeenth Army Corps in May 1863. When the Ninety-Fifth Illinois was selected for the Red River Expedition in the spring of 1864, the Seventeenth Wisconsin was left to perform garrison duty at Vicksburg. Wood, *History of the Ninety-Fifth Regiment*, 34, 72, 97.

35. Chilvers Family Papers, Letter from William B. Chilvers to George Burnham, 1864 undated.

36. Wood, *History of the Ninety-Fifth Regiment*, 92–93.

37. The Red River Campaign was the last victorious campaign for the South.

38. The Union forces of Gen. A. J. Smith plundered across Louisiana during the Red River Campaign and continued this activity when they were transferred to the east as part of "the March to the Sea," from November 15 through December 15, 1864.

39. The *Woodford* was a hospital ship that accompanied the Mississippi Marine Brigade. The ship grounded at the falls at Alexandria. "Its hull pierced, it sank, and had to be burned." Gary D. Joiner, *Mr. Lincoln's Brownwater Navy* (Lanham, MD: Rowman & Littlefield Publishers, Inc., 2007), 68, 96, 150.

40. Fort DeRussy was a fortification on the Red River that the Ninety-Fifth Illinois attacked and captured under Gen. A. J. Smith on March 14. The Ninety-Fifth and Col. Thomas

Humphrey were assigned the task of destroying the well-built structure. Three magazines, including one with fifty kegs of powder, were exploded. Wood noted that, "the magazineds blew up with a terrific explosion, sinking the earth beneath one's feet, and filling the air, for hundreds of yards, with timbers, huge lumps of hard, red clay, and other dangerous missiles." Several soldiers were wounded, including Lt. John D. Abbe from Company K. In a later explosion, Pvt. Samuel Jackson, Company C, Ninety-Fifth Illinois, was killed. Wood, *History of the Ninety-Fifth Regiment*, 98–100.

41. Sixteenth Army Corps furnished two divisions for the Red River Expedition. The Seventeenth Corps supplied one division which was under the command of Brig. Gen. Thomas Kilby Smith. The force from both corps was under the command of Gen. A. J. Smith. Wood, *History of the Ninety-Fifth Regiment*, 97.

42. Bayou De Glaize is a stream between Marksville and Simmesport, Louisiana, near the Mouth of the Red River. Gary D, Joiner, *Through the Howling Wilderness* (Knoxville, TN: University of Tennessee Press, 2006), 40, 60.

43. Wood, *History of the Ninety-Fifth Regiment*, 98–99.

44. Ibid., 102.

45. Pvt. Samuel Pepper, Company G, Ninety-Fifth Illinois wrote, "I had the pleasure to acknowledge the receipt of 4 letters from you at Alexandria La 3 or 4 weeks ago which I fear may have been captured on Red River by Rebs as they captured two mails of ours one on its way down & another on its way up . . . some of them got below us cut our long line of communication planted a battery that was to powerful for our Transport Steamers. Sinking and burning ensued we lost quite a number of Boats." Crawford, *My Dear Wife*, 179.

46. Chilvers Family Papers, Letter from George Burnham to William B. Chilvers, April 24, 1864. The Red River Expedition occurred in the spring of 1864 when Nathaniel Banks led his Army of the Gulf north in an attempt to enter Texas through Shreveport, Louisiana. The campaign was stopped at the Battle of Mansfield, or Sabine Cross Roads, on April, 8, 1865, followed by a draw at the Battle of Pleasant Hill on April 9. Joiner, *Through the Howling Wilderness*, 1–15. Battle of Balls Bluff in October 1861 was fought in Northern Virginia. "The news of this disaster spread a glom over the land. Not only was the fall of Baker, a gallant man, and senator of the United States, deeply lamented, but the destruction in the two Massachusetts regiments, composed as they were of some of the finest young men of the state, was felt to be a national loss. Added to this was the universal feeling that that they fell victims to an unpardonable blunder, or to treason. McClelland had never ordered a movement of this kind, and the blame was at first divided between [General Stone] and [Colonel] Baker, but finally settled on the former. The whole affair remains a mystery to this day." J. T. Headley, *The Great Rebellion; A History of the Civil War in the United States* (Hartford, CT: Hurlbut, Scranton, and Company, 1864), 175–82. Gen. John Fremont is not thought to be an exceptional general by most modern historians. Both Chilvers and Burnham were supporters of Fremont due his strong abolitionist position. "The last of August was signalized by a proclamation of Fremont, declaring martial law in Missouri, and that under the decree of confiscation the slaves were free . . . the President directed Fremont to modify his proclamation," by not freeing the slaves as "it would utterly destroy the Union cause in the border states." Fremont interpreted the design of the confiscation scheme to "embrace all the property of rebels, and it would be difficult to see what it could do with confiscated slaves but to give them their freedom." Headley, *The Great Rebellion*, 141. Through two phenomenal engineering feats, Nathaniel Banks led his army to the safety of occupied South Louisiana. Bailey rescued the Union fleet from capture by

building a dam to raise the water level to get the fleet across the rapids at Alexandria. The Southerners had cleverly lowered the depth of the Red River by bypassing some of its flow into the parallel Bayou Pierre. Later in the retreat Union forces had been trapped at Yellow Bayou but the resourceful Bailey tied the fleet together to make a pontoon bridge and allow the soldiers to cross the river. Joiner, *Through the Howling Wilderness,* 152–56, 161.

47. For the quotation located in the biographical sketch of Gen. Charles Pomeroy Stone, *see* Warner, *Generals in Blue,* 480-81. 1st Sgt. William Andrews, Company E, Ninety-Fifth Illinois, and another soldier were wounded. Wood, *History of the Ninety-Fifth Regiment,* 103.

48. Ibid.

49. John D. Weight, ed., *The Oxford Dictionary of Civil War Quotations* (Oxford: Oxford University Press, 2006), 367.

50. Col. Thomas W. Humphrey of the Ninety-Fifth Illinois fell mortally wounded, in the early part of the action, leading his men at the Battle of Guntown, June 10, 1864. Capt. E. N. Bush, of Company G, took command of the Ninety-Fifth Infantry Regiment after the death of Humphrey. After a short period, he was "stricken down and counted among the fallen and killed." Wood, *History of the Ninety-Fifth Regiment,* 111.

51. Sgt. Stephen Albert Rollins, Company B, Ninety-Fifth Illinois Infantry, died of wounds from the Battle of Guntown. Rollins was born in Belvidere, Illinois, and was a twenty-year-old student at the time of his enlistment. He was elected as corporal and later promoted to the rank of corporal. Wood, *History of the Ninety-Fifth Regiment,* 222, 233; Crawford, *My Dear Wife,* 186; Shannon, *The Civil War Letters of Sergeant Onley Andrus,* 61.

52. Pvt. Henry Williams, Company B, Ninety-Fifth Illinois Infantry, died of wounds sustained at the Battle of Guntown. Lt. James M. Tisdel, Company B, Ninety-Fifth Illinois Infantry, was wounded severely in the leg at the Battle of Guntown. Cpl. Joseph Sweetapple, Company B, Ninety-Fifth Illinois Infantry, was wounded at Guntown and did not muster out with his regiment. Pvt. Washington Porter, Company B, Ninety-Fifth Illinois Infantry, was wounded at Guntown and discharged prior to the end of the war. Wood, *History of the Ninety-Fifth Regiment,* 219, 220, 223, 233.

53. Pvt. Cordenio Bruce, Company K, Ninety-Fifth Illinois Infantry. Wood, *History of the Ninety-Fifth Regiment,* 230.

54. Chilvers Family Papers, Letter of William Chilvers to George Burnham, June 4, 1864. Pvt. Francis T. Houk, Company B, Ninety-Fifth Illinois Infantry, mustered out with the regiment in 1865. Pvt. Elisha N. Strong, Company B, Ninety-Fifth Illinois Infantry, died in the service. Pvt. James Goodman, Company B, Ninety-Fifth Illinois Infantry, was mustered out of the service but not with the regiment. Pvt. William N. Tyler, Company B, Ninety-Fifth Illinois Infantry, mustered out but not with the regiment. Pvt. Mort L. Powell, Company B, Ninety-Fifth Illinois Infantry, mustered out of the service but not with this regiment. Wood, *History of the Ninety-Fifth Regiment,* 219, 220.

55. Chilvers Family Papers, Letter from William B. Chilvers to George Burnham, June 22, 1864.

56. The Ninety-Fifth Illinois hobbled back into Memphis following the debacle at Brice's Crossroads (Guntown). The regiment "had been so much shattered by recent misfortunes that it was relieved . . . and allowed to recover from the severe shock it had received, before taking part in an expedition which was soon to set out from Memphis for Arkansas, under the command of General Mower." Wood, *History of the Ninety-Fifth Regiment,*

117. Under Sturgis' command were two Cavalry Brigades under the command of Gen. Benjamin Grierson, and three infantry divisions under Gen. William McMillen. The First Infantry Division was commanded by Alexander Wilkin and consisted of the 114th Illinois, Ninety-Third Indiana, Seventy-Second Ohio, and the Ninth Minnesota Infantry Regiments, along with the Sixth Indiana Battery. The Second Infantry Division (known as the Illinois division) was commanded by Col. George B. Hoge. The Third Infantry Division was commanded by Gen. Edward Bouton and consisted of the Fifty-Fifth U.S. Colored and Fifty-Ninth U.S. Colored Infantry Regiments, and the Second U.S. Colored Artillery, Company F. Michael Ballard, *The Civil War in Mississippi: Major Campaigns and Battles* (Jackson, MS: University Press of Mississippi, 2011), 195–219.

57. The Ninety-Fifth Illinois was part of the Illinois Brigade (which also included the Eighty-First, 108th, 113th, and the 120th Illinois Regiments, and Company B, Second Illinois Light Artillery) under Gen. George B. Hoge. This Second Brigade of McMillen's Infantry lost thirty-nine killed, 109 wounded, and 602 missing for a total loss of 750 men at the Battle of Guntown. Ballard, *The Civil War in Mississippi*, 195–219; Stewart L. Bennett, *The Battle of Brice's Crossroads* (Charleston, SC: The History Press, 2012), 67, 93, 127, 128.

58. Sgt. Stephen Albert Rollins' brother was John Rollins. There are five men with this name who were Illinois soldiers or perhaps this John was a civilian. Those named were members of the Twenty-Ninth, Forty-Fifth, Eighty-Fifth, and 136th Infantry Regiments, and the Second Light Artillery Regiment. *Dyer's Compendium.*

59. Capt. Joseph Nelson Harper, Ninth Illinois Cavalry Regiment, was mustered in as a second lieutenant and was promoted to colonel prior to being mustered out. M539/ roll 38. *Dyer's Compendium.*

60. Lt. James Milton Tisdel, Company B, Ninety-Fifth Illinois Infantry. Wood, *History of the Ninety-Fifth Regiment*, 219, 233.

61. Pvt. Daniel G. Winegar wrote his wife on June 10, 1864, that the regiment got its "teeth kicked in" at the fight at Brice's Cross Road, near Guntown, Mississippi. He followed, "I am back from the hardest trip we have had since I have been in the army." On June 14 he noted, "I came out safe but am badly used up. We left here June 1st and on June 10th got to Baldwin's Cross Road, which is about 40 miles below Corinth and 115 miles from here. We came on the rebels, they had a large force. We marched on a 'double quick' about 5 miles in the middel of the day, with the sun shining on our heads, hot enough to kill us – so we were whipped when we got in the fight, so we could not do anything with them." Letter from Pvt. Daniel G. Winegar, Company B, Ninety-Fifth Illinois Infantry, to his wife, Elvira Winegar, June 10 & 14, 1864. John R. Tripp, "The Ninety-Fifth Illinois faced illness, heat and Rebel bullets in its three-year tour of duty," *America's Civil War* (January 1991), 16, 69–70. Wales Wood blamed General Sturgis and not the troops on the defeat at Guntown. He noted "bravery on the part of our troops was not wanting . . . The true cause of the great misfortune was plainly *incompetency* and *lack of courage* on the part of one who should have been the leading spirit of the occasion." Wood, *History of the Ninety-Fifth Regiment*, 114. Pvt. Samuel Pepper, Company G, Ninety-Fifth Illinois Infantry, wrote, "This almost amounts to a stampede . . . we hve lost in the Regt on this last trip between 70 & 80 in Killed wounded and missing. There is another expedition going out but our Regt is reported unfit for duty at present." Crawford, *My Dearest Wife*, 187.

62. Sergeant Andrus wrote, "Gen Sturgis, who hsad grossly mismanaged the affair from the start remained during the battle at a safe distance & gave hardly any orders except the final one to retreat when his own hiding place was about to be overrun. Then he raced from the

scene leaving his army to get away the best it could." Shannon, *The Civil War Letters of Sergeant Onley Andrus*, 61–62.

63. Gen. Nathaniel Bedford Forrest had 4,900 troops compared to Union Gen. Samuel Sturgis' force of more than 8,100. Bennett, *The Battle of Brice's Crossroads*, 26–28.

64. "Some later claimed the black soldiers just threw down their weapons and ran as fast as they could, like many of the white Union troops. Doubtless some did, but most stood and fought. They were accused of throwing away some badges attached to their uniforms that said 'Remember Fort Pillow.' That was true, for Confederates found some of these badges. Some black troops likely thought that if they were captured with the badges still on their uniforms, they might be shot down, too. Forrest and his men had heard that Bouton's black soldiers had taken a vow of 'no quarter' toward white troops after what happened at Fort Pillow. After the campaign, Washburn protested to Stephen Lee that the black troops seemed to have suffered a larger number of casualties than should have been the case. Washburn linked the losses to Fort Pillow. Forrest and Lee replied, with Forrest assuring Blackburn that he viewed 'captured negroes' as any other property captured in battle and not as soldiers. He argued it was not the South's policy to eliminate blacks, but 'to preserve and protect' them. He went on to say all black troops 'who have surrendered to us received kind and humane treatment.' Lee supported Forrest's comments, and there the matter seemed to rest." Ballard, *The Civil War in Mississippi*, 213–14. Stephen D. Lee wrote to Union General Washburn in support of Forrest at both Fort Pillow and Guntown. In regards to Fort Pillow, Lee wrote, "the garrison never surrendered, the colors never struck the fort's commander issued all liquor rations he had before the fight, and the Negro troops displayed especial fanaticism; and in spite of all of this over two hundred prisoners-both black and some white-finally were taken and still remained in southern hands." Herman Hattaway, *General Stephen D. Lee* (Jackson, MS: University Press of Mississippi, 1976), 117.

65. Rollins description by others.

66. Chilvers Family Papers, Cousin Pvt. John Fulton Fillingham, Company F, Seventh Illinois Cavalry.

67. John C. Freemont ran for president in 1856, 1860 and 1864. He was known as "the pathfinder" due to his exploring ventures in the West prior to the Civil War. He was very well connected politically through his marriage to Jessie Benton, the intelligent daughter of Missouri Sen. Thomas Hart Benton. Warner, *Generals in Blue*, 160–61.

68. Lincoln chose Tennessee Sen. Andrew Johnson as his running mate for the 1864 election.

69. Gen. Samuel Sturgis was born on June 11, 1822, in Shippensburg, Pennsylvania, and graduated in the 1847 class at West Point. After earning a brevet at the Battle of Wilson's Creek in 1861 he was sent East. He took part in the Battles of Second Manassas, Sharpsburg, and Fredericksburg. He said of a fellow general, "I do not care for John Pope one pinch of owl Dung." He was sent West in command of an expedition to destroy Nathan Bedford Forest. He was badly defeated and was without a command until after the war. Sturgis surprisingly was given a high position, despite his failure at the Battle of Guntown, after the Civil War. Sturgis was assigned colonel of the Seventh Cavalry, where George Armstrong Custer became his lieutenant. Colonel Sturgis died on September 29, 1889, at St. Paul, Minnesota, and is buried at Arlington National Cemetery. Stewart Sifakas, *Who Was Who in the Civil War* (New York: Facts on File Publications, 1988), 632–33; Warner, *Generals in Blue*, 486–87.

70. Surgeon John W. Green, Ninety-Fifth Illinois Regiment, enlisted in Walnut Hills, Wisconsin, on May 14, 1863. His hometown was Marengo, Illinois. He was a forty-one-year-old physician at the time of his enlistment and reported to the regiment on June 9, 1863. He took Colonel Humphrey's body from the battlefield of Guntown to Memphis. He was later wounded in the neck at the Battle of Spanish Fort in 1865. He mustered out with the regiment on August 17, 1865. Quartermaster Gardner S. Southworth, Ninety-Fifth Illinois Infantry. Crawford, *My Dear Wife*, 110; Wood, *History of the Ninety-Fifth Regiment*, 212, 217, 232. Gen. Andrew Jackson Smith was the Sixteenth Corps commander. He fought under Grant and Sherman during the Vicksburg campaign. Warner, *Generals in Blue*, 454–55.

71. "Lincoln did not comment publicly on the treatment of USCT by the Confederates until late July 1863. He did so following allegations that black soldiers were murdered or enslaved after battles of Port Hudson (May 27), Milliken's Bend (June 7), Mound Plantation (June 29), in Louisiana, and Battery Wagner (July 18) in South Carolina." These troops performed well, and "convinced many skeptics, in both the North and the South, that African American soldiers would fight – and would fight bravely and with distinction . . . Confederate threats to give black troops and their officers 'no quarter' inspired the men of the USCT to become stubborn fighters who were loath to give up, fearful that southern troops would not take them alive . . . Colonel Daniels of the Second Louisiana Native Guard wrote that his troops, 'fight like bloodhounds, and never surrender. Defeat in our case is worse than Death. Victory the only alternative – my men are well aware of this and will vent themselves accordingly.' At Milliken's Bend USCT fought fiercely but suffered devastating loses '35 % of black troops were killed or wounded. The 9th Louisiana [Volunteers of African Descent] lost almost 45 percent of its men.'" John David Smith, ed., *Black Soldiers in Blue: African American Troops in the Civil War Era* (Chapel Hill, NC: University of North Carolina Press, 2002), 46–47, 55. At Fort Pillow, about forty miles north of Memphis, "a force of 1,500 Confederate cavalrymen under the command of Maj. Gen. Nathan Bedford Forrest demanded the surrender of the fort, manned by some 500 Federals, nearly half of whom were black soldiers. When the Union commander refused, Forrest's forces stormed the fort and killed, wounded, or captured almost the entire garrison. Some two-thirds of all black soldiers at Fort Pillow lost their lives, while Confederates killed 36 percent of all white troops." Joseph T. Glathaar, *Forged in Battle: the Civil War Alliance of Black Soldiers and White Officers* (Baton Rouge, LA: Louisiana State University Press, 1990), 156–57.

72. Hattaway, *General Stephen D. Lee*, 111–17.

73. Pvt. Samuel Pepper, Company G, Ninety-Fifth Illinois Infantry, wrote, "Col Humphrey after the engagement opened said to the men of the 95th {Remember Fort Pillow} which each Co Comdr passed along the line and the Rebels could hear the words plain." Crawford, *My Dear Wife*, 183. Sergeant Onley Andrus, Company D, Ninety-Fifth Illinois Infantry, noted that caring the black soldiers "has in effect raised the Black flag, and those who fight under that must bide the consequences. Our men were foolish enough to go into that fight with 'Remember Ft Pillow' for their battle cry, which being interpreted meant no quarter asked nor given." Shannon, *The Civil War Letters of Sergeant Onley Andrus*, 87.

74. Massacres occurred against the Southern soldiers at Tupelo and Fort Blakely. Pvt. Andrew Fern, Company E, Ninety-Fifth Illinois, wrote, "the[y] had a fight with General Forrest under General Lee and whipped them at Tupelo. They actually had three fights with him and whipped him each time. They took only about 60 prisoners that they brought in, the Rets [rest] of the prisoners were taken under negro guard to the rear. The Negro soldiers

came out all right [in the fight] but they woould [*sic*] not hear anything of the prisoners. The negroes would take them a little way from the train and stab them right through with the bayonet. This was an effect of the Fort Pillow scrape when they [the Confederates] commenced fighting they showed no quarters [on negro prisoners]. Our men [negro troops] thought they should show no quarters for them [Forrest's captured troops]. At Tupelo we killed about 4000 of them, our lost was about 150 killed and wounded." Letter of Pvt. Andrew Fern, Company E, Ninety-Fifth Illinois Infantry, to his brothers at home, James and George and Mother, Memphis, Tennessee, July 27, 1864. Union Engineer George P. Hunt of the U.S.S. *Metacomet* wrote about Fort Blakely, "our troops . . . about 35,000 strong . . . gave a yell and rushed headlong into their batteries and had little mercy, especially the colored troops as when they entered they discovered a Negro tied up by his thumbs and toes. This together with having lost so many men by torpedoes made them perfectly beyond control and they showed no quarter during the firsty [*sic*] part of the fight. Those who threw down their arms begged for mercy, the colored troops thought Forrest and his command were there. The whole garrison was marched down to the landing, guarded by Negro troops. Generals, Captains, and all hands, they appeared to take it very hard, but there was no help for them." Letter of Engineer George P. Hunt, U.S.S. *Metacomet*, from Mobile Bay, to Miss Earnes, April 16, 1865, Catalogue of the Historical Shop, New Orleans, item #5296. Pvt. William Wiley, Company F, Seventy-Seventh Illinois Infantry, also mentioned atrocities at Fort Blakely. He wrote, "the fort was a strong earthwork surrounded by a strong abatis of fallen trees, fallen with their tops from the fort and their limbs all turned up and sharpened and three or four lines of shividefrize. The ground around the fort litterly planted full of torpedoes. Gen. Steele assaulted the works with three divisions two whiote [*sic*] and one colored troops. Our loss was quite heavy as the rebels just mowed them down while they were making their way through the obstructions and a great many was blown up by the torpedoes. The colored troops so worked up by the time they got in the fort their officers couldn't control the[m]. They set up yell, Remember Fort Pillow. Kill them, surrender or no surrender! They had to bring up a division of white tro[o]ps to stop them." Terrence J. Winschel, ed., *The Civil War Diary of a Common Soldier: William Wiley of the 77th Illinois Infantry* (Baton Rouge, LA: Louisiana State University Press, 2001), 150. For more information about the massacre of Confederate soldiers at Blakely, *see* John S. Sledge, *These Rugged Days: Alabama in the Civil War* (Tuscaloosa, AL: University of Alabama Press, 2017), 188.

75. Surprisingly, there was at least one woman who was a member of the Ninety-Fifth Illinois Infantry. Pvt. Albert Cashier, Company G, Ninety-Fifth Illinois, was the tent mate of Pvt. Samuel Pepper. Apparently, neither Samuel Pepper, his wife, nor any of the other soldiers of the regiment knew of Cashier's identity as a woman. Pepper was a very religious man and wrote to his wife that he wore his clothes at night as items were often stolen. Crawford, *My Dear Wife*, 197. Jennie Hodgers, alias Albert Cashier, was one of the best documented woman soldiers of the Civil War. Hodgers, an illiterate immigrant, born on Christmas Day 1843, was thought to "have been born in Ireland (Clogherhead), came to the United States as a shipboard stowaway . . . and then drifted to Belvediere, arriving before the war dressed as a man." She worked as a laborer, farmhand, and shepherd prior to her enlistment from Boone County. She performed well in the service according to all reports. Pvt. Albert D. J. Cashier, Company G, Ninety-Fifth Illinois Infantry, and "his" comrades were all examined on the same day, were not stripped, and, testified one, "All that we showed was our hands and feet." After the war she worked several years with Pepper. In 1911, while "doing odd jobs for Illinois state senator, Ira Lish, Cashier's leg was fractured when the senator accidently backed over her in his automobile. The town doctor was summoned, and in the course of setting the broken thigh discovered that Albert

Cashier was a woman." The injury poorly healed and she was placed into the Illinois Soldier's and Sailors' Home in Quincy, Illinois. Her sexual identity remained secure until she mentally declined and proceedings began to declare her insane. The story leaked that she was a woman and "when word reached the Pension Bureau, they appointed a special examiner to investigate the case, convinced that Cashier had defrauded the government for the past twenty-four years." She was committed to the Watertown State Hospital on March 27, 1914. Former soldiers of the Ninety-Fifth Illinois Infantry rallied around her, with efforts led by Robert Horan and Charles W. Ives. In December 1914, the special examiner, after taking many depositions, declared that she was Pvt. Albert Cashier, had not defrauded the government, and her pension checks would continue. She died on October 15, 1915, at the Watertown State Hospital, of an unknown infection. Deanne Blanton and Lauren M. Cook, *They Fought Like Demons: Women Soldiers in the American Civil War* (Baton Rouge, LA: Louisiana State University Press, 2002), 16–21, 28, 60–61, 170–76, 184, 187, 196.

76. Shannon, *The Civil War Letters of Sergeant Onley Andrus*, 62.

77. Crawford, *My Dear Wife*, 183.

Chapter 6

1. Lt. John K. Newton, Company F, Fourteenth Wisconsin Infantry, was in the same brigade as the Ninety-Fifth Illinois Infantry. He wrote a summary of the Red River Campaign: "When I left here I never suspected that within three months I could count the number of battles I have been in by almost the dozen, but such is the case. I was in three battles on the march from Natchitoches to Alexandria, on the 22nd another, another on the 23rd, and another on the 24th of April. I was in three others on the retreat from Alexandria to Morganza, one on the 6th of May about 14 miles from Alexandria, another on the 16th at Marksville, and another one at Fort Morgan on the Yellow Bayou about three miles from Simmsborough." It was a "pretty hard campaign." Stephen E. Ambrose, ed., *A Wisconsin Boy in Dixie: the Selected Letters of John K. Newton* (Madison, WI: University of Wisconsin Press, 1961), 109, 111.

2. Chilvers Family Papers, Letter from William B. Chilvers to George Burnham, July 5, 1864.

3. 1st Lt. Asa Farnum, Company E, Ninety-Fifth Illinois Infantry. Wales Wood, *History of the Ninety-Fifth Regiment Illinois Infantry Volunteers* (Belvidere, IL: Boone County Historical Society, 1993), 223.

4. Chilvers Family Papers, Letter from George Burnham to William B. Chilvers, July 18, 1864.

5. Yankee shinplasters was a term for money.

6. The Battle of Guntown on June 10, 1864, is better known as Brice's Crossroads.

7. Chilvers is referencing Richmond, Virginia, and Atlanta, Georgia, in this passage.

8. Frank Blair, and his brother, Montgomery, were the sons of Frank Blair, Sr., who had "gained wealth and great national influence under Andy Jackson. Father and son knew instictively all angles of the political game." Jay Monaghan, *Civil War on the Western Border, 1854–1865* (Lincoln, NE: University of Nebraska Press, 1955), 118. Edward Bates of St. Louis was considered for nomination for president at the Republican Convention in Chicago for the election of 1860. The nomination was led by Missouri Republicans such

as Frank Blair. Monaghan, *Civil War on the Western Border*, 118. Salmon P. Chase served as secretary of the treasury where he oversaw funding of the war. He was named chief justice of the United States Supreme Court by President Abraham Lincoln. Margaret E. Wagner, Gary W. Gallagher, and Paul Finkelman, eds., *The Library of Congress Civil War Desk Reference* (New York: Grand Central Press Book, 2002), 174.

9.   "100-day men" were enlisted for 100 days of service. Three-year enlistments were for three years.

10. Chilvers Family Papers, Letter from William B. Chilvers to George Burnham, July 5, 1864.

11. William P. Fessenden became secretary of the treasury in 1864 when Salmon P. Chase was named chief justice of the Supreme Court. Wagner, eds., *The Library of Congress Civil War Desk Reference*, 174.

12. Chilvers Family Papers, Letter from William B. Chilvers to George Burnham, July 18, 1864.

13. Foreigner.

14. Chilvers Family Papers, Letter from George Burnham to William B. Chilvers, July 31, 1864.

15. Chilvers Family Papers, Letter from William B. Chilvers to George Burnham, July 24, 1864.

16. In letter from William B. Chilvers to George Burnham dated July 24, 1864, Chilvers mentioned that there were rumors suggesting the regiment might move to Memphis. Ibid.

17. Tupelo, Mississippi.

18. Chilvers is referencing the Fourteenth Wisconsin Infantry Regiment and the Thirty-Third Wisconsin Infantry Regiment in this passage.

19. Colonel Wilken. See Thomas E. Parson, "Thwarting Grant's First Drive on Vicksburg: Van Dorn's Holly Springs Raid," *Blue and Gray*, XXVII, no. 3 (2010), 23–24.

20. Believed to be the Ninth Illinois Infantry Regiment.

21. It is believed that Chilvers is referencing Andrew Jackson Smith in this passage.

22. Gen. James Birdseye McPherson was killed at the Battle of Atlanta on July 22, 1864. Ezra Warner, *Generals in Blue* (Baton Rouge, LA: Louisiana State University Press, 1964), 306–308.

23. Chilvers is probably referring to Capt. Alexander S. Stewart, Company A, Ninety-Fifth Illinois Infantry, and not Capt. William Stewart, Company F, Ninety-Fifth Illinois Infantry, as the later was wounded at the Battle of Guntown. Wood, *History of the Ninety-Fifth Regiment*, 213, 225.

24. 1st Lt. Asa Farnum, Company E, Ninety-Fifth Illinois Infantry Regiment. Ibid., 223.

25. Maj. William Avery. Ibid., 220.

26. Chilvers Family Papers, Letter from William B. Chilvers to George Burnham, July 27, 1864.

27. Ibid.

28. Ibid., Letter from William B. Chilvers to George Burnham, August 29, 1864.

29. "General Rosecrans need troops to check General Sterling Price's advance west of the Mississippi River." Ambrose, ed., *A Wisconsin Boy in Dixie*, 116.

30. Pvt. Julius C. Bishop, Company B, Ninety-Fifth Illinois Infantry; E. A. Tyler, Ninety-Fifth Illinois Infantry; Pvt. Charles Farnsworth, Company B, Ninety-Fifth Illinois died prior to the muster out of the unit. Wood, *History of the Ninety-Fifth Regiment*, 219, 220.

31. Duvall's Bluff was a base of supplies for Steele's Army. Ambrose, ed., *A Wisconsin Boy in Dixie*, 115.

32. Thirty-Seventh Illinois Infantry. *Dyer's Compendium*.

33. Chilvers Family Papers, Letter from William B. Chilvers to George Burnham, August 7, 1864.

34. Lt. James K. Newton, Company F, Fourteenth Wisconsin Infantry, mentioned this community: "It is a small town – or rather a good site for a town – on the west bank of the White River, about twenty miles from Duvall's Bluff, which is the base of supplies for Steele's Army at present. There is a railroad for the latter place to Little Rock. There are three other reg'ts here besides ours, & we're placed here to hold this position." Ambrose, ed., *A Wisconsin Boy in Dixie*, 115–16. For a detailed description of the campaign see Wiley Britton, "Resume of Military Operations in Missouri and Arkansas, 1864–1865," *Battles and Leaders*, Vol. IV (New York: Thomas Yoseloff, Inc., 1956), 374–77.

35. Sgt. Maj. Charley Curtis, Ninety-Fifth Illinois Infantry; Sgt. William Andrews, Company E, Ninety-Fifth Illinois Infantry. Wood, *History of the Ninety-Fifth Regiment*, 212, 223.

36. Chilvers Family Papers, Letter from William B. Chilvers to George Burnham, August 21, 1864.

37. Confederate Gen. John Sappington Marmaduke was born in Arrow Rock, Missouri. He led several raids into Arkansas in 1863 and 1864. Ezra Warner, *Generals in Gray: Lives of the Confederate Commanders* (Baton Rouge, LA: Louisiana State University Press, 1959), 211–12.

38. Chilvers Family Papers, Letter from William B. Chilvers to George Burnham, August 21, 1864.

39. Gen. John Anthony Mower was a division commander under Gen. A. J. Smith's corps during Sterling Price's raid through Missouri in 1864. Warner, *Generals in Blue*, 338–39; Wood, *History of the Ninety-Fifth Regiment*, 117, 119–21; Fred Shannon, ed., *The Civil War Letters of Sergeant Onley Andrus* (Urbana, IL: University of Illinois Press, 1947), 82–83, 96–97, 100.

40. Chilvers Family Papers, Letter from William B. Chilvers to George Burnham, September 13, 1864.

41. Ibid., Letter from William B. Chilvers to George Burnham, September 20, 1864.

42. Brownsville Station, Arkansas. Ambrose, ed., *A Wisconsin Boy in Dixie*, 120–21.

43. Chilvers Family Papers, Letter from William B. Chilvers to George Burnham, September 20, 1864.

44. Ibid.

45. Ibid., Letter from William B. Chilvers, September 13, 1864.

46. Pvt. John Martin, Company B, Ninety-Fifth Illinois Infantry. Wood, *History of the Ninety-Fifth Regiment*, 219.

47. Chilvers Family Papers, Letter from William B. Chilvers to George Burnham, August 29, 1864.

48. Pvt. James R. Manning, Company B, Ninety-Fifth Illinois Infantry, was wounded at Vicksburg in May 1863 and discharged in 1864. Wood, *History of the Ninety-Fifth Regiment*, 219, 233. Chilvers Family Papers, Letter from William B. Chilvers to George Burnham, undated.

49. Ibid., Letter from William B. Chilvers to George Burnham, August 7, 1864.

50. Ibid., Letter from George Burnham to William B. Chilvers, August 31, 1864.

51. Ibid., Letter from William B. Chilvers to George Burnham, September 13, 1864.

52. Ibid., Letter from William B. Chilvers to the Burnhams, written from Memphis, Tennessee, July 5, 1864.

53. Alexander, a neighbor farmer in Boone County.

54. Chilvers Family Papers, Letter from George Burnham to William B. Chilvers, July 18, 1864.

55. Ibid., Letter from William B. Chilvers to George Burnham, July 27, 1864.

56. Pat Flanery was a laborer and farmer in Boone County, Illinois.

57. Uncle Sam.

58. Chilvers Family Papers, Letter from George Burnham to William B. Chilvers, July 31, 1864.

59. Ibid., Letter from William B. Chilvers to the Burnhams, written from St. Charles, Arkansas, August 21, 1864.

60. Ibid., August 29, 1864.

61. Ibid., Letter from George Burnham to William B. Chilvers, September 11, 1864.

62. Ibid., Letter from George Burnham to William Chilvers, August 31, 1864.

63. Ibid., Letter from William B. Chilvers to George Burnham, undated letter.

64. Ibid., Letter from George Burnham to William Chilvers, October 1, 1864.

65. Ibid., Letter from George Burnham to William B. Chilvers, October 1, 1864.

66. Cpl. William Stevenson, Company B, Ninety-Fifth Illinois Infantry.

67. Chilvers Family Papers, Letter from George Burnham to William B. Chilvers, October 1, 1864.

68. Ibid.

69. Ibid.

70. Pvt. Ira Dean Hill, Company B, Ninety-Fifth Illinois Infantry, was born on December 25, 1823, in Stockton, New Hampshire, and mustered out with the regiment in 1865. Cpl. Paul

Hostrawser, Company B, Ninety-Fifth Illinois Infantry. Wood, *History of the Ninety-Fifth Regiment*, 218–19.

71. Chilvers Family Papers, Letter from William B. Chilvers to George Burnham, August 21, 1864.

72. Ibid., Letter from William B. Chilvers to George Burnham, undated.

73. Ibid., Letter from William B. Chilvers to George Burnham, July 5, 1864.

74. Col. Lawrence Church resigned his command of the Ninety-Fifth Illinois Infantry due to poor health on January 20, 1863. Wood, *History of the Ninety-Fifth Regiment*, 14, 18, 19, 24, 27, 70.

75. Chilvers Family Papers, Letter from George Burnham to William B. Chilvers, August 31, 1864.

76. Ibid., Letter from William B. Chilvers to George Burnham, September 13, 1864.

77. Ibid., Letter from George Burnham to William B. Chilvers, October 1, 1864.

78. The North's response to the Southern invasion of Arkansas and Missouri was delayed as both Rosecrans and A. J. Smith "were waiting for General Joseph A. Mower's division . . . it had turned up near Cape Girardeau with 4,500 infantry, 2,000 cavalry, and 2 six-gun batteries." Mark A. Lause, *Price's Lost Campaign: The 1864 Invasion of Missouri* (Columbia, MO: University of Missouri Press, 2011), 156.

79. Chilvers Family Papers, Letter from William B. Chilvers to George Burnham, September 20, 1864.

80. The steamer *Omaha* left Cape Girardeau on October 7, 1864, and arrived on October 10. "The troops were then transferred to the transport *Yellow Stone*, for a trip up the Missouri River to Jefferson City. After much delay in ascending this muddy stream, on account of numerous sand-bars in the river, the regiment reached that point October 16th, and on the 20th moved forward by railroad to Sedalia. It was here assigned to garrison duty, Colonel Blanded being in command of the post, and remained at Sedalia until the campaign against Price ended in the complete defeat and rout of that invader's army." Wood, *History of the Ninety-Fifth Regiment*, 123.

81. McAdamized is a term for a road composed of layers of small stones.

82. Gen. Sterling Price led a raid, with 14,000 cavalrymen and ten pieces of artillery, through Missouri in 1864. He initially sought to capture St. Louis but his efforts were slowed by the forces of Thomas Ewing defending Fort Davidson at Pilot Knob which allowed the Union to reinforce and strengthen the defenses of the city. Walter E. Busch, *Fort Davidson and the Battle of Pilot Knob: Missouri's Alamo* (Charleston, SC: The History Press, 2010), 72–77. General Price then followed the southern banks of the Missouri River and moved west to obtain supplies and recruits from Southern sympathizers. Gen. William S. Rosecrans mobilized more than 100,000 Union troops in an effort to destroy or capture the Confederates. Many Missourians who were supportive of the South had been enticed to join the Union army as a home guard to protect their homes from Kansas raiders. Many of these men switched sides and joined Price's Confederates. Price's army was slaughtered at the Battles of Westport, Marais des Cygnes, and Mine Creek. Soldiers of the Missouri Guard who wore some blue were immediately executed upon capture. Confederate generals William Cabell and John S. Marmaduke were captured. Only

through the heroics of Gen. J. O. Shelby were some of the Confederates able to escape. Howard N. Monnett, *Action Before Westport, 1864* (Kansas City, NE: Lowell Press, 1964), passim. Jeffrey D. Stalnaker, *The Battle of Mine Creek: The Crushing End of the Missouri Campaign* (Charleston, SC: The History Press, 2011), 67–72, 81–95.

83. Chilvers Family Papers, Letter from William B. Chilvers to George Burnham, October 8, 1864.

84. Gen. William Starke Rosecrans was transferred to command the Department of Missouri following his loss at the Battle of Chickamauga on September 19 and 20, 1863. Warner, *Generals in Blue*, 410–11.

85. Chilvers Family Papers, Letter from William B. Chilvers to George Burnham, undated.

86. Sgt. Charles Anderson, Company B, Ninety-Fifth Illinois Infantry, was wounded at Vicksburg in May 1863, and died in August 1864. Wood, *History of the Ninety-Fifth Regiment*, 219, 233.

87. Chilvers Family Papers, Letter from William B. Chilvers to George Burnham, August 21, 1864.

Chapter 7

1. Chilvers Family Papers, Letter from William B. Chilvers to George Burnham, January 17, 1865.

2. Chilvers Family Papers, Letter from George Burnham to William B. Chilvers, January 4, 1865.

3. Pvt. Cordenio Bruce, Company K, Ninety-Fifth Illinois Infantry. Wales Wood, *History of the Ninety-Fifth Regiment Illinois Infantry Volunteers* (Belvidere, IL: Boone County Historical Society, 1993), 230.

4. Timothy Bruce was the father of Cordenio Bruce.

5. Pvt. Cordenio Bruce, Company K, Ninety-Fifth Illinois Infantry. Cordenio Bruce owned section 35/80 acres in Caledonia Township, Boone Co, Illinois. L. Toeple owned section 30, 50 acres Belvidere, George Burnham, section 8/57 acres Belvidere, J. Robinson section 1/78 acres, section 6/80 acres, section 7/80 acres. *See* Culture and Heritage Museum, Boone County, Illinois. Chilvers Family Papers, Letter from William B. Chilvers to the Burnhams, January 17, 1865.

6. Ed Bruce, the father of Cordenio Bruce. Chilvers Family Papers.

7. Pvt. Cordenio Bruce, Company K, Ninety-Fifth Illinois Infantry. Wood, *History of the Ninety-Fifth Regiment*, 230, 236.

8. Pvt. Cordenio Bruce, Company K, Ninety-Fifth Illinois Infantry. Cordenio was born in about 1826 in Saratoga, New York. Bruce survived the war and apparently moved with his wife and family to Potosi, Linn County, Kansas. He married Maria Burroughs on February 9, 1853. According to Roll T 288_58 of the Kansas Pension he filed as an invalid – application # 91154 which was approved certificate # 05589. In the Kansas State Census of March 1, 1885, roll KS 1885_76, line 25, roll v 115-81, he was listed at sixty years old, Maria at fifty, Earnest at twenty, and Everitt J. at eleven years old. Everitt J. was buried at the Pleasanton Cemetery with a headstone reading 1875-1928. Cordenio Bruce was buried at the Pleasanton Cemetery and his headstone read, "Cordenio Bruce died February 3, 1898

aged 72." www.billion graves.com; Wood, *History of the Ninety-Fifth Regiment*, 230, 236; National Archives and Records Administration, www.NARA.gov, M539, Roll 11.

9. Chilvers Family Papers, Letter from William B. Chilvers to George Burnham, February 27, 1865.

10. Cpl. William R. Stevenson, Company B, Ninety-Fifth Illinois Infantry. Wood, *History of the Ninety-Fifth Regiment*, 218, 233.

11. H. Parsons is not listed in Company K. This entry probably references Pvt. John H. Parsons, Company B, Ninety-Fifth Illinois Infantry. He was transferred to another unit prior to the end of the war. Pvt. Moses C. Fitzer, Company E, Ninety-Fifth Illinois Infantry, was transferred prior to the end of the war. Wood, *History of the Ninety-Fifth Regiment*, 219, 224.

12. Chilvers Family Papers, Letter from William B. Chilvers to George Burnham, January 17, 1865.

13. Pulaski was the location "where the solid Pike on which troops had marched from near Nashville, terminated, and thence to the Tennessee river their course was to be over a dirt road, muddy, snowy, badly cut up, and difficult to travel at this inclement season of the year." "This place" referenced in the letter refers to Clifton, Tennessee. Wood, *History of the Ninety-Fifth Regiment*, 132, 143, 144–47, 149.

14. Chilvers Family Papers, Letter from William B. Chilvers to George Burnham, January 3, 1865.

15. Wood, *History of the Ninety-Fifth Regiment*, 146.

16. Chilvers Family Papers, Letter from William B. Chilvers to George Burnham, January 3, 1865.

17. Different commanders, including Gen. A. J. "Whiskey" Smith, wrangled with each other on obtaining boats for their troops at Clifton. "Soldiers were crammed into places where they perhaps had room to stand, but not to lie down; mules were knocked around and severely beaten, when, in fact, they knew more than those who were beating them; everything was in uproar, everybody was mad, and *somebody* must have been drunk." Wood, *History of the Ninety-Fifth Regiment*, 149, 150.

18. Ibid., 149–51.

19. Chilvers Family Papers, Letter from William B. Chilvers to George Burnham, January 17, 1865.

20. Wood, *History of the Ninety-Fifth Regiment*, 151–52.

21. Archduke Ferdinand Maximilian of Austria was named the Emperor of Mexico after the French invaded the country in 1863. "Louis Napoleon had secretly asked Seward at the end of 1865 whether the United States would recognize the validity of Emperor Maximilian's rule in Mexico in exchange for a complete withdrawal of the French army. Seward not only turned down the offer, but allowed General Grant to send thirty thousand U.S. troops under General Phillip Sheridan to the Rio Grande, where they provided arms and training to the Juarez rebels . . . Emperor Napoleon informed Maximilian that the French army would remain in Mexico only until March 1867, when he would have to choose between maintaining his throne unaided and abdicating . . . Maximilian would not hear of leaving . . . and within weeks of the French leaving Mexico, . . . Maximilian was captured and

executed by the victorious Benito Juarez on June 19, 1867." Amanda Foreman, *A World on Fire: Britain's Crucial Role in the American Civil War* (New York: Random House, 2010), 592, 798.

22. Chilvers Family Papers, Letter from William B. Chilvers to George Burnham, undated.

23. As late as March 2, 1865, newspapers in New York and Houston reported that, "a collision with France is inevitable: and means . . . a war with all the great Powers of Europe, excepting, perhaps Russia . . . The richest mineral territory of Mexico; Sonora, Sinaloa, and other Northern states, has been ceded to the Emperor, and a Southerner, Dr. William A. Gwin, has been selected as Governor-General of the French. Gwin is an 'ardent sympathizer' with the cause of the South . . . Napoleon is the arch intriguer of the world. When he offered the imperial crown of Mexico to Maximilian, he had already determined that the armies and navies of France should assist the Southern States to accomplish their independence . . . It is a *necessity* for France to recognize the South, or lose the prize that has cost so much labor, strategy, and treasure." J. E. Carnes, ed., "A Foreign War Inevitable: the South Master of the Situation," reprint from *New York News*, in *Texas Christian Advocate*, Vol. VIII, No. 25, Houston, Texas, March 2, 1865.

24. Chilvers Family Papers, Letter from George Burnham to William B. Chilvers, February 9, 1865.

25. The phrase "see the elephant" in this passage refers to combat. Chilvers Family Papers, Letter from William B. Chilvers to George Burnham, February 5, 1865.

26. Ibid.

27. Ibid.

28. Pvt. Samuel Pepper, Company G, Ninety-Fifth Illinois Infantry described the steamer, *Adam Jacobs*, as "a large and beautiful steamer gliding swiftly down the Mississippi for parts as yet to us unknown." Franklin R. Crawford, ed., *My Dear Wife: The Civil War Letters of Private Samuel Pepper. Company G – 95th Illinois Infantry 1862–1865* (Caledonia, IL: The Muffled Drum, 2003), 270.

29. Chilvers Family Papers, Letter from William B. Chilvers to George Burnham, February 13, 1865.

30. "While at New Orleans, General Smith's command underwent some changes in it's name and organization. During its operations in the Department of the Cumberland, at Nashville, and throughout the subsequent campaign, it as designated as the Detachment of the Army of the Tennessee. On its arrival within the Department of the Gulf, it was formed into the Sixteenth Army Corps, Maj. Gen. A. J. Smith commanding and was known as such in the campaign against Mobile and until the close of the war." The Ninety-Fifth Illinois was part of the Second Brigade of Colonel Moore's division. Wood, *History of the Ninety-Fifth Regiment*, 160, 161.

31. Memphis Hospital.

32. Eastport, Tennessee. Wood, *History of the Ninety-Fifth Regiment*, 147, 150–52, 154–57, 159.

33. Chilvers Family Papers, Letter from William B. Chilvers to George Burnham, February 13, 1865.

34. Gen. Edward Hatch commanded a division of cavalry under Gen. J. H. Wilson opposing John Bell Hood's invasion of Tennessee where he was brevetted as a major general for

gallantry. Ezra Warner, *Generals in Blue* (Baton Rouge, LA: Louisiana State University Press, 1964), 215–16.

35. Gen. Eugene Asa Carr commanded a division in the Seventeenth Corps which participated in the Mobile Campaign. Warner, *Generals in Blue*, 70–71. He took over command of Moore's Division at Dauphine Island on March 4, 1865. Colonel Moore became the commander of the First Brigade of that division. He replaced Col. Leander Blanden who then resumed command of the Ninety-Fifth Illinois Infantry Regiment in place of Lt. Col. William Avery. Wood, *History of the Ninety-Fifth Regiment*, 162–63.

36. Chilvers Family Papers, Letter from John Fillingham to William B. Chilvers, April 7, 1865.

37. Ibid., Letter from George Burnham to William B. Chilvers, January 4, 1865.

38. Ibid., Letter from George Burnham to William B. Chilvers, undated.

39. Pettit J. Sands.

40. Chilvers Family Papers, Letter from George Burnham to William B. Chilvers, January 20, 1865.

41. Quota.

42. Marengo, Illinois. Wood, *History of the Ninety-Fifth Regiment*, 14.

43. Chilvers Family Papers, John Ford was the brother of Ester Ford, a girlfriend of Chilvers.

44. "Snapt" in this passage refers to "snapped." "Dunham town" refers to Dunham, Illinois.

45. Topping, the mortgager, may reference Toefle.

46. Chilvers Family Papers, Letter from George Burnham to William B. Chilvers, February 14, 1865.

47. John Ford. Chilvers Family Papers, Letter from William B. Chilvers to George Burnham, February 27, 1865.

48. Matthew Twelves, uncle of William B. Chilvers. Chilvers Family Papers, Letter from William B. Chilvers to George Burnham, February 27, 1865.

49. Confederate Secretary of War Judah P. Benjamin wrote "The usages of civilized warfare require that the commanding generals on each side should agree on a cartel of exchange." However, the exchange collapsed in May 1863, and over the next twenty months general exchanges became nonexistent. Ulysses S. Grant wrote, "On the subject of exchange . . . every man we hold, when released on parole or otherwise, becomes an active soldier against us at once either directly or indirectly. If we commence a system of exchange which liberates all prisoners taken, we will have to fight on until the whole South is exterminated. If we hold those caught they amount to no more than dead men." Lonnie R. Speer, *Portals to Hell: Military Prisons of the Civil War* (Mechanicsburg, PN: Stackpole Books, 1997), 13, 97, 114–15, 130, 139.

50. Colliersville, Tennessee. Wood, *History of the Ninety-Fifth Regiment*, 51.

51. Chilvers Family Papers, Letter from James Fillingham to William B. Chilvers, January 27, 1865. War crimes trials were held after the war. The commander of the prisoner of war camp at Andersonville, Henry Wirz, was the only one executed. "When the defendant was called upon to plead he claimed that his case was covered by the terms of Johnston's surrender, and furthermore, that the country now being at peace, he could not be lawfully

tried by court-martial. These objections being overruled, he entered a plea of not guilty to all the charges and specifications . . . He denied all the specific acts of cruelty alleged against him . . . As to the lack of shelter, room, and rations for so many prisoners, he claimed that the sole responsibility rested upon the Confederate Government." John McElroy, *Andersonville: A Story of Rebel Prisons* (Washington, D.C.: The National Tribune, 1899), 639–44.

52. Pvt. Lawrence Fagan, Company B, Ninety-Fifth Illinois Infantry was transferred to another regiment prior to the end of the war. Wood, *History of the Ninety-Fifth Regiment*, 219.

53. Chilvers Family Papers, Letter from William B. Chilvers to George Burnham, February 13, 1865.

54. Chilvers was probably referencing his friend, Sgt. Maj. Charley Curtis, Ninety-Fifth Illinois Infantry. Wood, *History of the Ninety-Fifth Regiment*, 212.

55. Lake Pontchartrain, Louisiana, has a pass that leads to Lake Borgne and then through Grant's Pass to Dauphine Island. Fort Gaines was located on Dauphine Island. It was one of the Confederate forts which protected the opening of Mobile Bay, Alabama. On March 11, 1865, the Ninety-Fifth Illinois was moved from New Orleans to the old race track between the city and Lake Pontchartrain. On March 13, the Ninety-Fifth Illinois Infantry (except companies F, G, H, and K who remained) left on the steamship *Warrior* to be transported to Dauphine Island. Wood, *History of the Ninety-Fifth Regiment*, 161–62.

56. Chilvers Family Papers, Letter from William B. Chilvers to George Burnham, February 27, 1865.

57. Following the Battle of Mobile Bay, Fort Morgan was besieged and finally surrendered on August 23, 1864, when Brig. Gen. Richard L. Page determined that the fort "had no means left of defense." The operations in Mobile Bay with the occupation of Forts Gaines and Morgan resulted in the termination of blockade running at the port. Arthur W. Bergeron, Jr., *Confederate Mobile* (Jackson, MS: University Press of Mississippi, 1991), 149–51.

58. Diary of Pvt. Henry Andrus, Company C, Ninety-Fifth Illinois Infantry, March 23, 1865.

59. Cedar Point, Alabama, lay on the west side of Mobile Bay. On March 18, Col. Jonathan B. Moore's brigade composed of the Ninety-Fifth and Seventy-Second Illinois, Forty-Fourth Missouri, and Thirty-Third Wisconsin regiments. Moore was sent to Cedar Point as a feint, as General Canby transferred the Thirteenth and Sixteenth Army Corps (except Colonel Moore's brigade) to Dauley's landing on the Fish River. Cedar Point had been an encampment of Confederate soldiers as well as a military observation point where batteries had formerly been placed to attempt to protect Grant's Pass from entry by Union forces. Cedar Point had been evacuated by the Confederates during Admiral Farragut's successful attack on Mobile Bay in the summer of 1864. Wood, *History of the Ninety-Fifth Regiment*, 163, 167, 169.

60. The Fish River is located on the east side of Mobile Bay and close to Fort Spanish and Blakely. These formidable outposts were the keys to taking the city of Mobile. Wood, *History of the Ninety-Fifth Regiment*, 164. Henry Andrus wrote on March 25, 1865, "went on board steamer and sailed across part of Mobile Bay and six miles up Fish River we went into camp." Diary of Pvt. Henry Andrus, Company C, Ninety-Fifth Illinois Infantry, March 25, 1865.

61. The mouth of the Fish River. Wood, *History of the Ninety-Fifth Regiment*, 164.

62. Part of the Sixteenth and Thirteenth Corps were under the command of Gen. Edward Canby. The Sixteenth Army Corps was led by Gen. Andrew Jackson "Whiskey" Smith and the Thirteenth was commanded by Gen. Gordon Granger. Ibid., 169.

63. Cpl. William R. Stevenson, Company B, Ninety-Fifth Illinois Infantry. Ibid., 218, 233.

64. Chilvers Family Papers, Letter from William B. Chilvers to George Burnham, March 24, 1865.

65. Dabney Herndon Maury was born in Fredericksburg, Virginia, on May 21, 1822. He was a graduate of the University of Virginia before entering West Point where he graduated in 1846. He won brevet honors at the Battle of Cerro Gordo in the Mexican War. He was dismissed from the United States Army on June 25, 1861, as he was thought to have "entertained and had expressed treasonable designs." He was initially appointed colonel and chief of staff to Gen. Earl Van Dorn, who commanded the Trans-Mississippi Department. Maury was promoted to brigadier general following Battle of Pea Ridge on March 18, 1862. Following the Battles of Iuka and Corinth, he was appointed major general on November 4, 1862. He briefly served at Vicksburg and in East Tennessee, and then assumed command at Mobile, "which he most ably defended until its capture at the close of the war." After the war he was founder of the Southern Historical Society, an ambassador to Columbia, and an executive committee member of the National Guard. He died on January 11, 1900. Ezra Warner, *Generals in Gray: Lives of the Confederate Commanders* (Baton Rouge, LA: Louisiana State University Press, 1959), 215–16. Gen. Dabney H. Maury was quoted in the *Mobile Advertiser and Register* on March 12, 1865, "Our fortifications are strong—our stores are abundant and good—our troops are veterans—and with the cordial support of the people in all measures required for the public safety, and, with the blessing of Almighty God, are confident of victory." Bergeron, Jr., *Confederate Mobile*, 172.

66. Chilvers Family Papers, Letter from William B. Chilvers to Rebecca Burnham, March 30, 1865.

67. In March 1865, Gen. James H. Wilson led 13,480 horsemen through the deep South areas that had been agricultural and industrial bases previously untouched by the war. Wilson led his troops through Columbus, Georgia, and Selma, Alabama, which were two of the South's most productive industrial communities. "Wilson was able to supply almost his entire corps with the premier weapon of the day, the Spencer seven-shot repeating carbine . . . in addition each trooper carried a six-shot revolver and a saber . . . By April 1 Wilson's raid had produced a wave of fear across Alabama. Citizens eagerly awaited word of the Federal's repulse, but press information of the Battle at Ebenezer Church was conflicting . . . . The *Montgomery Daily Mail* reported a Confederate victory, while Greensboro's *Alabama Beacon* told of Forrest's wound and the rebel retreat." Unfortunately for the South the later report was true. "Wilson captured three hundred prisoners and three pieces of Forrest's artillery. Wilson's price was twelve killed and forty wounded." James Pickett Jones, *Yankee Blitzkrieg: Wilson's Raid Through Alabama and Georgia* (Athens, GA: University of Georgia Press, 1976), xi, 18–19, 73. Cavalry raiders under Gen. James H. Wilson captured Selma on April 2 by defeating Nathan Bedford Forrest's outnumbered Confederates. They moved into Montgomery on April 12, 1865. "The destruction conducted by Wilson's raid negated any last-ditch stand the Confederates in the West might have contemplated and made it unnecessary for Canby to move his army beyond Mobile." Bergeron, Jr., *Confederate Mobile*, 192–93.

68. Chilvers Family Papers, Letter from John Fillingham to William B. Chilvers, April 7, 1865.

69. Ibid., Letter from George Burnham to William B. Chilvers, April 9, 1865.

70. Calico fabric is a type of print on a dress.

71. Chilvers Family Papers, Letter from George Burnham to William B. Chilvers, April 15, 1865. Mobile, Alabama. Wood, *History of the Ninety-Fifth Regiment*, 84, 156, 160, 161, 163–65, 167, 169, 174–78.

72. The news of the death of Lincoln was received with sentiments of disbelief, anger, and of deep admiration of the president by the Union troops. Pvt. Henry Andrus, Company C, Ninety-Fifth Illinois Infantry, wrote in his diary, "hare Lincon is killed but don't hardly believe it." Pvt. Samuel Pepper, Company G, Ninety-Fifth Illinois wrote, "the wicked horrid murder of Abraham Lincoln which is received with feelings of sorrow and mingled feelings of indignation which only shows the true spirit of the Southern traitor Leaders . . . Abram Lincoln was the Glory and to a great extent an idol with our soldiers and I dont know but every lovr of his country and of the principles for which we are struggling are apt to look more at him than to god who made him and had he been permitted to live and finish the good work already begun the People might have given the glory to him that is due the Governor of the Universe." Crawford, *My Dear Wife*, 298.

73. Chilvers Family Papers, Letter from George Burnham to William B. Chilvers, April 14. 1865. President Abraham Lincoln was shot at Ford's Theater on April 14, 1865, by John Wilkes Booth. Booth was mortally wounded by Sgt. Boston Corbett when he was finally caught by Union troops at the Garrett Farm in Virginia on April 26, 1865. Michael W. Kauffman, *American Brutus: John Wilkes Booth and the Lincoln Conspiracies* (New York: Random House, 2004), 310–18.

74. On May 3, 1865, Pvt. Samuel Pepper, Company G, Ninety-Fifth Illinois Infantry, wrote his wife "we have heard officially of the surrender of Gen Lee to Gen Grant . . . and the Basis of a treaty has been agreed by both parties." Crawford, *My Dear Wife*, 298. On April 9, 1865, Robert E. Lee surrendered to Grant on the same day that Fort Blakely and Mobile were occupied. Fred Shannon, ed., *The Civil War Letters of Sergeant Onley Andrus* (Urbana, IL: University of Illinois Press, 1947), 125.

75. There were several theories of why Booth shot Lincoln including that the Confederacy had employed Booth. The South's motive against the Federal President was that Lincoln authorized the capture or murder of Jefferson Davis in the Dahlgren Raid of 1864. "No matter if Booth acted at Ford's Theater in accordance with what he thought would be in the interest of his country or under its order, there is much more to the history of the assassination than is encompassed by the simple conspiracy." William A. Tidwell, *April '65: Confederate Covert Action in the American Civil War* (Kent, OH: Kent State University Press, 1995), 13.

76. Gen. Joseph E. Johnston surrendered to William T. Sherman at Durham Station, April 26, 1865, after he disobeyed his orders from President Jefferson Davis to "retreat and fight on." Sherman issued the 25,000 paroled former Confederate troops ten days' rations and his field orders went out to "encourage the inhabitants to renew their peaceful pursuits and to restore relations of friendship among our fellow citizens and countrymen." Jay Winik, *April 1865: The Month that Saved America* (New York: Harper Collins, 2001), 318–19; Chilvers Family Papers, Letter from William B. Chilvers to George Burnham, May 9, 1865.

77. Bergeron, Jr., *Confederate Mobile*, 178.

78. Wood, *History of the Ninety-Fifth Regiment*, 174–75. Chilvers Family Papers, Obituary of William B. Chilvers.

79. For further information about the Blakely massacre, please see Chapter 5, note 74.

80. "The condition of the people of Alabama and Mississippi was at this time deplorable. The waste of war had stripped large areas of the necessaries of life. In view of this, I suggested to General Canby that his troops, sent to the interior, should be limited to the number required for the preservation of order, and be stationed at points where supplies were more abundant. That trade would soon be established between soldiers and people – furnishing the latter with currency, of which they were destitute – and friendly relations. These suggestions were adopted" and copies were forwarded to Generals Granger and Steele. Alexander K. McClure, ed., *The Annals of the War Written by Leading Participants North and South* (Philadelphia, PN: *Philadelphia Weekly Times*, 1879), 67–71.

81. Wood, *History of the Ninety-Fifth Regiment*, 178–82.

82. "On May 4 Taylor met with Canby at Citronelle, forty-mile north of Mobile. Conditions of surrender were speedily determined, and of a character to soothe the pride of the vanquished." T. Michael Parrish, *Richard Taylor: Soldier Prince of Dixie* (Chapel Hill, NC: University of North Carolina Press, 1992), 441. *See also* Wood, *History of the Ninety-Fifth Regiment*, 186.

83. Wood, *History of the Ninety-Fifth Regiment*, 188.

84. "Soon after the arrival of the troops at Opelika, the negro question became the principal subject of consideration, and gave the military commander much trouble and annoyance . . . Large numbers of the colored people flocked in daily, anxious to learn what rights they had under the altered conditions of affairs . . . They were told that they were perfectly free, but wre advised universally to seek employment immediately, either on the plantations where they had been living, or elsewhere . . . The relation of master and slave no longer existed in Alabama, and that while the negroes would not be allowed to roam about the country unemployed, they would still be protected in all their privileges as freeman." Wood, *History of the Ninety-Fifth Regiment*, 194–95, 197–98.

85. Stephen A. Townsend, *The Yankee Invasion of Texas* (College Station, TX: Texas A&M University Press, 2006), 132–37. Joseph T. Glathaar notes that the surrender occurred on the USS *Andrew Jackson*. Gary W. Gallagher and Joseph T. Glathaar, *Leaders of the Lost Cause: New Perspectives on the Confederate High Command* (Mechanicsburg, PA: Stackpole Books, 2004), 239.

86. Wood, *History of the Ninety-Fifth Regiment*, 206–209.

87. Ibid., 210.

88. Chilvers Family Papers, Letter from George Burnham to William B. Chilvers, January 4, 1865. "To take it very hard, but there was no help for them."

89. Topping owned the Burnham mortgage.

90. Chilvers Family Papers, Letter from George Burnham to William B. Chilvers, January 12, 1865.

91. Ibid., February 9, 1865.

92. Cairo, Illinois. Wood, *History of the Ninety-Fifth Regiment*, 26–28, 81,108, 121, 128, 131, 132, 158.

93. Kansas City, Missouri.

94. Warrensburg, Missouri.

95 Chilvers Family Papers, Letter from William B. Chilvers to George Burnham, February 13, 1865.

96. Ibid., February 14, 1865.

97. Nashville, Tennessee.

98. Chicago, Illinois. Wood, *History of the Ninety-Fifth Regiment*, 24, 26, 209.

99. Pacific Railroad.

100. Chilvers Family Papers, Letter from William B. Chilvers to George Burnham, February 27, 1865.

101. Proportion.

102. Chilvers Family Papers, Letter from William B. Chilvers to George Burnham, April 15, 1865.

103. Ibid., Letter from George Burnham to Rebecca Burnham, May 7, 1865.

104. Ibid., Letter from James Fillingham to William B. Chilvers, not dated.

105. Ibid., Letter from William B. Chilvers to Rebecca Burnham, May 9, 1865.

106. Gen. Eugene A. Carr. Wood, *History of the Ninety-Fifth Regiment*, 162, 170.

Chapter 8

1.   Chilvers Family Papers, Letter from James and Elizabeth Emery to William B. Chilvers, October 21, 1866; Letter from Mate Stork to Rebecca Burnham, November 15, 1870.

2.   Ibid. Stephen Stork, Chilvers and the Burnhams relative, moved from County Norfolk, England to Boone County, Illinois, and finally to Norfolk, Madison County, Nebraska. He married a woman named Ann, whose last name is lost to history. They had two daughters who were named Mate and Rebecca. He wrote a letter to George Burnham on November 15, 1870.

3.   Chilvers Family Papers, Letter from Stephen Stork to George Burnham, July 17 year not noted.

4.   Ibid.

5.   George Burnham.

6.   Rockford, Illinois, was within 20 miles from the Burnhams and Chilvers home in Belvidere. It was the location of Camp Fuller where Chilvers began his training in the Ninety-Fifth Illinois Infantry in September 1862. Fremont, Nebraska, was named for "the Pathfinder," John Fremont. The Burnhams and Chilvers were strong political supporters of General Fremont during his presidential bids of 1856–1864. Chilvers Family Papers. Mr. Phillips was an early settler in Nebraska.

7.   Stephen Stork, Chilvers friend (probably cousin) moved from England to Boone County, Illinois, then from Illinois to Norfolk, Madison County, Nebraska. He was married to Ann Stork. Bill (Will) Chilvers.

8. Government land.

9. The Union Pacific Railroad came to Omaha in July 1865 and the Nebraska Central Railroad to Norfolk, Nebraska, on December 1, 1879. For more information see the Union Pacific Railroad website: www.uprr.com.

10. Evert Point, Nebraska.

11. Norfolk, Nebraska.

12. Bill (Will) Chilvers.

13. George Burnham.

14. Union Creek.

15. Sioux Indians.

16. Chilvers Family Papers, Letter from Burnham's nephew, William Stork, to George and Rebecca Burnham, November 15, 1870.

17. Ibid., Letter from Mate Stork to Rebecca Stork, November 15, 1870. She mentions Grandpa, other family relatives, and difficulties in interpersonal relations between their English relatives.

18. Ibid. Rebecca Stork is the daughter of Stephen and Ann Stork.

19. "Beck" was the nickname of Rebecca Stork, who was named for her aunt, Rebecca Burnham. She was the sister of Mate Stork. They were the children of Stephen and Ann Stork. Chilvers Family Papers.

20. Ibid., Letter from Mate Stork to Rebecca Burnham, November 15, 1870.

21. Possibly Herndon.

22. George Burnham sold his farm.

23. Vegetables.

24. Bridge.

25. Prey.

26. Deers and antelopes.

27. Chilvers Family Papers, Letter from Stephen Stork to William Chilvers, February 5, 1871.

28. "Nellie" Irene Ellen Pilcher was born in Lancaster, Ohio, in 1854 and had lived in Bonus, Boone County, Illinois, by 1871. She died in Nebraska in 1917. *Pierce County Call,* December 24, 1914.

29. Chilvers Family Papers. Eliza Mae ("Aunt Lida") Pilcher is Nellie's younger sister.

30. Ibid., Letter from William B. Chilvers to Nellie Pilcher, December 7, 1871.

31. Will Chilvers helped erect the George D. Hetzel Hotel in 1871 which was the first commercial building in Pierce, Nebraska. The lumber was hauled from Sioux City, Iowa. This was followed by a schoolhouse in 1872. *Pierce County Call,* December 24, 1914. In an undated letter to Nellie Chilvers, Will wrote, "The building I am at work at is the first one in the City of Pierce, Neb. although it is laid off the pattern [illegible] in big style I am

right in front of the Court House Square." Chilvers Family Papers, Letter from William B. Chilvers to Nellie Pilcher of Bonus, Illinois, from Pierce, Nebraska, undated.

32. Ibid. Will moved back to Chicago in the spring or summer of 1872.

33. Ibid. Eliza Mae, "Aunt Lida," was Nellie (Irene Ellen) Pilcher's younger sister.

34. Ibid., Letter from William B. Chilvers to Nellie Pilcher, September 17, 1872.

35. Roseville, a hamlet located in Pierce County, Nebraska, was founded on April 1, 1872. The name of the town was changed to Plainview within a few years as the original name gave to much credit to Charlie Rose who was an early settler. Interview with Tom Chilvers, the grandson of William B. Chilvers, September 2012.

36. Chilvers Family Papers, Letter from George Burnham to William B. Chilvers, January 22, 1873.

37. Ibid., Letter from George Burnham to William B. and Nellie Pilcher, December 29, 1873.

38. Ibid. William W. Cones (1840–1922) was a businessman and may have been a major source of disagreement between Will Chilvers and his Uncle George Burnham. Burnham did not like Cones. Cones owned businesses and banks in eastern Nebraska. He eventually moved back east to Indianapolis, Indiana, where he was buried.

39. Ibid. Apparently Chilvers had been successful in his construction work in Chicago.

40. Ibid., Letter from George Burnham to William B. Chilvers, from Plainview, Nebraska, January 28, 1874.

41. Ibid., Letter from George Burnham to William B. Chilvers, February 19, 1874.

42. William Washington Cones appears to be an individual that Will Chilvers and his uncle, George Burnham, felt very differently. Cones was born in Cincinnati, Ohio, on February 1, 1820. He initially worked as a banker and when the bank failed he moved to Iowa in the 1850s. He built the first gas works in Iowa City in 1857 and was elected a member of the Iowa State Senate for Scott County in 1858. In 1870, he moved to Pierce, Nebraska, and helped organize Pierce County. He was a banker and arranged financing for farmers and merchants. In 1875, the family moved to West Point, Nebraska, as his wife "was not willing to live in this wild country" after some of her relatives were killed by Indians. Two years later he sold his banking interests and moved to Wisner, Nebraska, and built the first bank in that town. He retired in 1886 and moved to Council Bluffs, Iowa, the following year. He was married twice. He married Elizabeth L. Cones and after her death in 1856 to Lorinda Wood Cones. He had six children. According to his obituary dated January 17, 1907, he was "known not only in Pierce but all the counties in Northeast Nebraska. He was a man of strict business integrity and had the esteem and respect of all he came in contact with." *Omaha Daily Bee*, January 17, 1907; *Wabash Express*, Vol. 15, No. 1, Terre Haute, Vigo County, December 12, 1855; *Compendium of History, Reminiscence and Biography of Nebraska: Containing a History of the state of Nebraska; Also a Compendium of Reminiscence and Biography Containing Biographical Sketches of Hundreds of Prominent Old Settlers and Representatives of Nebraska* (Chicago: Alden Publishing Company, 1912), 417; *Appendix of the Journal of the Senate to the State of Ohio Containing Report of Investigating Committee for the 2nd Session of the 52 General Assembly Commencing Monday, June 5, 1857* (Columbus, OH: Statesman Steam Press, 1857), 420.

43. Chilvers Family Papers. Mr. Pilcher was the father of Nellie Pilcher Chilvers and Eliza Pilcher. He lived in Lancaster, Ohio, before he came to Boone County, Illinois.

44. Ibid., Letter from Eliza Pilcher to Nellie and William B. Chilvers, September 29, 1874.

45. Part of the timber claim was donated to the city of Plainview by Chilvers' sons. It is known as Chilvers Park and is located in the center of the community. Interview with C. Richard Chilvers, the great-grandson of William B. Chilvers, September 2012.

46. Chilvers Family Papers, Letter of W. W. Cones to William B. Chilvers, undated.

47. The lumber to build the Mewis Hotel was hauled from Wisner which was the terminus of the nearest railroad. *Pierce County Call*, December 24, 1914.

48. Chilvers Family Papers. Nellie (Irene Ellen) Pilcher Chilvers was born in 1854 and died in Nebraska in 1914. Her father, "Grandpa Pilcher, moved to Nebraska to live with his daughter and family sleeping in the downstairs southeast bedroom. He enjoyed sitting on the front porch." According to Tom Chilvers, in a note, his Aunt Frances told him that Grandpa Pilcher made several trips to England to visit relatives. Tom Chilvers wrote on July 15, 2015, that, "the house set on a town block. The southeast corner was in flowers mostly and perennial crops like gooseberries, and raspberries. The north half and the area south of the tennis court was mostly hand dug and planted to potatoes. The north was 2/3rd in grass (supporting a milk cow a year or so). The west of the garage was planted as a garden as well with chokeberries, currants, gooseberries, red and black raspberries, strawberries, grapes, rhubarb, and annual garden crops." Eliza Mae was in the first graduating class of Pierce High School, attended college at Plainview Normal School, and graduated from Wayne College.

49. Ibid. Charles attended college in Red Wing, Minnesota, where he lived with Eliza, "Aunt Lida" and "Uncle Charlie" Dana.

50. *Pierce County Call,* December 24, 1914.

51. Ibid.

Appendix A
Chronology of Service of
Ninety-Fifth Illinois Infantry

August 15–30, 1862: Enlistment of volunteers into Ninety-Fifth Infantry Regiment

September 4, 1862: Nine local companies "mustered in" at Camp Fuller, Rockford, Illinois.

November 4, 1862: The soldiers left Rockford (Camp Fuller) by North Western Depot and arrived in Chicago by rail. Maj. Leander Blanton loses his horse as it was killed in an accident with rail cars.

November 5, 1862: Left on Illinois Central Railroad to Toloma, Arcola, Effingham, and Centralia, Illinois.

November 6, 1862: Arrived at Cairo, Illinois, and "saw 200 secess in cars bound south for the exchange." Went to Columbus, Kentucky, on the steamer *Decotah* boat that afternoon.

November 7, 1863: Moved by rail to Jackson, Tennessee. Were placed under the command of Gen. Stephen Hurlbut of Belvidere, Illinois.

November 23, 1862: Marched to Grand Junction, Tennessee, and to the command of Gen. John McArthur of Chicago.

November 28, 1862: Marched to Waterford, Mississippi, arriving on November 30 which was ten miles south of Holly Springs.

December 3, 1862: Arrived at Abbeville, Mississippi, after a twenty-mile march. Assigned to work on railroad bridge across the Tallahatchie River which had been destroyed previously by the Southerners.

December 18, 1862: Marched through Oxford to Yockena Station, Mississippi.

December 20, 1862: Gen. Earl Van Dorn leads raid on Holly Springs, Mississippi, destroying Gen. Ulysses S. Grant's supply depot.

January 5, 1863: Marched to Collierville, Tennessee.

January 16, 1863: Camp near Memphis after twenty-two-mile march.

January 20, 1863: Left Memphis upon the steamer *Maria Denning* to travel south 400 miles to area near Vicksburg. Many soldiers, horses, wagons, ambulances, and equipment crowded on to boats.

January 24, 1863: Col. Lawrence S. Church resigns. He was replaced as commander of the Ninety-Fifth Illinois Infantry by Col. Thomas W. Humphrey.

January 26, 1863: Landed at Milliken's Bend or Landing, Mississippi, many in regiment quite ill.

February 6, 1863: After a sixty-mile ship ride north, arrived at Lake Providence.

April 22, 1863: Reached Richmond, Louisiana.

May 5, 1863: Marched fifteen miles to Smith's Plantation, Louisiana, to build a bridge across a bayou. Smith's Plantation was located fifteen miles from Richmond, Louisiana. The Ninety-Fifth Illinois was assigned to Brig. Gen. T. E. G. Ransom, Sixth Division, Seventeenth Corps.

May 19 and 22, 1863: The Ninety-Fifth Illinois Infantry was involved in two attacks on the Vicksburg defenses. They lost sixty-five men in the first attack, and ninety-eight men in the second attack. Twenty-five men were killed but only one from Company B—Job Westbury. The company built roads and worked nights on fortifications and rifle pits.

July 4, 1863: Gen. John C. Pemberton surrendered the Confederate forces at Vicksburg. The Ninety-Fifth Illinois Regiment was one of the first units inside the Vicksburg defenses.

July 12, 1863: Embarked to Natchez, Mississippi, under Gen. T. E. G. Ransom's brigade.

October 18, 1863: The Ninety-Fifth Illinois was transferred back to Vicksburg and into the first division of the Seventeenth Corps under the command of Brig. Gen. Thomas Kilby Smith.

March 9, 1864: The Ninety-Fifth Illinois Infantry was temporarily detached from the Second Brigade, Seventeenth Army Corps, and assigned to a brigade made up for the Red River expedition consisting of the Fourteenth Wisconsin, Eighty-First Illinois, and Ninety-Fifth Illinois commanded by Col. L. M. Ward. They embarked aboard the steamer *John Raines* on a thirty-day expedition down the Red River.

March 14, 1864: Union forces capture Fort DeRussy, Louisiana.

April 5, 1864: Union fleet arrived at Campte, Louisiana. The Ninety-Fifth was assigned and divided up to serve on the steamers *Sioux City*, *Black Hawk*, *Meteor*, and *Shreveport*.

April 8, 1864: Battle of Mansfield, Louisiana.

April 9, 1864: Battle of Pleasant Hill, Louisiana.

April 22, 1864: The Ninety-Fifth Illinois embarked upon the steamer *Golden Era* reaching Vicksburg on April 23.

May 31, 1864: Arrived by ship in Memphis, Tennessee, and was assigned to Gen. Samuel D. Sturgis.

June 10, 1864: Battle of Guntown (Brice's Cross Roads). Colonel Humphrey killed in action.

August 3, 1864: Left Memphis on the steamer *White Cloud* and arrived at St. Charles, Arkansas, under the command of Gen. Joseph A. Mower.

September 8, 1864: Left St. Charles by ship and traveled twenty miles to Brownsville, Arkansas.

September 17, 1864: Marched from Brownsvillle, Arkansas, nineteen days to Cape Girardeau, Missouri, arriving on October 4. They were following Confederate Gen. Sterling Price's army.

October 7, 1864: Left Cape Girardeau on the steamer *Omaha*.

October 10, 1864: Landed at St. Louis and were transferred to the steamer *Yellow Stone* for a trip up the Missouri River to Jefferson City.

October 16, 1864: Arrived in Jefferson City, Missouri, following Price's raid.

October 23, 1864: Marched to Sedalia, Missouri.

November 6, 1864: Left Sedalia by railroad to Jefferson City, then by ship to Hermann, and finally by railroad to Benton Barracks in St. Louis.

November 13, 1864: Abraham Lincoln re-elected president of the United States.

November 23, 1864: Left St. Louis on the steamer *Isabella* to Cairo, Illinois, and then to Nashville, Tennessee.

December 2, 1864: Arrived at Nashville, Tennessee. According to Winegar, "the Rebels are advancing at this place, - hear cannonading and muskets all night."

December 14–15, 1864: Battle of Nashville. "[Gen. John Bell] Hood got the worst thrashing he ever had." The Ninety-Fifth Illinois Regiment only lost one man by having "one of his legs was shot off with a cannon ball."

December 20, 1864: The Ninety-Fifth Illinois marched to Spring Hill, Tennessee, in pursuit of General Hood's troops.

December 28, 1864: Marched to Pulaski, Tennessee.

January 2, 1865: Arrived that evening in Clifton, Tennessee. "The weather has been very cold." Winegar noted they had traveled about 2,500 miles since they left Memphis on August 4.

January 12, 1865: Traveled by boat to Eastport, Mississippi.

January 17–21, 1865: Went on a four-day scouting expedition to Iuka and Corinth. According to Winegar, the "Rebels left when they saw us."

February 7, 1865: Boarded the steamer *A. Jacobs* bound for Cairo, Illinois, and eventually Memphis, Tennessee.

February 14, 1865: In camp near Vicksburg.

February 22, 1865: Arrived in New Orleans, Louisiana.

March 5, 1865: In camp at Chalmette, Louisiana, four miles south of New Orleans on the old Jackson battlegrounds of 1812.

March 17, 1865: Sailed to Dauphine Island, Alabama, at the entrance of Mobile Bay.

March 21, 1865: Moved by boat to Daniels Mill, which was twenty-five miles east of Mobile. Winegar noted that we "can hear heavy cannonading at Mobile."

March 29, 1865: "twelve miles east of Mobile. Quite a number of our Reg't. wounded," Winegar wrote.

April 3, 1865: Arrived at Spanish Fort. Winegar transcribed, "hard fighting, - we are mounting more guns every night. Fort covers two square miles, east side of Mobile Bay."

April 9, 1865: Capture of Spanish Fort. Cpl. William B. Chilvers carried the flag of the Ninety-Fifth Illinois Infantry over the parapet.

April 13–25, 1865: Marched 200 miles from Spanish Fort to Montgomery, Alabama. Learned that Gen. Robert E. Lee had surrendered. "We think the war is over," wrote Winegar.

May 2, 1865: Built a bridge twelve miles south of Montgomery on Tickolly Creek. "Received official announcement of Assassination of our President a few days ago. His loss will be felt by the Army because they thought there was no man like 'Old Abe,'" Winegar noted.

May 28, 1865: A Division Review was held at Montgomery.

July 28, 1865: Left Montgomery on board ships *Red Chief* and *Coquette* to Selma, Alabama. Traveled through Demopolis, Meridian, Jackson, and Clinton, Mississippi.

August 2, 1865: Arrived in Vicksburg, Mississippi.

August 3, 1865: Boarded the steamer *Mollie Able* to go up the Mississippi River.

August 10, 1865: Arrived in St. Louis, Missouri.

August 11, 1865: Went by train to Camp Butler near Springfield, Missouri.

August 15, 1865: Received complete muster out rolls. William B. Chilvers moved to Chicago.

Appendix B
Chronology of William B. Chilvers
after the Civil War

Spring 1871: Chilvers moved to Nebraska and worked as a carpenter.

December 7, 1871: Chilvers proposed to Nellie Pilcher, and after completion of the Hetzel Hotel, moved back to Illinois by the summer of 1871.

October 6, 1872: William B. Chilvers and Nellie Pilcher married in Sharon, Wisconsin, and the couple lived in Chicago.

Summer 1874: William B. and Nellie Chilvers moved back to Nebraska.

December 16, 1914: Death of William B. Chilvers.

Appendix C
Ninety-Fifth Illinois Infantry Soldiers Diaries and Letters used in Annotation

Onley Andrus, Company D

Fred Shannon, ed. *The Civil War Letters of Sergeant Onley Andrus*. Urbana, IL: University of Illinois Press, 1947.

Andrew Fern, Company E

Samuel Pepper, Company G (Tent mate was Albert Cashier)

Franklin R. Crawford, ed. *My Dear Wife: The Civil War Letters of Private Samuel Pepper, Company G – 95th Illinois Infantry 1862-1865*. Caledonia, IL: The Muffled Drum, 2003.

Daniel G. Winegar, Company B

Sewell Van Alstine, Company K

Wales Wood, regimental adjutant

Appendix D
Regimental Index

First U.S. Cavalry
Second U.S. Cavalry
Thirteenth U.S. Army Corps
Fifteenth U.S. Army Corps
Sixteenth U.S. Army Corps
Seventeenth U.S. Army Corps
First U.S. Infantry Division
Second U.S. Infantry Division
Third U.S. Infantry Division

ALABAMA
Infantry
First (Fifty-Fifth U.S. Colored Infantry Regiment)

ILLINOIS
Infantry
Ninth, Eleventh, Twelfth, Fifteenth, Thirtieth, Thirty-Sixth,
Thirty-Seventh, Forty-Fifth, Forty-Sixth, Forty-Seventh, Sixty-
Fifth, Sixty-Sixth, Sixty-Ninth, Seventy-Second, Seventy-Seventh,
Eighty-First, Ninetieth, Ninety-Fifth, 108th, 113th, 114th, 120th,
136th, 142nd, 153rd
Artillery
Second Light
Cavalry
Second, Third, Seventh, Ninth

INDIANA
Infantry
Seventeenth, Ninety-Third
Battery
Sixth

IOWA

> **Infantry**
> Eleventh, Thirteenth, Fifteenth, Sixteenth, Thirty-Fourth
> **Cavalry**
> Second

KANSAS

> **Infantry**
> First

LOUISIANA

> **Infantry**
> Third, Ninth (African Descent), Eleventh

MINNESOTA

> **Infantry**
> Ninth

MISSISSIPPI

> **Infantry**
> First (African Descent), Third (African Descent), Sixth (Fifty-
> Eighth U.S. Colored Infantry Regiment)

MISSOURI

> **Infantry**
> Eighth, Forty-Fourth

TENNESSEE

> **Infantry**
> First (Fifty-Ninth U.S. Colored Infantry), Second (African Descent)
> **Artillery**
> Second (U.S. Colored Artillery)

WISCONSIN

> **Infantry**
> Fourth, Eighth Volunteer, Eleventh, Fourteenth, Sixteenth,
> Seventeenth, Thirty-Third, Seventy-Second

Bibliography

Primary Sources Unpublished

Chicago Historical Society Papers.

Chilvers Family Papers [Manuscript]. In the collection of C. Richard Chilvers, Shreveport, LA.

Hunt, George P. Letter of Engineer aboard *Metacomet* to Miss Earnes, April 16, 1865. Catalogue of the Historical Shop, New Orleans, LA. Item # 5296.

Illinois Adjutant General Records. Muster Rolls for Illinois Regiments in the Civil War. National Archives and Records Administration. Washington, D.C. Roll #47-15.

Kansas Pension Files. Roll T 288_58, Application # 91154, Certificate # 05589.

Kansas State Census. Untabulated returns. March 1, 1885. Roll KS 1885_76, Line 25, Roll V 115-81.

Massachusetts Historical Society Papers.

National Archives and Records Administration. Washington, D.C. Record Group 94, Service and Pension Records.

Vermont Historical Society Papers.

Winegar, Pvt. Daniel G. Letters. Company B, 95th Illinois Regiment. To his wife Elvira Winegar. Compiled by Mrs. Leon Tripp, Belvidere, IL. Collection of Boone County, Illinois Historical Museum.

Primary Sources Published

Ambrose, Stephen E., ed. *A Wisconsin Boy in Dixie: The Selected Letters of John K. Newton.* Madison, WI: University of Wisconsin Press, 1961.

Burke, W. S. *Military History of Kansas Regiments During War for the Suppression of the Great Rebellion.* Leavenworth, KS: Adjutant General's Office, 1870.

Cassidy James T., Ross E. Petty, Ronald M. Laxer, and Carol B. Lindsley. *Textbook of Pediatric Rheumatology.* Philadelphia: Elsevier Saunders, 2005.

Crawford, Franklin R., ed. *My Dear Wife: The Civil War Letters of Private Samuel Pepper. Company G – 95th Illinois Infantry 1862–1865.* Caledonia, IL: The Muffled Drum, 2003.

Cutrer, Thomas and Michael T. Parrish, eds. *Brothers in Gray: The Civil War Letters of the Pierson Family.* Baton Rouge: Louisiana State University Press, 1997.

Davenport, Edman. *History of the Ninth Regiment Illinois Cavalry.* Chicago: Donohue & Henneberry Printers, 1888.

Dyer, Frederick H. *A Compendium of the War of the Rebellion.* New York: Thomas Yoseloff, 1959, 3 vols.

The Factory Act of 1833 [3 & 4, Will. IV c. 103], *British Parliamentary Papers* (1836) No 356.

Greiner, James M., Janet L. Coryell, and James R. Smither, eds. *A Surgeon's Civil War: The Letters and Diary of Daniel M. Holt, M.D.* Kent, Ohio: Kent State University Press, 1994.

Headley, J. T. *The Great Rebellion: A History of the Civil War in the United States.* Hartford, CT: American Publishing Company, 1863.

Illinois. *Report of the Adjutant General of Illinois,* Vol. 4. Springfield, IL: State of Illinois, 1863.

Kelley, William N. *Textbook of Internal Medicine.* Philadelphia: J. B. Lippincott, 1884–1887

Kirkland, Frazier. *The Book of Anecdotes of the War of the Rebellion.* Hartford, CT: Hartford Publishing Company, 1866.

Poor Law Act of August 14, 1834. *An Act for the Amendment and better Administration of the Laws relating to the Poor in England and Wales.* 4 & 5 Will. IV c.76.

Representation of the People Act of 1832. The Reform Act of 1832. Act of Parliament. 2 & 3 Will. IV c. 45.

Roberts, Clayton, David Roberts and Douglas R. Bisson. *A History of England, Volume II: 1688 to the Present*, 5th Edition. Upper Saddle River, NJ: Prentice Hall, 2002. Two Vols.

Slavery Abolition Act 1833. 3 & 4 Will. IV c. 73.

Shannon, Fred Albert, ed. *The Civil War Letters of Sergeant Onley Andrus.* Urbana: University of Illinois Press, 1947.

Tanner, H. S. *The New Universal Atlas of the World.* Philadelphia: H. S. Tanner Publishers, 1836.

U.S. Department of Commerce. Eighth Decennial Census (1860). Boone County, Illinois. Untabulated returns in the National Archives and Records Administration. Washington, D.C.

U.S. Department of Commerce. Tenth Decennial Census (1880). Jackson County, Missouri. Untabulated returns in the National Archives and Records Administration. Washington, D.C.

U.S. Department of Commerce. Eighth Decennial Census (1860). McHenry County, Illinois. Untabulated returns in the National Archives and Records Administration. Washington, D.C.

U.S. Department of Commerce. Tenth Decennial Census (1880). Pierce County, Nebraska. Untabulated returns in the National Archives and Records Administration. Washington, D.C.

U.S. War Department. *War of the Rebellion: The Official Records of the Union and Confederate Armies*. Washington, D.C.: United States Government Printing Office, 1890–1901. 128 vols.

Way, Frederick, Jr. *Way's Packet Directory, 1848–1994*. Athens: Ohio University Press, 1994.

Winschel, Terrence J., ed. *The Civil War Diary of a Common Soldier: William Wiley of the 77th Illinois Infantry*. Baton Rouge: Louisiana State University Press, 2001.

Wood, Wales. *History of the Ninety-Fifth Regiment Illinois Infantry Volunteers*. Belvidere, IL: Boone County Historical Society, 1993.

Secondary Sources

Adams, George Worthington. *Doctors in Blue*. Dayton, OH: Morningside Press, 1985.

Alfriend, Frank H. *The Life of Jefferson Davis*. Cincinnati, OH: Caxton Publishing House, 1868.

Ballard, Michael B. *The Civil War in Mississippi: Major Campaigns and Battles*. Jackson, MS: University of Mississippi Press, 2011.

Bearrs, Edwin C. *The Battle of Wilson's Creek*. Springfield, MO: Battle of Wilson's Creek Foundation, 1985.

Bennett, Stewart L. *The Battle of Brice's Crossroads*. Charleston, SC: The History Press, 2012.

Bergeron, Arthur W., Jr. *Confederate Mobile.* Jackson, MS: University Press of Mississippi, 1991.

Bernstein, Iver. *The New York City Draft Riots: Their Significance for American Society and Politics in the Age of the Civil War.* Oxford, U.K.: Oxford Press, 1990.

Blanton, Deanne and Lauren M. Cook. *They Fought Like Demons: Women Soldiers in the American Civil War.* Baton Rouge: Louisiana State University Press, 2002.

Bollet, Alfred Jay. *Civil War Medicine: Challenges and Triumphs.* Tucson, AZ: Galen Press, 2002.

Bowman, John S. *Who Was Who in the Civil War.* East Bridgewater, MA: World Publications Group, 2011.

Brinton, John H. *Personal Memoirs of John H. Brinton: Civil War Surgeon, 1861–1865.* Carbondale, IL: University of Southern Illinois Press, 1996.

Brockett, Linus Pierpoint. *The Camp, the Battlefield, and the Hospital: Or Lights and Shadows of the Great Rebellion.* Philadelphia, PA: National Publishing Company, 1866.

Brooksher, William Riley. *Bloody Hill: The Civil War Battle of Wilson's Creek.* Dulles, VA: Brassey's 1995.

Brown, D. Alexander. *The Galvanized Yankees.* Urbana, IL: University of Illinois Press, 1963.

Buck, Irving. *Cleburne and his Command.* Wilmington, NC: Broadfoot Publishers, 1991.

Burroughs, Kevin, Curtis Reimer, and Karl B. Fields. "Lisfranc Injury of the Foot: A Commonly Missed Diagnosis," *American Family Physician,* 58 (1) m (July 1993), 118–24.

Busch, Walter E. *Fort Davidson and the Battle of Pilot Knob: Missouri's Alamo.* Charleston, SC: The History Press, 2010.

Carnes, J. E., ed. "A Foreign War Inevitable: The South Master of the Situation." *Texas Christian Advocate: Published by a Joint Committee of the Texas Conference of the Methodist Episcopal Church.* Houston, TX: March 2, 1865.

Christ, Mark K. *Civil War Arkansas 1863: The Battle for the State*. Norman,
    OK: University of Oklahoma Press, 2010.

Cisco, Walter Brian. *War Crimes Against Southern Civilians*. Gretna, LA:
    Pelican Press, 2007.

Clausius, Gehard P. "The Little Soldier of the 95th: Albert D. J. Cashier,"
    Journal of the Illinois State Historical Society, 51 (Winter 1958), 380–87.

Cole, Arthur Charles. *The Centennial History of Illinois, Volume 3: The Era
    of the Civil War, 1848–1870*. Chicago: A. C. McClurg & Co., 1922.

Cunningham, H. H. *Doctors in Gray: The Confederate Medical Service*.
    Baton Rouge: Louisiana State University Press, 1958.

Cunningham, O. Edward. *Shiloh and the Western Campaign of 1862*. Gary
    D. Joiner and Timothy Smith, eds. New York: Savas Beattie, 2007.

Denny, Robert E. *Civil War Medicine: Care and Comfort of the Wounded*.
    New York: Sterling Publishing, 1994.

DeStoop, H. Goossens N. "LisFranc's Fracture-Dislocations: Etiology,
    Radiology, and Results of Treatment: a Review of 20 Cases." *Clinics in
    Orthopedics and Related Research*. (June 1983), 176.

Dufour, Charles. *The Night the War was Lost*. Garden City, NY: Doubleday
    & Company, 1960.

Duke, John K. *History of the Fifty-Third Ohio Regiment, During the War of
    the Rebellion*. Portsmouth, UK: The Blade Printing Company, 1900.

East, Charles, ed. *Sarah Morgan: The Civil War Diary of a Southern
    Woman*. New York: Simon and Schuster, 1991.

Egnal, Marc. *Clash of Extremes: The Economic Origins of the Civil War*.
    New York: Hill and Wang, 2009.

Ehle, John. *Trail of Tears: The Rise and Fall of the Cherokee Nation*. New
    York: Anchor, 1988.

Eicher, David J. *The Longest Night: A Military History of the Civil* War.
    New York. Simon & Schuster, 2001.

EuDaly, Kevin, Mike Schafer, Jim Boyd, Steve Jessup, Andrew McBride,
    and Steve Glischinski. *The Complete Book of American Railroad*.
    Minneapolis, MN: Voyageur Press, 2009.

Fly, George W. "Feminine Fortitude in War Times," *Confederate Veteran*,
    XI (1903).

Foote, Shelby. *The Beleaguered City: The Vicksburg Campaign.* New York: The Modern Library, 1995.

_____. *The Civil War: A Narrative.* Alexandria, VA: Time-Life Books, 1998.

Foreman, Amanda. *A World on Fire: Britain's Crucial Role in the American Civil War.* New York: Random House, 2010.

Fox, Adam T., Michael Fertleman, Pauline Cahill, and Roger D. Palmer. "Medical Slang in British Hospitals." *Ethics and Behaviour.* Vol. 13, No. 2 (2003), 173–89.

Gallagher, Gary W. and Joseph T. Glatthaar, eds. *Leaders of the Lost Cause: New Perspectives on the Confederate High Command.* Mechanicsburg, PA: Stackpole Books, 2004.

Glatthaar, Joseph T. *Forged in Battle: The Civil War Alliance of Black Soldiers and White Officers.* Baton Rouge: Louisiana State University Press, 1990.

Gates, Henry Louis, Jr. and Donald Yacovone, eds. *Lincoln on Race and Slavery.* Princeton, NJ: Princeton University Press, 2009.

Gibson, Charles Dana and E. Kay Gibson. *The Army's Navy Series: Dictionary of Transports and Combatant Vessels, Steam and Sail, Employed by the Union Army 1861–1868.* Camden, ME: Ensign Press, 1995.

Goodwin, Doris Kearns. *Team of Rivals.* New York: Simon and Schuster, 2005.

Grear, Charles D., ed. *The Fate of Texas: The Civil War and the Lone Star State.* Fayetteville, AR: University of Arkansas Press, 2008.

Hattaway, Herman. *General Stephen D. Lee.* Jackson, MS: University Press of Mississippi, 1976.

Headley, J. T. *The Great Rebellion: A History of the Civil War in the United States.* Hartford, CT: Hurlbut, Scranton, and Company, 1864.

Hess, Earl. *The Civil War in the West: Victory and Defeat from the Appalachians to the Mississippi.* Chapel Hill: University of North Carolina Press, 2012.

Hopewell, Clifford. *James Bowie: Texas Fighting Man, a Biography.* Austin, TX: Eakin Press, 1994.

Hunt, Roger and Jack R. Brown. *Brevet Generals in Blue*. Palmyra, VA: Olde Soldiers Books, 1990.

Jacobs, Lee. *The Gray Riders: Stories from the Confederate Cavalry*. Shippensburg, PA: Burd Street Press, 1999.

Joiner, Gary D. *One Damn Blunder from Beginning to End: The Red River Campaign of 1864*. Wilmington, DE: SR Books, 2003.

_____. *Through The Howling Wilderness: The3 1864 Red River Campaign and Union Failure in the West*. Knoxville: University of Tennessee Press, 2006.

_____. *Mr. Lincoln's Brown Water Navy: The Mississippi Squadron*. New York: Scholarly Resources, 2007.

Jones, Harold Webster, Norman L. Hoerr, and Arthur Oso. *Blakiston's New Gould Medical Dictionary*. New York: Blakiston Company, 1949.

Jones, James B., Jr. *Tennessee in the Civil War: Selected Contemporary Accounts of Military and Other Events, Month by Month*. Jefferson, NC: McFarland & Company, 2011.

Jones, James Pickett. *Yankee Blitzkrieg: Wilson's Raid Through Alabama and Georgia*. Athens: University of Georgia Press, 1976.

Jones, Howard. *Blue and Gray Diplomacy: A History of Union and Confederate Foreign Relations*. Chapel Hill: University of North Carolina Press, 2010.

Kauffman, Michael W. *American Brutus: John Wilkes Booth and the Lincoln Conspiracies*. New York: Random House, 2004.

Kelley, William N. *Textbook of Internal Medicine*. Philadelphia: J. B. Lippincott, 1992.

Klement, Frank L. *The Limits of Dissent: Clement L. Vallandigham and the Civil War*. New York: J. Walter & Co., 1864. Reprint, Lexington: University Press of Kentucky, 1970.

Korn, Bertram Wallace. *American Jewry and the Civil War*. Philadelphia: Jewish Publication Society of America, 1951.

Lause, Mark A. *Price's Lost Campaign: The 1864 Invasion of Missouri*. Columbia: University of Missouri Press, 2011.

Lowry, Thomas P. *Tarnished Eagles: The Court-Martial of Fifty Union Colonels and Lieutenant Colonels*. Mechanicsburg, PA: Stackpole Books, 1997.

Johnson, Robert Underwood and Clarence Clough Buel. *Battles and Leaders of the Civil War*. New York: Thomas Yoseloff, 1956. 3 vols.

Lord, Francis A. *Civil War Collector's Encyclopedia: Arms, Uniforms, and Equipment of the Union and Confederacy*. Harrisburg, PA: The Stackpole Company, 1963.

Loughborough, Mary Ann. *My Cave Life in Vicksburg, With Letters of Trial and Travel by a Lady.* New York: D. Appleton & Co., 1864.

Marvel, William. *Tarnished Victory: Finishing Lincoln's War*. New York: Houghton Mifflin Harcourt Publishing, 2011.

Marx, Karl and Frederick Engels. *The Civil War in the United States*. New York: International Publishers, 1937.

Mathless, Paul, ed. *Vicksburg: War, Terrible War had Come to our very Hearthstone.* Richmond, VA: Time-Life, 1997.

_____. *Voices in the Civil War: Vicksburg.* Richmond, VA: Time-Life Books, 1997.

McClure, Alexander K., ed. *The Annals of the War Written by Leading Participants North and South.* Philadelphia: *Philadelphia Weekly Times*, 1879.

McElroy, John. *Andersonville: A Story of Rebel Prisons.* Washington, D.C.: *The National Tribune*, 1899.

McPherson, James M. *Illustrated Battle Cry of Freedom: The Civil War*. Oxford, UK: Oxford University Press, 2003.

Miles, Jim. *A River Unvexed.* Nashville: Rutledge Hill Press, 1994.

Miller, Edward A. *The Black Civil War Soldiers of Illinois: The Story of the Twenty-Ninth U.S. Colored Infantry.* Columbia, SC: University of South Carolina Press, 1998.

Mitcham, Samuel W., Jr. *Richard Taylor and the Red River Campaign of 1864*. Gretna, LA: Pelican Publishing Company, 2012.

Monahan, Jay. *Abraham Lincoln Deals With Foreign Affairs: A Diplomat in Carpet Slippers.* New York: Bobbs-Merrill Company, 1945.

_____. *Civil War on the Western Border, 1854–1865.* Lincoln, NE: University of Nebraska Press, 1955.

Monnett, Howard N. *Action Before Westport, 1864.* Kansas City, MO: Lowell Press, 1964.

Moore, Frank. *Women of the War: Their Heroism and Sacrifice.* Hartford CT: S. S. Scranton, 1867.

Morgan, Winifred. *An American Icon: Brother Jonathan and American Identity.* Wilmington: University of Delaware Press, 1988.

Numbers, Ronald L. and Todd L. Savitt. *Science and Medicine in the Old South.* Baton Rouge, Louisiana State University Press, 1989.

Overdyke, Darrell. *The Know-Nothing Party in the South.* Baton Rouge: Louisiana State University, 1950.

Parrish, T. Michael. *Richard Taylor: Soldier Prince of Dixie.* Chapel Hill: University of North Carolina Press, 1992.

Parson, Thomas E. "Thwarting Grant's First Drive on Vicksburg: Van Dorn's Holly Springs Raid" *Blue and Gray.* XXVII. No. 3. (2010), 23–24.

Prokopowicz, Gerald. *All for the Regiment: The Army of the Ohio, 1861–1862.* Chapel Hill: University Of North Carolina Press, 2001.

Roberts, A. Sellew. "The Federal Government and Confederate Cotton," *American Historical Review.* 32 (January 1927), 262–75.

Rosen, Robert N. *Confederate Charleston: An Illustrated History of the City and the People During the Civil War.* Columbia: University of South Carolina Press, 1996.

Rutkow, Ira M. *Bleeding Blue and Gray: Civil War Surgery and the Evolution of American Medicine.* New York, Random House, 2005.

Shea, William L. and Terrence J. Winschel. *Vicksburg is the Key: The Struggle for the Mississippi River.* Lincoln, NE: University of Nebraska Press, 2003.

Shoaf, Dana. "Luck of the Draw." *America's Civil War.* (July 2003), 48–49.

Sifakas, Stewart. *Who Was Who in the Civil War.* New York: Facts on File Publications, 1988.

Silber, Nina. *Daughters of the Union: Northern Women Fight the Civil War.* Cambridge, MA: Harvard University Press, 2005.

Silverstone, Paul H. *Warships of the Civil War Navies.* Annapolis, MD: Naval Institute Press, 1989.

Simpson, Brooks D., Stephen W. Sears, and Aaron Sheehan-Dean, eds. *The Civil War: The First Year Told by Those Who Lived It.* New York: Penguin, 2011.

Simpson, Brooks D., ed. *The Civil War: The Third Year Told by Those Who Lived It*. New York: Penguin, 2013.

Smith, John David. *Black Soldiers in Blue: African American troops in the Civil War Era*. Chapel Hill: University of North Carolina Press, 2002.

Smith, Timothy B. *Champion Hill: Decisive Battle for Vicksburg*. New York: Savas Beattie, 2004.

Speer, Lonnie R. *Portals to Hell: Military Prisons of the Civil War*. Mechanicsburg, PA: Stackpole Books, 1997.

Stalnaker, Jeffrey D. *The Battle of Mine Creek: the Crushing End of the Missouri Campaign*. Charleston, SC: The History Press, 2011.

Stern, Phillip Van Doren, ed. *Soldier Life in the Union and Confederate Armies*. New York: Bonanza, 1961.

Tidwell, William A. *April '65: Confederate Covert Action in the American Civil War*. Kent, OH: Kent State University Press, 1995.

Townsend, Steven A. *The Yankee Invasion of Texas*. College Station, TX: Texas A & M Press, 2006.

Tripp, John R. "The 95th Illinois faced illness, heat and Rebel bullets in its three year tour of duty." *America's Civil War*. (January 1991), 16, 69–70.

Trowbridge, J. T. *The South: a tour of its Battlefields and Ruined Cities, A Journey Through the Desolated States and Talks With Its People*. Hartford, CT: L. Stebbins Publisher, 1866.

Wagner, Margaret E., Gary W. Gallagher, and Paul Finkelman eds. *The Library of Congress Civil War Desk Reference*. New York: Grand Central Press Book, 2002.

Warner, Ezra. *Generals in Blue*. Baton Rouge: Louisiana State University Press, 1964.

_____. *Generals in Gray*. Baton Rouge: Louisiana State University Press, 1959.

Way, Frederick Jr. *Way's Packet Directory, 1848–1994: Passenger Steamboats of the Mississippi River System Since the Advent of Photography in Mid-Continent America*. Athens: Ohio University Press, 1994.

Weber, Jennifer. *Copperheads: The Rise and Fall of Lincoln's Opponents in the North*. New York: Oxford University Press, 2006.

Weight, John D., ed. *The Oxford Dictionary of Civil War Quotations.* Oxford, U.K.: Oxford University Press, 2006.

Whitley, Edythe Johns. *Sam Davis: Hero of the Confederacy.* Nashville, TN: Blue and Gray Press, 1971.

Wiley, Bell Irvin. *The Life of Billy Yank: The Common Soldier of the Union.* Garden City, NY: Doubleday and Company, 1971.

_____. *Confederate Women.* Westport, CT: Greenwood Press, 1975.

Williams, John Hoyt. *Sam Houston: The Life and Times of the Liberator of Texas an Authentic American Hero.* New York: Promontory Press, 1993.

Welsh, Jack D. *Medical Histories of Union Generals.* Kent, OH: Kent State University Press, 1996.

Winik, Jay. *April 1865: The Month that Saved America.* New York: Harper Collins, 2001.

Winschel, Terrence J. *Triumph and Defeat: The Vicksburg Campaign,* Two vols. New York: Savas Beatie, 2006.

Winters, John D. *The Civil War in Louisiana.* Baton Rouge: Louisiana State University Press, 1963.

Woodworth, Steven E. *Jefferson Davis and His Generals: The Failure of Confederate Command in the West.* Lawrence, KS: University of Kansas Press, 1990.

_____. *Nothing But Victory: The Army of the Tennessee 1861–1865.* New York: Alfred A. Knopf, 2005.

Wright, John D., ed. *The Oxford Dictionary of Civil War Quotations.* Oxford, UK: Oxford University Press, 2006.

Young, Bennett. *Confederate Wizards of the Saddle.* Boston: Chapple Publishing Company, 1914.

Newspapers

Belvidere [Illinois] *Daily Standard*, June 29, 1864.

Mobile Advertiser and Register, March 12, 1865.

New York Times, July 11, 1884.

Pierce County [Nebraska] *Call*, December 24, 1914.

Philadelphia Enquirer, December 24, 1863.

Texas Christian Advocate, March 2, 1865.
Washington National Tribune, June 1884.

Websites

A Compendium of the War of the Rebellion [online]: https://archive.org/details/08697590.3359.emory.edu

"The History of Canton, Illinois" [online]: http://illinois.outfitters.com/illinois/fulton/history_canton.html

"The National Map" [online]: http://nationalmap.gov

"Illinois: 7th Regiment Cavalry." Civil War Archive [online]: http://www.civilwararchive.com/Unreghst/unilcav1.htm#7th

Index

CPSIA information can be obtained
at www.ICGtesting.com
Printed in the USA
LVHW010710271118
597809LV00001B/5/P